On Sonic Art

This book is accompanied by 1 CD-ROM(s)
Check on Issue and Return

TION

ONE WEEK LOAN

Contemporary Music Studies

A series of books edited by Peter Nelson and Nigel Osborne, University of Edinburgh, UK

Please see the back of this book for other titles in the Contemporary Music Studies series.

On Sonic Art

by
Trevor Wishart

A new and revised edition

Edited by
Simon Emmerson

ho **ap** harwood academic publishers

Australia • Canada • China • France • Germany • India • Japan • Luxembourg
Malaysia • The Netherlands • Russia • Singapore • Switzerland

First published 1996
Second printing 1998

Amsteldijk 166
1st Floor
1079 LH Amsterdam
The Netherlands

British Library Cataloguing in Publication Data

Wishart, Trevor
    On Sonic Art, – New and Rev. ed. –
    (Contemporary music studies; V. 12)
    1. Computer composition 2. Computer music
    3. Music – Philosophy and aesthetics
    I. Title II. Series III. Emmerson, Simon
    781.3′4

    ISBN 3-7186-5847-X (paperback)
    ISBN 3-7186-5848-8 (CD)

CONTENTS

CODA 323

INTRODUCTION TO THE SERIES

The rapid expansion and diversification of contemporary music is explored in this international series of books for contemporary musicians. Leading experts and practitioners present composition today in all aspects — its techniques, aesthetics and technology, and its relationships with other disciplines and currents of thought — as well as using the series to communicate actual musical materials.

The series also features monographs on significant twentieth-century composers not extensively documented in the existing literature.

Nigel Osborne

EDITOR'S INTRODUCTION

It is a dilemma for Trevor Wishart that so many people appreciate and demand his writings rather than just simply *listen to the music*. But luckily for us, providing the music is not compromised, he has consistently agreed to put his thoughts to paper. In this book there is an advocacy and an evangelism which is characteristically direct and uncompromising. *On Sonic Art* is a demand for a renewal, not just a personal credo. Also — notwithstanding a forthright statement on the very first page that the book is about the 'why' and not the 'how' of sonic art — there are clear insights into methods and means which will help attain these aims.

It was sometime in 1993 that Trevor Wishart said in an aside that, due to work on a new (self-published) book,[1] he was having difficulty financing and organizing a reprint of *On Sonic Art*. By good chance I was due to discuss another project with Robert Robertson of Harwood Academic Publishers and added the suggestion of a newly edited edition of this work to the agenda. To my surprise and delight, Robert had known the book for some years and accepted the project with enthusiasm. He was, in fact, one of an enormous group throughout the world for whom this text had been an inspiration, a stimulus and a constant reference.

The problems of editing were several. I wanted to preserve Trevor Wishart's idiosyncratic style and have only altered to clarify or correct. I decided that with a few minor exceptions the 'datedness' of some of the text was a strength. There are elements of the book that remain '1985'; to have updated these would have been difficult without major rewriting. By that time, while PCs and mainframes may yet have remained substantially separated and a great deal less powerful, the landscape we have today (of music software tools, at least) was largely formed. But in fact, and more importantly, many critical points which Wishart made remain unaddressed more than a decade later. A very high proportion of the book remains as

---

[1] *Audible Design (A Plain and Easy Introduction to Practical Sound Composition)*. York: Orpheus the Pantomime Ltd., 1995.

relevant now as then, while the remainder may be seen in clear perspective as a historical document.[2]

I intend the suggestions on the production of sound and music examples to represent a challenge to the reader, the listener and the teacher. The recording accompanying this book was produced by Trevor Wishart and myself and is largely of otherwise unavailable material. But increasingly the expanded ideal list of examples will be available through the development of on-line facilities: *On Sonic Art* suggests — even foretells — the development of this new resource. It is a key text for the *aurality* of the network.

Simon Emmerson
London, 1995

---

[2] For this reason added footnotes only reference more recent developments where this helps clarify a point.

PREFACE[1]

This book was written in a period of six weeks whilst in residence as the Queen's Quest Visiting Scholar in the Music Department of Queen's University, Kingston, Ontario. It is a very much expanded version of a series of lectures given in the Department on the subject of electronic music, though in fact it ranges over a field much wider than that normally encompassed by this term. The book grows out of my own musical experience over the past twenty years. Some of the ideas which I had been developing were fully confirmed during my experience of the course in computer music at the Institut de Recherche et Coordination Acoustique/Musique (IRCAM) in Paris during the summer of 1981.

I would particularly like to thank the Queen's University Music Department for their generous invitation to me which made the writing of this book possible. In addition I am particularly indebted to Professor Istvan Anhalt and to Jean-Paul Curtay for the sharing of ideas and insights into the field of human utterance. I am also indebted to the Yorkshire Electro-Acoustic Composers' Group (previously the York Electronic Studio Composers' Group) for the various debates and discussions on musical aesthetics in which I have been involved over the years.

In a way this book has grown out of a profound disagreement with my friend and fellow-composer, Tom Endrich, whose very thorough aesthetic research is founded primarily upon the properties of pitch and duration organization in different musical styles, both within the Western tradition and from different musical cultures. I hope that this book will present a

---

[1] The original edition of this book was produced entirely by the author. There were two additional paragraphs in the Preface of 1985. The first included a pessimistic prediction about the development of (open access) computer music facilities in Britain which Wishart's own participation in the foundation and development of the Composers' Desktop Project in subsequent years was at least partly to prove wrong. A final paragraph apologized for some of the literary and editing problems inherent in a self-produced publication which we trust this new edition has addressed. *(Ed.)*

rigorous complement to those ideas and look forward to further intense debate.

In addition, I would particularly like to thank Richard Orton, Peter Coleman, Philip Holmes, Simon Emmerson, David Keane, my wife Jackie for her continuing support and Jane Allen who typed the [original edition of this] book.

Trevor Wishart
York, 1985

ACKNOWLEDGEMENTS

Permission for the use of copyright material is gratefully acknowledged for the following:

Figure 4.10   Calycles of Campanularia

Figure 4.11   Patterns of growth compared
From D'Arcy Thompson *On Growth and Form* (pp. 68, 294, 299, 318, 319) © 1961 Cambridge University Press. Reprinted by permission of the publisher.

Figure 4.12   Two examples of 'catastrophes'
From René Thom *Structural Stability and Morphogenesis* (pp. 66, 67, 72) © 1989 by Addison-Wesley Publishing Company, Inc. Reprinted by permission of the publisher.

Figure 7.3   Layout of the orchestra in Stockhausen's *Trans*
From Karlheinz Stockhausen *Trans* (score) (p. xv) © 1978 Stockhausen Verlag. Reprinted by permission of the publisher.

Figure 10.1   The Gmebaphone (schematic)
Courtesy of the Groupe de Musique Expérimentale de Bourges.

Figure 10.3   The spherical auditorium Osaka World's Fair
From Karlheinz Stockhausen *Spiral* (score) (p. ii) © 1973 Universal Edition. Reprinted by permission of the publisher.

Figure 11.9   Spectrograms of rhesus monkey sounds
Reprinted by permission of the Zoological Society of London.

Figure 12.15   Examples of Jean-Paul Curtay's iconic notation. Reprinted by permission of Dr Jean-Paul Curtay.

Figure 13.2   Example of notation from Roland Sabatier's aphonic poem *Histoire*. Reprinted by permission of Dr Jean-Paul Curtay.

Attempts have been made to locate the present copyright-owners of the following figures: **4.8, 4.9, 11.1, 11.2, 11.3, 11.4, 11.5, 11.6, 11.7**. The author and editor would be happy to receive any information to allow due acknowledgement in future editions.

The Editor acknowledges with thanks the assistance of Hugh Davies in the location of material by Jean-Paul Curtay, and of Bob Cobbing for the loan of the rare Kostelanetz *Text-Sound Texts*; also the continued support of Harwood Academic Publishers.

Prelude

Chapter 1

WHAT IS SONIC ART?

This book is based on a series of lectures given whilst in residence at Queen's University, Kingston, Ontario in the Autumn of 1983. The inspiration for this series of lectures was the new control possibilities opened up by digital analysis, synthesis and processing of sound-materials. Whilst attending the IRCAM[1] computer music induction course in the summer of 1981, I had many of my ideas about the internal structure of sounds confirmed through the research on psycho-acoustics then going on at IRCAM and also discovered an instrument — the computer — through which I could realise some of the concepts of musical transformation I had been dreaming of for some years.

This book is not about *how* to do it, though I will be discussing at some stage new techniques such as frequency modulation synthesis, cross-synthesis and model-building. Rather it is about *why*. Faced with all the new possibilities for structuring sound and sequences of sound-events thrown up by digital synthesis, analysis and control, what might be the effect of ordering sounds in one way rather than another, and what might be fruitful avenues for exploration?

This book is also essentially speculative, though I should stress it is based on my own experience of working with sounds over many years. I intend to throw up various possible options which might prove fruitful in the future, and discuss some of my attempted solutions to these problems. In so doing I am attempting to draw together various theoretical threads which have emerged from fifteen years experience of working in music, music-theatre and electro-acoustic music. Some of the material in this book has appeared elsewhere in similar form (Shepherd, Virden, Vulliamy and Wishart (1977); Wishart (1979)), but the majority of it is entirely new.

My own experience as a composer is quite broad. I have worked in the spheres of music-theatre and environmental music events and, of particular relevance to this book, free improvisation, electro-acoustic music, both live and in the studio, and with extended vocal techniques. I have also

---

[1] IRCAM, the *Institut de Recherche et Coordination Acoustique/Musique*, is part of the *Centre Pompidou* in Paris and was directed by Pierre Boulez from 1974–1992.

spent a good deal of time listening to the world, observing natural landscapes and events and their structure and interaction, observing speech and verbal communications and working with the calls of animals and birds. Although I will refer a great deal in the first part of the book to the work done by the *Groupe de Recherches Musicales*,[2] I should emphasise that I read their work (Schaeffer, Reibel and Ferreyra (1983)) only a few weeks before presenting the series of lectures which form the basis of this book. I quote extensively from it as it is both very thorough and it confirms my own experience up to a point. But, although I admire the French group's general refusal to present any written down theory of sound organisation, preferring to rely exclusively on the ears and direct aural feedback, I would like to go a small step further here and attempt to theorise about these matters. I would stress, however, that my theories remain heuristic tools, and not a means to replace intuition by an overall *logos* such as the serial principle (which I shall criticise in detail later).

One essential aim of this book is to widen the field of musical debate. One problem I have had in my own musical career is the rejection by some musicians and musicologists of my work on the grounds that 'it is not music'. To avoid getting into semantic quibbles, I have therefore entitled this book *On Sonic Art* and wish to answer the question what is, and what is not, 'sonic art'. We can begin by saying that sonic art includes music and electro-acoustic music. At the same time, however, it will cross over into areas which have been categorised distinctly as *text-sound* and as *sound-effects*. Nevertheless, focus will be upon the structure and structuring of sounds themselves. I personally feel there is no longer any way to draw a clear distinction between these areas. This is why I have chosen the title *On Sonic Art* to encompass the arts of organising sound-events in time. This, however, is merely a convenient fiction for those who cannot bear to see the use of the word 'music' extended. For me, all these areas fall within the category I call 'music'.

Of the eight sound examples[3] which illustrate this chapter, only the fifth was originally presented *not* as music. Example 1.1, from *Pentes* by Denis Smalley, is at first glance a piece of pure electro-acoustic music on tape, into which live-performance instrumental material has been integrated. The second (Example 1.2) from my own *Menagerie* (the section called *Musical Box*), uses the accident of interruption of another piece of music as a starting

---

[2] The *Groupe de Recherches Musicales* (GRM), is the current name of the organisation (the originators of *musique concrète*) originally founded by Pierre Schaeffer in 1948 within Radio France, now part of the *Institut National Audiovisuel*.

[3] See the introductory note to the sound examples list.

point for structuring an electro-acoustic piece. Example 1.3, from *Concrète PH-II* by Iannis Xenakis is the most persistently abstract example on first hearing. Example 1.4, from Michael McNabb's *Dreamsong* uses computer technology to transform representational and vocal material. Example 1.5 is an extract from BBC Radio's *Goon Show (Napoleon's Piano)*. Although the use of sound-effects here is essentially humorous, this is an early example of the creative use of sound-effects to do more than merely set a scene for an essentially verbal presentation. Example 1.6 is by Bernard Parmegiani, *Étude elastique* from *De Natura Sonorum*. Although at first hearing no two examples could seem more different than the previous two, I will show in a later chapter of the book how certain aspects of these two approaches to the organisation of sound are in fact very similar. Example 1.7, from *Thema — Omaggio a Joyce* by Luciano Berio, could hardly be rejected for inclusion in a text-sound collection, though it has always been presented as music. The final example (Example 1.8) is from an album of free improvisation by the English guitarist Richard Coldman.

From the final quarter of the twentieth century, it now seems clear that the central watershed in changing our view of what constitutes music has more to do with the invention of sound recording and then sound processing and synthesis than with any specific development within the language of music itself. These latter developments have vastly expanded our knowledge of the nature of sounds and our perception of them and contradicted many nineteenth century preconceptions about the nature of pitch and its relationship to timbre. Computer technology, offering us the most detailed control of the internal parameters of sounds, not only fulfils the original dream of early electronic music — to be able to sculpt all aspects of sound — but also (as evidenced by the McNabb piece) makes the original categoric distinctions separating music from text-sound and landscape-based art forms invalid. We can no longer draw these lines of division. In future it might therefore be better if we referred to ourselves as *sonic designers* or *sonic engineers*, rather than as composers, as the word 'composer' has come to be strongly associated with the organisation of notes on paper.

Looking around for a more general definition of the task of the composer, we are faced with the following definitions of what music might be. John Cage, for example:

> *Music is sounds, sounds around us whether we're in or out of concert halls: cf. Thoreau. (Personal communication to Murray Schafer (Schafer 1969: 1)).*

This is certainly a good definition to open our minds to the new possibilities but unfortunately it is much too wide to offer us any advice or sense of direction in our approach to the vast new world of sounds at our disposal. At the other extreme Lejaren Hiller remarks, perhaps inadvertently, in an article in *Computer Music Journal*:

> [...] *computer-composed music involves composition, that is note-selection.*
> *(Hiller 1981: 7)*

Clearly for the contemporary composer, this is a uselessly narrow definition of composition. It does not even apply to the structuring of the extended drone sound in our first example *Pentes*. In fact, long ago, with the advent of the voltage control synthesiser, it was possible to generate a piece consisting of a singly attacked event which then proceeded to transform timbrally and perhaps split into a number of lines without ever re-attacking, i.e. a piece involving musical evolution, but without any 'notes'.

These narrow conceptions can equally be found on the other side of the fence. Richard Kostelanetz, in his compilation *Text-Sound Texts* (Kostelanetz 1980), makes the following distinction between text-sound and music:

> *The first exclusionary distinction then is that words that have intentional pitches, or melodies, are not text-sound art but song. To put it differently, text-sound art may include recognizable words or phonetic fragments; but once musical pitches are introduced, or musical instruments are added (and once words are tailored to a pre-existing melody or rhythm), the results are music and are experienced as such.*
> *(Kostelanetz 1980: 15)*

This definition is too narrow from the opposite point of view, as a listening to both the Berio and the McNabb examples will evidence.

A more sophisticated series of specifications for the boundaries between music and other disciplines is provided by Boulez in the book *Boulez on Music Today* (Boulez 1971). In some ways *On Sonic Art* can be viewed as a reply to Boulez's proposed limitations on the sphere of what constitutes music. Here is what Boulez has to say:

> *Pitch and duration seem to me to form the basis of a compositional dialectic, while intensity and timbre belong to secondary categories. The history of universal musical practice bears witness to this scale of decreasing importance, as is confirmed by the different stages of notational development. Systems of notating both pitch and rhythm always appear highly developed and coherent, while it is often difficult to find codified theories for dynamics or timbre which are mostly left to pragmatism or ethics [...].*
> *(Boulez 1971: 37)*

In this book I will suggest that the logic of this assertion is inverted. It is notatability which determines the importance of pitch, rhythm and duration and not vice versa and that much can be learned by looking at musical cultures without a system of notation.

> *What is the series? The series is — in very general terms — the germ of a developing hierarchy based on certain psycho-physiological acoustical properties, and endowed with a greater or lesser selectivity, with a view to organising a FINITE ensemble of creative possibilities connected by predominant affinities, in relation to a given character; [...].*
> (Boulez 1971: 35)

In this book, I will suggest that we do *not* need to deal with a finite set of possibilities. The idea that music has to be built upon a finite lattice and the related idea that permutational procedures are a valid way to proceed will be criticised here and a musical methodology developed for dealing with a *continuum* using the concept of *transformation*.

> *When noise is used without any kind of hierarchic plan, this also leads, even involuntarily, to the 'anecdotal', because of its reference to reality. [...] Any sound which has too evident an affinity with the noises of everyday life [...], any sound of this kind, with its anecdotal connotations, becomes completely isolated from its context; it could never be integrated, since the hierarchy of composition demands materials supple enough to be bent to its own ends, and neutral enough for the appearance of their characteristics to be adapted to each new function which organises them. Any allusive element breaks up the dialectic of form and morphology and its unyielding incompatibility makes the relating of partial to global structures a problematical task.*
> (Boulez 1971: 22–23)

This is a rather eloquent example of the ideology of instrumental puritanism — *thou shalt not represent anything in music*. In this book I will propose:

(1) that pitch-free materials can be structurally organised, though not in the hierarchic fashion used in lattice pitch music;

(2) that anecdotal aspects of sound-material can also be organised coherently and in a complex manner and even enter into our perception of the most supposedly abstract pieces. We are not talking here about the concept of association which is often used in reference to nineteenth century programme music, but about much more concrete things which I will describe as *landscape* and *gesture*.

As has already been pointed out, sound-art can no longer be confined to the organisation of notes. Even this original conception had already been broadened to include at least three areas:

(1) the instrumental approach where pitched sound-objects of short duration and fixed timbre were organised into larger structures through the medium of conventional notation;

(2)   *musique concrète*, using instead a vocabulary of sound-objects of various types categorised according to a phenomenological description of their properties and organised using studio techniques without (necessarily) any reference to the notated score;

(3)   voltage control synthesis techniques, giving us the possibility of sustained yet transforming streams of sound.

The power of the computer to help us construct the internal architecture of sounds from first principles allows us to broaden the concept of composer to include the notion of sonic sculpture. At the same time the use of sound-materials whose source is apparent or materials which, however abstract they may appear to the composer, suggest a source to the listeners, means that we may concern ourselves as composers with a landscape of the sound-world we are creating. The ability to capture and manipulate text or other vocal utterance (whether it be of human beings or other living creatures) brings into consideration other aspects of the presentation of sound-material which overlap almost completely with the concerns of text-sound-artists and in fact links us into the sphere of animal communication.

An additional reason that this book is called *On Sonic Art* is that, as I shall explain further, conventional music theories, dealing with the organisation of pitch in finite sets, rhythms using summative notation and most usually in fixed tempi, and sets of instruments grouped into clearly differentiated timbre-classes, I shall call *lattice sonics*. Everything from isorhythm through Rameau's theory of tonality to serialism comes under the general heading of lattice sonics and is adequately dealt with in existing musical text-books. I therefore intend to concentrate on areas that have conventionally fallen outside the scope of these theories. Hence *On Sonic Art*. I must stress, however, that I am not underrating the organisation of pitch and duration parameters as discussed in conventional theories. I am merely assuming that all this is by now common knowledge.

Also, one further important point, in contradistinction to what is implied in *Solfège de l'objet sonore* (Schaeffer, Reibel and Ferreyra (1983)[4]) this book assumes that there is no such thing as an *unmusical* sound-object.

---

[4] An earlier identical LP version was issued to accompany Schaeffer (1966).

Part 1

The Sonic Continuum

Chapter 2

BEYOND THE PITCH/DURATION PARADIGM

This chapter is an expansion and development of ideas first put forward in my contribution to the book *Whose Music? A Sociology of Musical Languages* (Shepherd, Virden, Vulliamy and Wishart (1977)). The principal point I am going to develop is that the priorities of notation do not merely reflect musical priorities — they actually create them. It is fundamentally important to grasp this point if we are to understand an approach to music based on our listening experience. In order to develop this particular point, we shall begin with a digression into media sociology. Our aim will be to draw a distinction between what our notation system puts an emphasis upon and what truly contributes to sound experience.

Three fundamental perspectives will be developed in this chapter. The first of these is that notation is *lattice-oriented*; there are fundamental aspects of sound experience even in the most highly notation-structured music, which are not conventionally notatable and therefore are not in the score. In fact music does not need to be lattice-based at all. Secondly, pitch and duration do not need to be the primary parameters in musical organisation. Thirdly, a perception and conception of music focused through notation can lead to an abstract formalist approach. What I am looking for are experientially verifiable criteria for making music. A preoccupation with conventional notation can lead us into formalism, a situation where there is no longer any experiential verification of our theories about how to compose music.

Writing, speaking

Since very ancient times, human thought and communication has been inextricably bound up with the use of the written word. So much so that it becomes almost impossible for us to disentangle ourselves for a moment from the web of written wisdom and consider the problems of meaning and communication *in vitro*, so to speak. Ever since the ancient Egyptians developed pictures into a viable form of hieroglyphic notation, our world has been dominated by a class of scribes, capable of mastering and hence

capable, or deemed capable, of controlling what was to be written down
and stored in the historical record. Although this function was often
delimited or occasionally usurped by illiterate or semi-literate political
supremos, such tyrants have usually succumbed to the literate scribehood's
cultural web as evidenced by the 'barbarian' invasions of the Roman and
Chinese empires and to some extent by the Moslem conquest of Persia and
Byzantium which generated a novel cultural epoch by throwing together
the divergent scribehoods of these two long-established cultures under the
unifying banner of Islam.

In the long era of scribery, all people regarding themselves as
'cultured' or 'civilised', as opposed to illiterate peasants or craftsmen, have
lived within the confines of an enormous library whose volumes have laid
down what was socially acceptable and, in effect, possible to know and to
mean. Whilst those lying on the margins of 'civilisations' retain some
subcultural independence — variously labelled as 'ignorance',
'backwardness', 'superstition', 'folklore' or 'folkculture' — they equally had
no access to the pages of history, and hence whatever the significance of
their cultural world, it was devalued by default. The vast growth in literacy
in the last century, with its numerous undoubted social advantages, has,
however, further increased the dominance of our conception and perception
of the world through that which can be written down.

So here we are in a library, and I would like to convey to you what I
mean. If, for a moment, we could put all these volumes of words on one
side, if we could face each other across a table and engage in the immediate
dialectic of facial and bodily gestures which accompany face-to-face speech
communication, perhaps you could appreciate that what I intend to mean is
not necessarily reducible to the apparent meanings of the words I employ
during the interchange; perhaps you could reach through my words to my
meanings.

Writing, originally a clever mnemonic device for recording the
verbal part of important speech communications between real individuals,
soon grew to such a degree as to dominate, to become normative upon, what
might properly be said. Divorced from the immediate reality of face-to-
face communication, it became objectified, generalised, and above all,
permitted the new class of scribes (whether priests, bureaucrats or
academics) to define and control what might 'objectively' be meant. Max
Weber's conception of the advance of Western civilisation, spearheaded by
a specialist rational bureaucracy, is a natural outgrowth of this simple
development. In fact, Weber devoted a small volume to a discussion of the
'rationalisation' of musical systems embodied in the Western European
tempered scale (Weber 1958).

For Plato, the *idea* of the object, which took on a new historical permanence in its notation in the written word, came to have more 'reality' than the object-as-experienced. The commonplace tables and chairs which we experience in the course of our everyday life were mere pale reflections of the ideal table and chair existing in some Platonic heaven. (This heaven in fact was to be found between the covers of books.) This radically new stance reflects a permanent tendency of scribe-dominated cultures towards the reification of ideas and the undervaluing of immediate non-verbal experience, which has special relevance to the history of music. Even for the average literate individual it might at first sight appear that what we can think is commensurate with what we can say, and hence to appear verbally confused or elliptical is easily interpreted as a failure of clear thought, rather than a difficulty of verbal formulation of a perfectly clear non-verbal idea. For example, the idea of a good 'break' in improvised musical performance is clearly understood by any practitioner but has never been adequately reduced to a verbal description.

I am going to propose that words never 'mean' anything at all. Only people 'mean' and words merely contribute towards signifying peoples' meanings. For the scribe meaning appears to result as the product of a combinatorial process; broadly speaking, various words with more or less clearly defined reference or function are strung together in a linear combination to form sentences, paragraphs, etc., which have a resultant clearly specified meaning. For the individual speaker, however, meaning is a synthetic activity. She or he *means*. Not merely the combination of words but a choice from an infinitude of possible inflections, tones of voice and accents for their delivery, together with possibilities of movement, gesture and even song, enter into the synthesis of the speech-act which attempts to convey what he or she means. In this way a speech act may uniquely convey quantities of information about the state of mind of the speaker and his relationship to what is said (for example irony and so on) which would be entirely lost if merely the words used were transcribed, but is certainly not lost on the person spoken to. It is clear that not meaning, but signification, resides in the words and that the mode and context of use of these significations all contribute towards the speaker's meaning. These two quite different conceptions of the meaning of words contribute differently to our experience. The idea of meaning as a synthetic activity is most significant in direct communications with other human beings, which might be mediated through musical instruments or recording. The idea of meaning as a structural property of written words governed by rules of combination is the basis for the operation of our system of law. Law codes are in a sense seen as existing transcendentally and having a meaning independent of the original creators of the legal documents — though of course this does in time lead to difficulties of interpretation.

Now immediately we become aware of a problem, for all that remains of what we or anyone else ever meant, once committed to parchment or print, is these marks on the paper. Here in the library, we *see* love, tragedy, joy, despair, lying silently on the shelves, the entire history of the word. Occasionally, a gifted scholar does appear to question the very basis of a writing-dominated world-view. Lao Tse, the Chinese philosopher, resorted to extreme verbal ellipsis in a late attempt to notate his philosophical stance. At the other extreme, Marx, whose principal commitment lay outside the scholarly profession, still felt impelled to justify his world-view before the international scribehood and committed to paper the astonishing theory that the world is shaped by human *activity*, whilst talking, writing and the resulting development of ideas, constitute only one particular type of human activity, and this of secondary importance to materially productive economic activity. What had usually been regarded as history-as-such was, in his view, merely one particular reified result of human activity. The enscribed verbalisations of certain mortals with certain preconceptions, economic interests and systems of relevance.

Unfortunately, Marx's great scholarly erudition won for his radical works a more or less permanent place on the library shelves, but in so doing it delivered his work into the hands of the scribehood, who would promulgate his writings, but not very often their significance. The up-and-coming would-be radical scholar would learn about 'praxis' as a concept in 'Marxist epistemology', his understanding of alienation or class-consciousness would be understood by its verbal competence.

Music and social control

At the other extreme, we have music! Ever since the world library opened, there have been problems in this department. Somehow it seemed that music could mean something to people, judging by their reactions, but this something rarely seemed reducible to any definite verbal equivalent. Music as an alternative mode of communication, however, has always threatened the hegemony of writing and the resultant dominance of the scribehood's world-view. Therefore, from the earliest times, attempts have been made to lay down what could and could not be accepted as 'correct' musical practice. Both Plato and Confucius recognised the threat posed by uncontrolled musical experience to the 'moral fibre' of the rationalistic scribe state, and advised the exclusive adoption of forms of music which seemed to them to be orderly in some kind of verbally explicable way. As, for the moment, there was no way of capturing music in the same way as speech — no notation procedure — it seemed safest to adhere absolutely to previous musical practice, while often ensuring that the music itself was subservient to an approved text. The codification and standardisation of church chant by Pope Gregory in post-Roman Europe may be seen as but one example of a tendency which is exemplified by the Chinese emperor's great concern for the 'correct' tuning of the imperial pitch-pipes at the beginning of his reign, the execution of performers who made mistakes during ceremonial performances in the Aztec world and in many other cultures, and so on.

With the appearance of musical notation, new factors came into play. However, a rapid glance at the syllabuses of most Western universities (centres of writing dominated culture) will reveal the tremendous emphasis placed upon the study of composers who employed a clearly, rationally codifiable (verbalisable) musical praxis, in particular the work of Palestrina (the champion of the Council of Trent), J. S. Bach and, of course, Schoenberg and his '12-tone technique'. Even so, music continued to convey its alternative messages and holy men (like St. Augustin) were obliged to admonish themselves before God for being seduced by the 'mere sensuous quality of musical sounds'. This feeling that attention to aspects of sound beyond those which are capable of description, and hence prescription, in writing (and later in musical notation), is lascivious or morally harmful is a recurring theme of scribe-dominated societies.

Committed verbalists will not be convinced by anything I have to say about the separation between 'meaning' and 'signification'. For the linguistic philosopher all problems are reducible to problems of signification within language and such a philosopher will merely deny the validity of our problem. However, if you are capable of imagining that talking to your lover is not merely an exchange of syntactically-related arbitrary signs and bodily gestures, but an essentially non-verbal communion between two people, mediated and articulated through word and gesture, but not constituted by them, then you may understand what I have to say.

Firstly, if this communion exists, surely it can be named. This is perfectly true; however, the point remains that its *articulation* is not the articulation of *signs*. We must not assume that we can notate its articulation by attaching signs to different parts of it and then articulating the signs. Written language constitutes what I will call a discrete/combinatorial system. Written words are strictly delimited, distinct and repeatable entities which form the finite elements of a combinatorial process of structure-building. Our internal 'state' (whether a 'bio-emotional state' or 'intellectual-physiological state' — but let us not be deceived by a label) constitutes a holistic/

processual system. The distinction between these two systems can be hinted at by reference to analogies. First of all we have the distinction between an analogue and a digital system. In an analogue system the state of the system can be represented by continuously varying parameters (corresponding to the holistic/processual system) whereas in the digital system the state is broken up into discrete samples which have discrete values (corresponding to a discrete/combinatorial system). Of course, with modern digital technology, the discrete states can be made so close together, particularly in terms of time that the distinction between a discrete and a holistic representation ceases to be of importance. However, on the grosser level of representation that we find in the discrete/combinatorial system of language, the distinction is absolutely crucial. A second, though more tenuous, analogy might be seen in the distinction between particulate and wave descriptions of phenomena such as the behaviour of light, though again these have a point of reconciliation in modern quantum theories.

The distinction between these two systems is perhaps one reason why our vocabulary for referring to internal states is so vague and ill-defined. Furthermore, there is an important distinction between the experience (the state) as the state of ourselves, and the mere notations of it, the arbitrary labels assigned to bits of the ongoing process; or between the most immediate reality of me, now, and the reality of socially interdefinable name-plates and syntactic laws. We may reach some agreement on how to use these name-plates, but that does not touch the heart of the matter. This problem is with us as soon as we begin to speak. But it is writing, with the consequent reification of ideas in written reportage and the scribal control of world-view that forces the problem to the centre of civilisation. Very soon we are beginning to deny the existence of any sub-label reality at all, and such things that we have called 'the emotions', or the highly articulate gestural response in improvised music which we may vaguely refer to as 'spontaneity', become as mysterious as Platonic ideals.

What the aural-tradition musician takes on faith is that music does touch the heart of the matter. With language, the actual medium may not be of special significance; it may be spoken (sound), written (visual), touched (Braille) and so forth. In a certain sense, a significant part of the message transcends the immediate concrete experience of the medium which carries it. Music, however, cannot be divorced from the medium of sound[1] and enters into our experience as part of an immediate concrete reality; it impinges on us and in so doing it effects our state. Furthermore, as Susanne

---

[1] Though various scribe-philosophers and aesthetes have attempted to declare that music is essentially abstract — we shall return to this point later.

Langer remarks in *Feeling and Form*, in its articulation of the time-continuum of concrete experience, it corresponds directly with the continuum of our experiencing, the continuous flux of our response-state (Langer 1953: chapter 7).

Hence, our pre-notation musician takes on faith that the way his musical articulation of sound impinges upon his own state is in many ways similar to the way it impinges upon the state of others. He seeks no verbal confirmation (except indirectly), understanding that there can be none. We might say that there is no divorce between the syntax of musical activity and the syntax of musical experience. Whatever is played is directly monitored, by the ears, by the player's immediate response to it. There is an immediate dialectic of musical action and experience by which music reaches directly to us in a way which language can never do, communicating powerful messages which are not refutable within the socially-approved categorical systems of any scribe-culture. It is music's intrinsic irrefutability, its going behind the back of language, which has caused it to be viewed with so much suspicion and disdain by guardians of socially-approved order.

Musical gesture

The essential feature of this direct musical communion is what I shall describe as *musical* gesture. In a sense it would be more logical to drop the qualifying adjective 'musical' as the concept of gesture has much more universal application both to other art-forms and to human experience in general. In Chapter 6 I will be discussing in greater detail this concept of gesture. Here I will confine myself to a few important observations. Gesture is essentially an articulation of the continuum. It is therefore of special relevance to any art-form or approach to an art-form which attempts to deal with the continuum. Conventional music theory (at least in the West) deals almost exclusively with the properties of sounds on a *lattice*. We will discuss this concept a little further on.

Secondly, musical gesture is evidenced in the internal morphology of sound-objects and also in the overall shaping of groups, phrases, etc.. In fact, the morphology of intellectual-physiological gestures (an aspect of human behaviour) may be translated directly into the morphology of sound-objects by the action of the larynx, or the musculature and an instrumental transducer. The translation of performance-gesture into the gestural-structure of the sound-object is most complete and convincing where the technology of instrument construction does not present a barrier. Thus vocal music where there is no socially-constructed mechanical intermediary — and particularly where performance practice has not become dominated by a notation-based system of theory — is the most sensitive carrier of gestural information. This reaches down to the level of timbre modulation, as well as amplitude and frequency modulation (vibrato and tremolo and *articulation* of all these) and up to all higher levels of sound ordering. All wind instruments having a direct and continuous connection with the physiological breathing of the player are similarly gesturally-sensitive transducers although technology and performance practice can get in the way — compare, for example, typical contemporary performance practice on the flute and the saxophone. Bowed instruments, similarly, where sound is produced by a continuing physiological action, are also gesturally sensitive. Percussive instruments (from drums to pianos) are not gesturally sensitive at the level of the individual sound-event, except in the elementary sense that more energy in the gestural input leads to a louder sound, but gestural information may be carried by groupings of individual sound-objects.

It is this immediate dialectic, however, which is broken asunder by the advent of musical notation, causing a fundamental reorientation of musical conception and perception in the West, and rendering music susceptible to new verbal definitions and hence subjecting it to increasing interference from the 'verballigentsia'. Gestural structure is the most immediate and yet notationally the most elusive aspect of musical communication. One important feature of this book will be to suggest means whereby gestural structures may be both notated and harnessed to contrapuntal musical ends. Furthermore, in music which attempts to deal with the continuum (rather than the lattice), gestural structure becomes the primary focus of organisational effort.

Ideograms and alphabets: neumes and notes

Undoubtedly, musical notation, like 'speech-notation', originated first as a mnemonic device for already well-established musical practice, but, like writing, it quickly grew to dominate that musical practice. Just as the original form of writing, the ideogram (see Figure 2.1), did not attempt to convey the sound of words (as with alphabetic writing) but the ideas which were expressed through the word-sounds and hence demanded a familiarity with, and an adherence to, the sphere of those ideas, so the neume did not attempt to mark out what we have now come to regard as individual pitches and units of rhythm but only shapes and contours of melodic line customary in current practice, and hence also requiring a complete familiarity with that practice, and an adherence to it, before becoming usable.[2] In this way these

---

[2] An interesting example of this is to be found in the neumic notation of Tibetan chant (see Kaufmann 1967), in which a single curvilinear neume might indicate changes in pitch, duration and timbre. See Figure 2.2a.

Mayan hieroglyphs   Ancient Egyptian hieroglyphs

Khitan characters, from ⑩ China   Ancient Egyptian Hieratic (curvilinear hieroglyphs)

Ideograms

Hebrew syllabary: there are no vowels

ア	イ	ウ	エ	オ	カ	キ	ク	ケ	コ
a	i	u	e	o	ka	ki	ku	ke	ko
サ	シ	ス	セ	ソ	タ	チ	ツ	テ	ト
sa	shi	su	se	so	ta	chi	tsu	te	to
ナ	ニ	ヌ	ネ	ノ	ハ	ヒ	フ	ヘ	ホ
na	ni	nu	ne	no	ha	hi	hu	he	ho
マ	ミ	ム	メ	モ	ヤ	イ	ユ	エ	ヨ
ma	mi	mu	me	mo	ya	i	yu	e	yo
ラ	リ	ル	レ	ロ	ワ	ヰ	ウ	ヱ	ヲ
ra	ri	ru	re	ro	wa	i	u	e	o
ガ	ギ	グ	ゲ	ゴ	ザ	ジ	ズ	ゼ	ゾ
ga	gi	gu	ge	go	za	ji	zu	ze	zo
ダ	ヂ	ヅ	デ	ド	バ	ビ	ブ	ベ	ボ
da	ji	zu	de	do	ba	bi	bu	be	bo
パ	ピ	プ	ペ	ポ	ン				
pa	pi	pu	pe	po	vu	n			

Japanese Katakana script

Syllabaries

A	B	C	D	E	F	G	H	I	J	K	L	M	N	O	P	Q	R	S	T	U	V	W	X	Y	Z
a	b	c	d	e	f	g	h	i	j	k	l	m	n	o	p	q	r	s	t	u	v	w	x	y	z

А	Б	В	Г	Д	Е	Ё	Ж	З	И	Й	К	Л	М	Н	О	П	Р	С	Т	У	Ф	Х	Ц	Ч	Ш	Щ	Ъ	Ы	Ь	Э	Ю	Я
а	б	в	г	д	е	ё	ж	з	и	й	к	л	м	н	о	п	р	с	т	у	ф	х	ц	ч	ш	щ	ъ	ы	ь	э	ю	я

Alphabets

Figure 2.1   Forms of script.

first notation procedures tended to stabilise, if not to atrophy, the pre-existing ideological and musical praxes. A more significant breakthrough occurs with the emergence of analytic notation systems (see Figures 2.2b and 2.2c). Here the verbal or musical praxis is analysed into constituent elements which are notated, and the notations combined to form the meaningful or characteristic units of verbal or musical praxis. In terms of language, the earliest examples were afforded by the syllabary, as in Hebrew, where constituent, but meaningless, syllables are assigned separate written signs, and these strung together to form the combined sounds of meaningful words and utterances. However, the most significant form of analytic notation for language was the alphabet, probably invented in the Middle East but taken up by the Greeks as the foundation of the first literate, critical culture.[3] The alphabet takes the principle of the syllabary one stage further, notating the (idealised) sound-constituents of the syllables themselves, and in so doing achieving such a considerable economy of means — for example 26 letters in the English version of the Roman alphabet as compared to tens of thousands of Chinese ideograms — that universal literacy became a practical possibility for the first time (see Figure 2.1).

Particularly in relation to the further development of ideas in this book, it is important to bear in mind that even in almost entirely phonetic languages, like Finnish, there is not a one-to-one correspondence between the spoken sound-object and the notation of it. The distinction we have made earlier between the sequence of combinatorial sound-units in speech and the use of inflection, tone of voice, etc. in the conveying of meaning is only one level at which this comment is true. This distinction has been raised as an issue within the sphere of linguistics. The original theorists of language seem to have been committed to the discrete/combinatorial view of the subject, but the conflict between 'discreteness' and 'gradience' is now an issue. At a deeper level, computer analyses of the sounds of speech show that the individual sound constituents (phonemes) are not spliced onto each other in a way one might achieve in an editing studio but in most cases elide into one another very rapidly in the course of the speech-act. Even more fundamental, as will be discussed later, many consonants are characterised by their morphology — the way in which they change form — rather than by their spectrum (their particular frequency or formant characteristics). All this relates very strongly to what I shall be saying about the architecture of music.

The ideogram-writer had attempted to write down what was meant by the speaker in terms of the ideograms which were notations of

---

[3] A fuller discussion of these issues is to be found in Goody and Watt (1963).

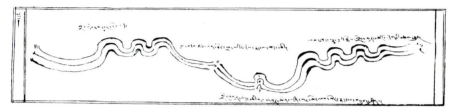

Figure 2.2a Tibetan neumes.

Figure 2.2b 10th century European neumes.

Figure 2.2c Modern European analytic notation.

conventionalised and traditional ideas; by the intrinsic nature of the system, novel ideas were extremely unlikely to be recorded, even if they did arise in speech-discourse. With the alphabet, however, the notation of the constituent *sounds* of language made possible the recording of what was actually *said* and hence made possible the recording of conflicting statements and the emergence of the critical tradition (see Goody and Watt 1963). Whilst this freed language from the domination of the tradition-bound ideas of a tiny elite of priest-scribes, it vastly expanded the spread and domination of writing as a vehicle for mediating and explaining human experience, and hence led to the devaluation by default of all non-verbal modes of action and communication and all non-notatable aspects of discourse — the ultimate triumph of a newly-expanded secular scribehood.

The effect of analytic notation of music in the context of a writing-dominated world was much more fundamental. Arising only in Western Europe, it developed considerably later than alphabetic writing. The fundamental thesis of this system is that music is ultimately reducible to a small, finite number of elementary constituents with a finite number of 'parameters', out of which all sounds possibly required in musical praxis can be notated by combination. *It must be noted from the outset that this finitistic thesis is a requirement of notation rather than fundamentally necessary to conceivable musics.* For a notation procedure to be of any use it must use only a manageable (small) number of constituents which are then permuted; notation of the continuum is necessarily approximate. This is the same problem we have met with verbal categorisation of the internal experiential state (and also in the discreteness/gradience issue) and is very important in relation to my discussion of gesture.

The two features of sound used in tenth century Western musical practice which appeared most accessible to analytic musical notation were pitch-level and rhythm. Timbre was not tackled in this way, up until the twentieth century being limited by the available instrument technology; the continuum of possible dynamic levels has never been remotely accurately categorised, despite attempts to give it a notational rationale in some integral serial composition; while dynamic balance — remaining largely a matter of unspoken convention — and acoustics — usually the accident of performance location — have only come under accurate control with the advent of electronic sound-recording techniques.

However, even pitch and rhythm could only be captured in a very particular way, determined by the exigencies of analytic notation itself. Thus, whereas aural rhythm takes place against the silent backdrop of somatic rhythm, enabling the aural musician to indulge in the most intricate articulations of time, notated rhythm is limited by the problem of notational economy. We can divide time infinitely and in performance can judge directly the effectiveness of the most subtle placements of sounds. But analytic notation is a finitistic procedure. We must be able to count the divisions in order to write them down — but not necessarily in order to judge aurally what is effective. Hence, analytically notated music is bound within the limitations of summative rhythm (see Figure 2.3).

Similarly, discrete fixed pitches are idealisations of acoustic reality. In practice there are only sounds in their infinite variety of possible frequency, spectrum, timbre, dynamic-envelope, and change (dynamic morphology) and combinations of all these. Consider the irreducible infinitude of tones of voice. But the infinite is not simply notatable. What notation demands is a finite set of pitch-levels which we can permute and combine. The refinement of instrument technology attempts to impose this discrete permutational rationality upon the very production of sounds, and our ears learn to approximate our acoustic experience to the discrete steps of our imposed logic.

Lattice and continuum; on instrumental streaming

We are now in a position to describe the concept of a *lattice* and its bearing on conventional music theory. For anyone who has ever heard a pitch portamento or a tempo accelerando, both pitch and tempo can take on an infinitude of possible values and may vary continuously over this continuum. Notation, however, imposes a finite state logic upon the two domains. The result is that music, at least as seen in the score, appears to take place on a two-dimensional lattice (see Figure 2.4a). Two things should be said about this lattice formulation. First of all it is our conception of what constitutes a valid musical object which forces 'musical sounds' onto this lattice; secondly, despite our intentions, the lattice only remains an approximate representation of what takes place in actual sound experience (except in the extremely controlled conditions of a synthesis studio).

The technology of instrument design underlines and reinforces this lattice conception of musical architecture. First of all, on keyed, holed or fretted instruments, the discrete logic of the pitch lattice is imposed on the production mechanism of sound-objects. Secondly, the concept of the instrument itself further expands the lattice notion. Conceptually, at least, an instrument is a source of stable timbre, but variable pitch. The essential function of an instrument is to hold timbre stable and to articulate the pitch parameter. This conception contributes to the myth of the primacy of pitch (and duration) in musical architecture. The grouping of instruments into families of distinct timbral type and the development of music based upon

Figure 2.3 Summative rhythm: each note value can be expressed as the sum of smaller equal note values.

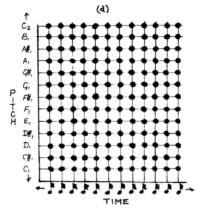

Figure 2.4a   Music on a two-dimensional lattice (schematic representation).

fixed-timbre (or instrumental) streaming develops the lattice one stage further.

Hence music can now be viewed as taking place on a three-dimensional lattice (Figures 2.4b–2.4d). The three dimensions being made up of discrete pitch-levels, discrete durational values, and discrete timbral objects (or instrumental types). In fact, the concept of the instrumental stream is perhaps the most persistent in conventional musical thought — the lattice of both pitch and duration have been challenged by composers working within conventional notation. Even in the classical voltage control studio it was possible to conceive of a musical composition in which a single sound stream evolved, possibly diverged into separate streams which might be separately articulated, might reconverge and continue thus to the end of the piece (see Figure 2.5). The evolving streams within such a piece might be continually changing their timbral characteristics, even though they were continuously connected to the opening event (i.e. the piece need only have one attack — at its opening — and therefore in the conventional musical sense contain only one 'note'). The conception of music as consisting of fixed-pitch, fixed-timbre entities called 'notes' is extremely persistent.[4] It even imposes conceptual limitations upon the design of digital musical instruments (where such traditional conceptions are no longer necessary). Computer music machines such as the Fairlight and Synclavier with their keyboard input and instrument definition, and even the more general Music 11 program, carry with them into the digital

---

[4] See the quote from Lejaren Hiller in Chapter 1 (Hiller 1981: 7).

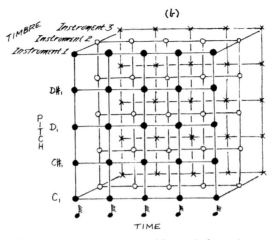

Figure 2.4b   Music on a three-dimensional lattice (schematic representation).

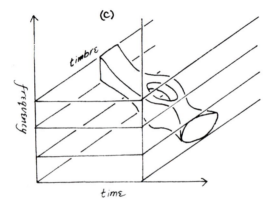

Figure 2.4c   A complex sound-object moving in the continuum (schematic representation).

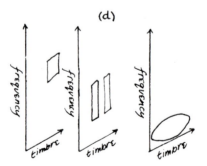

Figure 2.4d   Frequency/timbre cross-section of sound at start, mid-point and end.

Figure 2.5 Evolving timbre-stream composition (schematic representation).

world the concept of instrumental streaming from conventional musical practice.[5] It is of course possible to subvert the various systems but it is a struggle against the design concepts of the instrument or software.

We can, however, perceive important distinctions within lattice-based musical conventions. The major distinction — though this is usually a matter of degree — is between music 'hung around' a lattice and music developed 'on' the lattice. Examples 2.1, 2.2, 2.3 and 2.4 illustrate Japanese *joruri* singing (*gidayu* style used as part of the *bunraku* (puppet) and *kabuki* theatres), North Indian singing, jazz singing and part of a Haydn mass. In certain musical cultures, the pitch lattice (which might also be referred to as a *harmonic* field so long as we do not connect this with Western harmonic thinking) may be regarded as a framework around which the music takes place, thus in the example of *joruri* singing, the pitch set (or rather the pitches which can be identified as being on a lattice) is fairly limited and does not change its general character. However, the focus of attention of the performer (and of the listener) is heavily weighted towards aspects of the sound articulation which cannot be related directly to the lattice. Thus there is a complex articulation of portamento structures leading onto or away from the lattice pitches, the control of articulation of vibrato (frequency modulation) — in Western art music vibrato is usually a relatively constant parameter of a particular type of vocal production rather than a parameter which one articulates through time — and focusing on the evolution of timbre within individual events (particularly the development of sub-harmonic colouration). These aspects of musical articulation are carried over into the more speech-like sections of *gidayu* style presentation. An attempt to capture the essence of this music in conventional Western notation would clearly fail miserably.

In North Indian music concepts of pitch (or more precisely pitch on lattices), as opposed to the kind of subtle portamento articulation found in

---

[5] This situation has only partly been alleviated in the years since this was written and was certainly reinforced by the Midi protocol, relatively new at the time of writing (*Ed.*).

the Japanese example, are more highly developed, although musical development still takes place over a fixed pitch-set (harmonic field). Even here, however, we find the use of subtle sliding inflections onto and away from the lattice pitches and the internal articulation of the sound-objects which make up the ululation-based runs. Again, these cannot be approximated by conventional Western notation procedures but are clearly a fundamental aspect of the musical structure. Jazz is clearly much more strongly influenced by the lattice-based approach of Western harmony. Yet typical jazz vocal and wind instrument production is very heavily concerned with the internal articulation of sound-objects including sliding ornamentations and careful control of vibrato and other timbral modulations of the sound. All these features can now be clearly described — they are not mysterious in any way — but again would be lost in conventional Western notation.

Finally, the example from Haydn illustrates what happens to vocal production when musical conception is focused upon the lattice itself. Vocal production becomes conventionalised and aims at an idealised type of production focusing on the lattice pitches. Idiosyncratic developments of timbral and pitch articulation, which serve to identify and project particular jazz singers, for example, are to be rejected in favour of a universally stereotyped *bel canto* production. Vibrato is no longer a parameter for musical articulation but a relatively fixed feature of the required sonority. The latter example typifies music developed on a lattice where development of the parameters of the lattice itself dominate all other types of musical articulation. If we now turn to the instrumental Examples 2.5, 2.6 and 2.7 which are of Japanese shakuhachi playing, a classical chamber work (using wind instruments) and a piece of jazz, we will hear a similar development in the use of wind instruments. In fact, it is the combination of a conception of music focusing on the parameters of the lattice and the developing technology of instrument design going along with this developing conception which leads us away from the multi-dimensionally rich articulation of the shakuhachi towards the timbral uniformity of the present-day Western keyed flute.[6] Despite these developments, however, articulation of the continuum is still present in performance practice. As we have discussed earlier, the articulation of the continuum in intellectual-physiological gesture is transferred directly to the sound-object by the player of a wind instrument. Even in the most rationally developed notated scores,

---

[6] Contemporary instrumental composers have, of course, sought to counteract the stranglehold of technological rationalisation by exploring non-conventional modes of sound production on the Western instrument (flutter-tonguing, key-slapping, whistle-tones etc.).

aspects of performance gesture, often loosely referred to under the term 'interpretation', still have an important bearing on our musical experience. In certain types of music, articulation of the continuum plays a much more significant role as can be discerned by comparing the typical use of the trombone, trumpet and particularly the saxophone in jazz with the typical use of the keyed flute in classical Western music.

In this continuing technological development, the voice and the keyboard may be seen as occupying the two opposite ends of the musical spectrum. Voice, the immediate source of intellectual-physiological gesture, will be seen as an important focal model for music throughout this book. The keyboard on the other hand represents the ultimate rationalisation of a lattice-based view of music. Timbre is fixed; pitches are incapable of any sort of inflection, physiology is only allowed one single point of contact with the sound-object, at the initiation of the note, and thereafter can have no impact on the internal morphology of the sound. This distance can perhaps best be appreciated by comparing the ululated trill articulation of the North Indian vocal music example with the typical trills and turns on a keyboard instrument. Vocal articulations such as trills and turns are semi-unified objects, the apparent pitch-elements of which are bonded by subtle internal portamenti and timbre transitions. On the keyboard instrument the individual notes of the trill or turn are as close as we can possibly approximate to the individual notes on the page. It is interesting and ironic in this respect that the computer, in some senses the ultimately definable and controllable musical instrument, has for the first time begun to reveal to us the subtle inner architecture — the continuum architecture — of sounds.

It is very important to understand that the lattice is a conceptual construct. It is we who have decided to construct our musical architecture on the lattice. Because we do, however, it is very easy to fall into the mental trap of observing the world of sounds as if it divided up neatly on a three-dimensional lattice. Thus for anyone with a conventional musical training — and particularly for those with no studio experience — sound-objects appear to be divisible into three distinct categories of pitch, duration and timbre. This is of course true of most sound-objects appearing in conventional music — they have been constructed on the lattice and are therefore divisible in terms of that lattice. In fact as we proceed we shall see how the conventional (Helmholtzian) view of acoustics tends to fall into the same trap. At this stage we will merely note that lattice notation encourages the following connections:

(1)   instrumental streaming leads us to suppose that timbre is a simple category like frequency;

(2)   focus on pitch leads us to suppose that pitch itself is a simple category (though it is in fact simpler than timbre);

(3)   viewing duration through lattice notation leads some members of the musical community to view Dave Brubeck's excursion into 5/4 metre as a major breakthrough in jazz rhythm (rather than the minor excursion on the lattice which it is), while entirely overlooking the highly articulate development of phrase-structures against the lattice (Charlie Parker) or placement of individual events or groups against the lattice (the essence of 'swing').

Even where it is clear that the lattice is only an approximation to musical reality, notation focuses our attention on the lattice. In the long run, all 'respectable' theory is based on the lattice (see below).

Pitch versus timbre: primary and secondary qualities

In the West, the rationalisation of music on a lattice is taken to its extreme. First from the infinitude of possible pitch levels which could give rise to numerous subtly different musical scales, such as the scales of the ragas of Indian music and probably those of Western medieval pre-notation chant — though this we will never know — a small set of twelve clearly specified pitch-levels is gradually selected. Then partly through the tendency — intrinsic in the notation system and its realisation in the technology of instrument (especially keyboard instrument) design —towards a rational simplicity, a notational economy, the well-tempered scale arrives, permitting a considerable opening up of the field of harmonic inter-relations among a limited set of fixed pitches as Bach and composers through Wagner and Schoenberg were to demonstrate.[7]

In similar ways to alphabetic writing, analytic notation is in many ways a liberating invention. It frees composers from the established norms of a musical tradition and permits him or her to explore new and unheard possibilities. At the same time it is this very malleability of the *notatable*

---

[7] Bach's Art of Fugue, arguably one of the finest achievements of the traditional art music of Europe, illustrates our thesis in an interesting way. Bach confines himself to the notation of pitch and 'summative' rhythm, leaving unspecified dynamics and even timbre (instrumentation), both of which are usually notated (or at least indicated in the score). Although this approach may appear to approximate very closely to the 'abstract' view of music, we would argue that the work is, however, not an illustration of 'rational formalism' as discussed below, as the score notates sets of relations between sound-qualities which are experientially valid (see text), even if the range of possibilities is necessarily restricted by the nature of the notation system itself.

parameters which enables and encourages the one-sided, two-dimensional expansion of musical possibilities. This eventually leads to Boulez's theoretical distinction between primary and secondary qualities in music.[8] The primary qualities are those which have been accurately notated — in a certain limited sense — the secondary qualities those which have not.

There is a striking parallel here with the distinction made by Descartes between primary and secondary qualities of perceived natural phenomena. For Descartes, a phenomenon such as motion which could be given a direct quantitative mathematical description was regarded as primary, whereas qualitative phenomena such as colour were seen as secondary qualities and ultimately reducible to descriptions in terms of primary qualities. Exact mathematical representation, at least in theory, here plays the same role as accurate score-notation plays in Boulezian music theory. An interesting sidelight on this parallel is thrown up by the recent development of 'catastrophe theory' which will be discussed more fully below. Very briefly, physicists have tended to confine themselves to a study of equilibrium situations where in most cases precise quantitative mathematical formulation of the problem is possible. Note that most musical objects may be considered as examples of stable equilibria (for example after the initiation of a flute tone, a stable resonance is set up within the body of the instrument which constitutes the sound-object which we hear). Recently, however, attention has been focused on the study of more complex regimes whose stability may vary along with small changes in the parameters which define the situation. The study of such situations has established the first essentially qualitative branch of mathematics — differential topology. This branch of mathematics may give us some insight into the structure of the continuum and therefore has a bearing on the study of sound-objects in the continuum that we are pursuing in this book. In a similar way, the Helmholtzian theory of timbre may be seen as an attempt to reduce the qualitative (timbre) to the quantitative (frequency) which has in fact proved untenable (see Helmholtz (1954 originally 1877)).

In its constant search for new modes of expression, the Western classical music tradition was, however, constrained by its very concentration upon relationships of a limited set of thus notatable 'pitches' to extend the notatable field of harmonic relationships to the limit. The final step into a twelve-tone and thence 'integral' serial technique, rather than being a liberation from this restricted-set tonality, should be seen in historical perspective as the final capitulation to the finitistic permutational dictates of

---

[8] See the quotation in Chapter 1 (Boulez 1971: 37).

a rationalised analytic notation system. Within this same tradition, however, composers have made attempts to abandon the lattice-dominated aesthetic.

Consider now Examples 2.8, 2.9, 2.10 and 2.11. In Example 2.8, from the Webern *Symphonie*, we hear the apotheosis of the rational extrapolation of lattice aesthetics. In Example 2.9, from Penderecki's *Polymorphia*, we have a fairly typical example of this composer's approach to composing music which no longer conforms to the traditional lattice. In particular, he uses thick groupings of pitches only a quarter-tone apart (thus destroying the twelve-note chromatic lattice) and also textural aggregates of sounds with no, or ambiguous, pitch content. The sonorities are very striking, but the overall architecture does not seem so strong. The music seems to develop monophonically and tends to fall into long blocks of a particular sonority. We can say that the composer has broken free quite successfully from the domination of the lattice but as yet no strong and sufficiently articulate means of organising the new material has emerged.

In Example 2.10, from the end of Xenakis' *Pithoprakta*, we have a more interesting example of non-lattice-based musical organisation. The written score for this piece is superficially impenetrable, but if we sketch out the various notated pitch glissandi on a sheet of graph paper in which pitch and time form the axes the architecture of this particular section is quickly revealed (see Figure 2.6). Xenakis has grouped individual short glissandi on the string instruments into larger arching glissandi (glissandi of glissandi!).[9] At the same time the sounds are grouped into three contrasting string sonorities and the three resulting timbre streams arch up and down independently. In this way a pitch-based counterpoint of timbre streams is created which in no sense depends on the typical pitch lattice of conventional music. At the end of the section, as will be seen clearly from the figure, the glissandi of glissandi thicken out and unfold into a sustained chord, a wonderful process of pitched evolution which has no real parallel in typical lattice aesthetics. Although the processes of musical organisation here seem more articulate and evolved than in the Penderecki example, they have what Pierre Schaeffer has described as an architectural feel, that is to say that the gestural unfolding of events is quite slow and controlled. There is as yet not a moment-to-moment feeling for the gestural development of musical form. This is partly due to the essentially cumbersome nature of the orchestra when it comes to attempting to define non-lattice structures. Inevitably such structures must be constructed from individual elements which are notated on the lattice or in relation to the lattice and it becomes difficult to notate a

---

[9] Figure 2.6 is from Trevor Wishart's PhD Thesis (University of York, UK 1973).

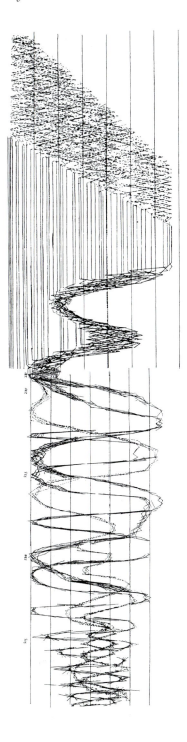

Figure 2.6 Glissandi of glissandi in Iannis Xenakis's *Pithoprakta*.

rapidly evolving event. Such events with rapidly involving internal morphologies are much more easily accessible in the electro-acoustic studio and it is here where the problem of their organisation begins to confront traditional musical aesthetics.

Then finally in this group, Example 2.11, from Stockhausen's *Carré*, illustrates yet another attempt to deal with the internal morphology of sound-objects. Stockhausen's piece is largely concerned with relatively sustained events in which there is internal motion, for example the slow glissandoing of trombones and voices in the opening moments. The larger-scale relationship between these individually articulated 'moments' is still governed by serial permutational criteria which, in my view, are an outgrowth of lattice-oriented thinking, and not on a gestural interaction between the individual sound-events which would generate a truly dynamic non-lattice-based musical form.

It is interesting in this respect that a composer like Boulez, who seems so adamantly committed to a lattice-based view of musical aesthetics produces music which is, from the listener's point of view, much more clearly gesturally articulate. In Example 2.12 we may consider a section from *Don* (from *Pli selon Pli*). The pitch and durational characteristics of this section are no doubt exceedingly carefully worked out, but in practice what one hears is its gestural structure. The music is dominated by sustained but hovering — and by implication pregnant — events. The initial loud attack and the mode of sustainment suggest that the events will burst forth into something else. This feeling is underlined both by the fact that separate events enter on different, though related, harmonic fields and particularly by the brass event, which, after its initial attack, begins to die away and then crescendos. This emergence verifies the pregnancy of the other (sustained) gestures. I will not attempt to give a more detailed gestural analysis of this particular passage here, but even this much serves to underline the significance of musical gesture, even where a lattice-based aesthetic appears to dominate through the score.

Musical values distorted; the emergence of formalism

As we have mentioned previously analytic notation is in many ways a liberating phenomenon; it permits us to explore new possibilities for musical expression. Using it we may, but need not, discover new modes of musical experience. However, this begs the central question of what defines a musical experience and this very concept has been fundamentally twisted by the impact of musical notation itself, gradually forcing music to kow-tow to the verbally definable. In fact, with the increasing domination of notation, there has been a move towards Platonic idealism in our conception of what music is. In the most extreme cases, music is viewed as an essentially abstract phenomenon and the sound experience of essentially secondary importance. More commonly the score is seen as normative on the musical experience.

The split in conception between what are seen as primary and secondary aspects of musical organisation leads to a split between composer and performer, between composition and interpretation and the gradual devaluation of non-notatable formations. This development leads directly to the attitudes expressed by Boulez and to the intellectual devaluation of forms of music (such as jazz improvisation) where non-notatable aspects of musical form have greater importance than in conventional classical music. At the same time, the spatialisation of the time-experience which takes place when musical time is transferred to the flat surface of the score leads to the emergence of musical formalism and to a kind of musical composition which is entirely divorced from any relationship to intuitive gestural experience.

What takes place is not merely a focusing of our *perception* upon the notatable and the consequent feedback upon our musical praxis, but a reorientation of our conception of music. Whereas previously verbal discourse had little of permanence to grasp onto in music except the very continuity and unity of established practice, which it could reinforce and stabilise by verbal decree, now musical process appeared to reveal itself concretely in the form of musical scores. A fleeting succession of musical experiences in time appeared to be captured in a continuously present spatial representation which could be studied at any time, at any speed and in any order. Just as the immediate dialectic of speech had been fundamentally subverted and devalued by the permanent monologues of the written word, so an intuitive and unverbalisable knowledge of music as an immediate dialectic of musical action and the fleeting, inscrutable musical experience was to be fundamentally challenged by the permanence and scrutability of the score. Permanently available and amenable to rationalistic verbal explication the score rapidly usurps the sound experience of music as the focus of verbal attention and becomes the keystone of an eminently verbalisable conception of what 'music' is.

The most obvious consequence of the discovery of analytic notation is the emergence of the *composer*, who is able to challenge and expand existing musical praxis through creating notations of novel musical activities, his original scores. The novel split which gradually emerges between composer and performer, between a score and its 'interpretation' is the concrete realisation in music praxis of the perceptual focusing upon notatable 'parameters'.

Interpretation, still a semi-intuitive discipline, remains of great importance in the education of the musical performer, who remains somewhat outside the sphere of intellectual respectability. For the music scholar, however, raised in primarily verbally-based institutions, especially the new European 'university', the focus of attention is on that musical syntax which can be discovered *in the score*. At the same time, the composer, whose musical tools are the notations at his disposal, will clearly tend to develop a musical syntax based on the organisation of these notatables. Hence, whilst ever the musical scholar concerns himself with notation-composed works, there will be a congruence of attention upon analytically notatable syntax, as scholar and composer have the same vested interest in notatability. The concatenation of scribal domination, compositional necessity and the limitations of analytic notation, however, elevate the organisation of a certain limited range of musical variables to the status of 'music' as such and leads to an inevitable clash of values when the classically trained musician comes into contact with music from an alien tradition.

We have already listened to and discussed music from the Japanese *joruri* tradition and from jazz, musics which to some extent develop their form outside the notatable lattice. A more radical example of such a music can be found in *free improvisation*. In Example 2.13 (free improvisation) we are faced with a musical experience where reference to the notational lattice is completely useless. The reaction of classically trained musicians to free improvisation, often on the basis of limited experience, can be quite negative. In fact the lack of explicit criteria in the field of free improvisation does lend itself to exploitation by mediocre performers. 'Spontaneity' is taken by some to mean self-indulgence, arbitrariness or whimsicality and in a typical bad performance, the participants ignore each other for most of the time, except at points where they all get louder and then (hopefully) all get quieter again. In a performance, however, where the participants have absorbed themselves in the technique of this kind of improvisation and freed themselves from conventional response and musical clichés, what we hear is a rapid and highly articulate gestural interaction between the performers. The ebb and flow of musical tension can be exceedingly rapid and the music highly articulate in its impact. Because of its essentially highly gestural basis, free improvisation need not confine itself to the use of conventional sound sources. Any sound-producing object may be turned to musical advantage[10] — an interesting parallel with *musique concrète*. The use

---

[10] Such as paper bags, soft trumpets (Martin Mayes, Trevor Wishart), amplified springs (Hugh Davies), or long pieces of elastic (Paul Burwell) (see discography).

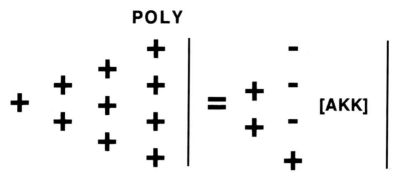

Figure 2.7 An example of 'plus/minus' notation (after Stockhausen).

of simple and non-prestructured sound-sources allows, in fact demands, strong gestural input from the performer. Experience from the free-improvisation forum can be extended into the electro-acoustic studio, as is shown by Example 2.14 from my own *Anna's Magic Garden* where the use of sounds of a piece of elastic is extended by simple *musique concrète* techniques.

Free improvisers in general make no attempt to notate the gestural structures and interactions which underlie their musical activity. Stockhausen, during his short digression into the sphere of improvised music, did attempt to develop some kind of simple notation to give form to otherwise freely-improvised music pieces. The '+/-' notation of this period (see Figure 2.7)[11] is an interesting early attempt to impose some sort of compositional rationale upon this basically intuitive discipline. Its simplicity and rationality meant, however, that not very much of what actually happens in the musical unfolding is really captured in the score and in some ways it seems to function more as an enabling device for permutational procedures to be imposed at least on the notations if not on the actual musical experience!

I shall have much to say about the sphere of electro-acoustic music elsewhere in this book, but in this particular context it is interesting to note the relative failure of electro-acoustic music to achieve academic respectability. This can to some extent be put down to the fact that no adequate notation exists for it — in fact many composers have actively avoided developing notational parallels to their musical events. But scholars like to see the music! The arrival of vast reams of computer print-out will

---

[11] For an explanation of Stockhausen's '+/-' notation system and some examples of its application see the introduction to the score of *Spiral* (Universal Edition).

no doubt put an end to this lacuna. Even the skills of the professional mixing engineer in achieving balance and artificial acoustic in the typical rock recording would not normally be considered 'musical' by the traditionally trained musical scholar, though composers who have worked in the electro-acoustic studio have come to see this rather differently.

A further, somewhat negative effect of the focus on lattice aesthetics is the destruction of the lively non-lattice aspects of various folk music cultures by concerned composers anxious to preserve these traditions in conventionally scored arrangements. In the extreme case, the combination of pitch, rhythm and timbre inflection in jazz and rock music is seen as lascivious, sexually suggestive and ultimately a threat to social order. As we can now see, this is more than a mere rejection of that which falls outside the clearly-definable limits of a long-established notation (perception and conception) procedure with its verbal-explicability and hence its social controllability. In a narrow sense, this attitude is correct, for musical experience, even where apparently constrained by clearly explicable notation-based procedures, is ultimately irreducible to verbalisations and hence beyond any direct social control.

The most radical impact of analytic notation on musical praxis is to transfer the musical structure out of the uni-directional continuum of experiential time, in which the musical dialectic takes place and in which musical gestures unfold, into the spatialised, perfectly reversible (Newtonian) time of the printed page.[12] In sound, the musical experience begins at the beginning and must be taken in the irreversible order and at the rate at which it comes to the listener. Furthermore, our experience of what arrives later is modified by our (perhaps inaccurate) memories of what has passed and, in this sense, there can never be a clear-cut 'recapitulation'; everything is modified by the context of what went before. In the score, however, the whole span of the music appears to exist in a timeless, spatialised, present. We may peruse its contents at any rate, in any order. In this way we may be able to see relationships, for example of recapitulation, which, however, after repeated and thorough aural experience of the music as sound we may never be able to hear. Can we thus treat such a recapitulation as an element of *musical structure*? This, of course, begs the central question of what constitutes music, what we experience in the sounds, or what we might theoretically appreciate of the score through the sounds, if our aural selectivity were more finely developed.

---

[12] I am indebted to Jan Steele for the following line of argument concerning the problem of musical retrogrades.

The best example of the split between a view of music based in uni-directional experiential time, and one based on spatial reversibility of time as represented in the score, is found in the concept of the *retrograde* as found in serial music, and also in some medieval and renaissance polyphony. Here the notational view is that by reversing the order of a group of notatable pitches we arrive at a pitch-set which is merely a derived form of the original. In the immediately present and spatially reversible time of the printed page the relationship of the two sets may be abundantly visually clear, but in the uni-directional and memory-dependent time of musical experience, considerable aural retentivity and the performance of a rapid feat of mental inversion is necessary to grasp this relationship. This may be a simple matter if the sequence of pitches is quite short or very fast. It is also true that if we conceive of the pitch set as a harmonic field the relationship between the two sets may be easier to grasp. With long and complex structures, however, the difference in perception between the sound experience in time and the visual scanning of the score is extremely marked. When we consider extended use of retrograde or cancrizans form, such as the perfect arch-form of *Der Mondfleck* from Schoenberg's *Pierrot Lunaire*, where the entire movement runs in reverse order of pitches and durations from the centre point — except, to complicate matters, the voice and piano, the latter having an elaborate fugato at the same time! — we must declare that experiential structure has been sacrificed to notational 'conceptual art'. The retrograde of a 'duration series' as used in 'integral serial' composition, is even more experientially problematic. All this then begs the question. What *is* music? The time-based experience in sound? Or an essentially abstract entity existing outside time, a Platonic conception of music?

Thus, just as the permanence of the written word 'table' appeared to Plato to project something more permanent and more 'real' than the many experienced tables of a concrete reality, so, to the Western musical scholar, musical notation can appear to project something more permanent and more 'real' than the direct, but fleeting, experiences of the sound of a musical performance. Music may hence be regarded as a phenomenon which transcends immediate sense-experience. With the accompanying dominance of composed music, 'music' and its 'interpretation' can hence be distinguished from one another and notatable syntax, discussible in a verbal space divorced from direct sense-experience, elevated to the position of *musical syntax* itself.

Schoenberg, the originator of the serial method, was clearly not unaware of the notational ideal/experiential dichotomy we have discussed. In actual practice the 'harmonic style' of his later serial works is not greatly dissimilar to that of his pre-serial 'expressionist' works, where the harmonic tensions characteristic of tonal music can still be felt even though traditional tonal progressions have disappeared. Having abandoned tonality as a basis it would seem that Schoenberg still felt the need to rely on an intuitive feel for harmonic relationships, and this approach is characteristic of his musical language with or without serialism. This fact is underlined by the rejection of Schoenberg's 'backward-looking' approach by proponents of the post-Webern school of serial (and integral serial) composition.

The fundamental conflict between the two views of music is in fact most clearly expressed in the symbology of Schoenberg's serial opera *Moses and Aaron*. The conflict between Moses' view of God as the all-pervasive, yet ultimately intangible, *idea* and Aaron's desire to relate God to *tangible experience*, is represented at a surface level by a verbal/musical dichotomy — Moses' part is confined to heightened speech (*Sprechstimme*), while Aaron sings expressive melodic lines — and at a deeper level by a notational/experiential dichotomy — the tone-row is all-pervasive in the score as the structural material out of which the opera is built but is not generally audible as such.

The second act (the end of the opera as it exists) ends with a dramatic duologue in which Moses (the speaker) holding the tablets of the written law, confronts Aaron (the singer) and finally breaks the tablets declaring "0 Wort, du Wort, das mir fehlt" ("Oh word, you word, which has failed me"). In the archetypal ideology of Schoenberg's biographer,

> *[…] in contrast to Moses the thinking character who clings to eternity, metaphysics and* real *values, Aaron is a materialist of everyday life* who is impressed by the glitter of gold and the successes of the moment.
> (Stuckenschmidt 1959: 151, my emphasis)

However, the fact that Schoenberg felt unable to write the third act of the opera, in which Moses' view triumphs has, in the light of the present discussion, far-reaching significance for an understanding of contemporary avant-garde music.

Where concrete musical relationships — at least originally based on their experiential success — are represented by their notations in the score, and study and conception focuses upon this structure, divorced from the experiential immediacy of the sound itself, these relationships, as *rediscovered* in the score, may be mistaken for *conventional* relationships. In other words, what to direct gestural experience may appear as a *necessary* relationship — in that it is only through that particular musical structure that a successful communication of the kind intended can take place — can come to appear in the score as merely *arbitrary* permutations of 'notes' and 'time-values'. On the timeless flat surface of the score the visual-spatial relationships of the notes (used to represent real time) may be changed at will to produce arbitrarily arrived-at visual-spatial structures, all having equal validity in visual space, but not necessarily so in experiential time.

Once, however, we demand that music be heard in terms of the score, then it is no longer experiential success which justifies notational visual-spatial arrangements, but notational arrangements become their own justification. Hence, 'musical form' may become freed from any restriction of direct experiential success in our original terms. This leads ultimately to a rational formalism in music. The composer establishes certain visual relationships between entities in his notation, the musical scholar is trained to listen for these relationships, he hears them and a successful 'musical' communication is declared to have taken place.

This beautifully closed rationalist view of music is the ultimate in scribal sophistication, it is complete and completely unassailable in its own terms. Music is hence completely socially definable and musical success may almost be measured with a slide rule. How much more tidy and convenient such a norm-adherent view of music than one bringing in the messy business of inter-personal, yet unverbalisable, gestural dialectics. The rationalist view of music fits ideally into a technocratic age with its linguistic and positivist ideologies. What we cannot talk about we cannot know, only that which we can talk about is real — so much for music!

Thus, ultimately, the score becomes its own rationale. It is what it is, and there is nothing more to say about it. The composer cannot be in error.[13] We see this spatial score-based focus in preoccupations with such two-dimensional visual forms as the golden section in analytical articles, but it is *permutationalism* which is the ultimate notation-abstracted procedure. Because musical notation presents music to us outside of time in an essentially two-dimensional scannable score, it does not seem immediately unreasonable to extract various parameters of the sound and arrange these into various other patterns. The most thorough-going way of going about this is the technique of the permutation of parameters as used in much serial composition. The technique of permuting objects is very general and is in fact a principle of ordering which does *not* relate to the materials being permuted directly. We may permute pitches, dynamic levels or, for that matter, sizes of shoes, using exactly the same criteria. Applications of the principle can be very sophisticated, based upon analysis of the nature of sound-objects. The principle problem from our point of view is that being an outside-time procedure, there is no reason why the resulting

---

[13] Although of course, not all composers, even today, accept this absurd view! There are often other criteria involved in composition, even where composers refuse, in a strictly positivist way, to talk about them.

sequences of sounds should have any dynamism. The parameters, separated through a lattice-based conception of musical structure, cease to have any meaningful linkage or gestural continuity and serve merely as evidence that the permutational procedure has taken place. This abstract architecture, therefore, reduces all objects which it touches to the same rather empty non-dynamic experience. There is no rationale beyond the arrangement of the bricks; the nature of the bricks becomes irrelevant so long as they fit into the pattern. The committed permutationalist is the musical (or artistic) equivalent of the linguistic philosopher. He or she cannot understand that there is a problem inherent in this approach.

A much more sophisticated and satisfactory approach can be seen in the work of Brian Ferneyhough. Ferneyhough is clearly (from my listening to the music) concerned with musical gesture and in a piece such as his *Second String Quartet* the interaction of musical gestures between the four players is of primary importance in our apprehension of the music. In works for a greater number of performers, however, (such as *Time and Motion Study III* for sixteen amplified voices) the sheer density of musical gestures leads to a process of self-cancellation. The individual details of each part are extremely interesting but an overall sense of direction is lost in the welter of interaction. In 1981 I had the pleasure of meeting Brian Ferneyhough over dinner in Paris and the ensuing conversation may serve as an interesting footnote to our discussions of idealism and materialism in the conception of music. Ferneyhough and myself both declared that we were anarchists but on further discussion it transpired that our conceptions of anarchism could not have been more different. Ferneyhough's view was that he could take the strongest stand against the system by not voting. In this way he symbolically denied the relevance of the system and therefore in some way negated it. My more pragmatic view was that it was important to vote in order to keep out the worst possible contender. These conflicting idealist and materialist views of anarchist action had an interesting parallel in our discussions about musical structure. Ferneyhough noted that a particular passage in one of his works sounded pretty well aleatoric and that this was interesting because it was the result of a multi-layered process of complex compositional decisions. He seemed to be saying that the methodology of composition was the principle object, not the effect on the listener. The composition is more like a document which evidences the composer's methodology and it is evident in the particular case under discussion that the methodology will only become apparent through detached analytical study of the document, not directly through the effect of the music. Thus *a priori* design, not directed pragmatically to some practical sonorous end, has become the principal focus of the composer's interest. The concept of musical experience has been redefined as rediscovering the composer's methodology through the musical experience (or rather through the score) rather than feeling the gestural structure in time of the music in the listening experience, and hence directly understanding, through the gestural experience, the composer's design.

For me, on the other hand, a musical experience which appears aleatoric *is* aleatoric. The experience that the listener has *is* the music and the composer's methodology, no matter how rational it may be, is a heuristic device realising the source of that experience in sound. In Ferneyhough's case it would seem that music is an idealist object defined essentially by the composer's intention (just as the political stance is defined by the intention of the act of not voting). In my case, music is a material entity which is socially defined and judged by its results (similarly the political act must be an action taken in the world that will be judged by its success there). This being said, one must not confuse materialism with populism, but that is the subject of another essay and I will not pursue it here.

A fundamental thesis of this book is that, in order to understand and control the musical continuum, we will have to appeal to time-based notions like gesture and not only at the level of the individual musical event. Although a formalist, permutationalist approach can be applied to literally anything, including a particular classification of gestural types, we cannot ultimately learn anything from it because it is not open to any experiential verification (except in the tautologous sense that it evidences the permutations made). What I am searching for in this book are criteria for composing music with non-lattice materials which 'work' in some experientially verifiable sense that is not merely circular.

A final comment: it is clear that the separation of notation and actuality is of great value for the purposes of scholarship, even though it does lead to a distortion of our understanding of the object of study. The advent of digital recording and analysis of sound opens up a wonderful new opportunity for such scholarship. In one sense it can be very negative as this is a heaven-sent opportunity for formalism to run riot with a new ultra-powerful permutational tool. To date, however, computer technology seems to have been used in a much more sensitive way in the exploration and understanding of the inner details of sound architecture. The preliminary results of this exploration have been a source of inspiration for this particular book and the control which the computer will give us over this inner architecture makes the control of the details of gestural structure a compositional possibility for the first time. With musical sensitivity we may allow the computer to do the number-crunching and with real-time, or at least acoustic, feedback we can begin to make more refined aesthetic decisions about the gestural structure of sound on its most refined levels.

Chapter 3

PYTHAGORAS, FOURIER, HELMHOLTZ:
TOWARDS A PHENOMENOLOGY OF SOUND

Pythagoras, that grave and venerable personage, reproved all judgement of Musick which is by the eare, for he said that the intelligence and vertue thereof was verie subtile and slender, and therefore he judged thereof, not by hearing, but by proportionall harmonie: and he thought it sufficient to proceed as farre as to Diapason, and there to stay the knowledge of Musick. [Plutarch][1]

Pythagoras: stable vibrations and the *Harmony of the Spheres*

The preceding chapter sought to account for the ideology of musical praxis which sees pitch and duration as primary musical qualities, timbre as a distinct and secondary musical quality and takes instrumental streaming and the generation of music on a lattice for granted. The philosophy of the musical practice based upon establishing elementary relationships between stable vibrating systems has a very ancient and respectable pedigree. Pythagoras himself is believed to have first noted the fact that there is a simple relationship between the lengths of vibrating strings and the perceived quality of musical consonance between them. Given two strings[2] of the same material at constant tension then if one is stopped exactly half-way along its length it will produce a note sounding one octave above the other string (which is not stopped). The octave itself is qualitatively perceived to be the most stable or consonant of music intervals. With a length ratio of 3:2 the musical interval of a fifth is perceived which is also very stable and consonant. In general, the relative consonance of an interval is seen to be directly relatable to the simplicity of the ratio of lengths of the strings (or columns of air) which produce it (see Figure 3.1). This was not only the first important contribution to music theory but also had a significant role to play in the development of a scientific view of the world. It was the first clear demonstration that qualitative aspects of nature

---

[1] The author can no longer recall where he came upon this quaint translation into Elizabethan English (*Ed.*).

[2] The argument applies equally well to the lengths of columns of air.

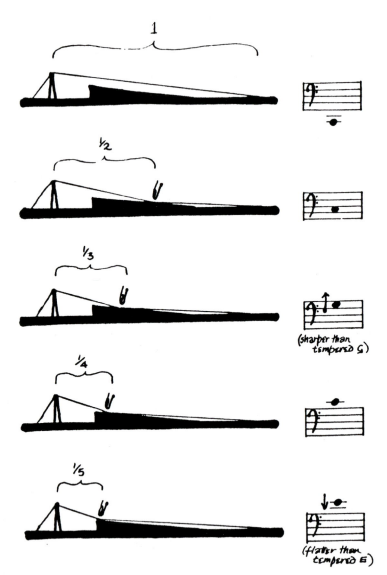

Figure 3.1   Relation between string length and 'consonantly' related tones.

could be reduced (apparently) to simple numerical relationships. This general view has been exceedingly fruitful but on occasions misleading. It led indirectly to the concept of the *Harmony of the Spheres*, one of the most persistent and misleading conceptions ever to animate the human mind: the heavenly bodies were assumed to be transported around the earth on giant spheres whose motion generated a heavenly music, governed in some way by the Pythagorean laws of proportion. The desire to find 'celestial harmony' in the world of nature persists even into the work of the astronomer Kepler, who was obsessed by the desire to fit the (assumed) spheres of planetary motion (Figure 3.2) around the Platonic solids (Figure 3.3).

It is important to point out that, important though these elementary physical relationships are in the underpinning of various musical languages, music in general is a cultural construct. Although the primacy of the octave and the fifth is preserved in most musical cultures (though not everywhere), we would have great difficulty in explaining away all the subtle ramifications of the North Indian scale system in terms of Pythagorean interval theory. More significantly, perhaps, for the subject of this book, the Western tempered scale in fact preserves only the true octave in its structure. All other

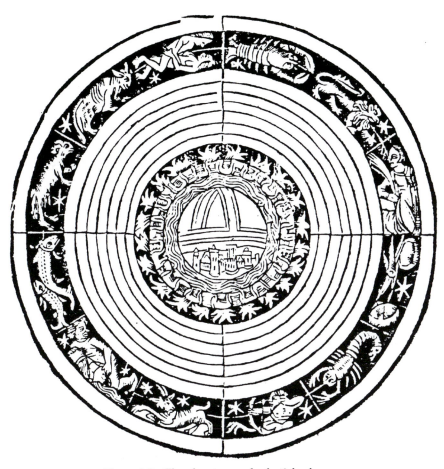

Figure 3.2 The planetary and celestial spheres.

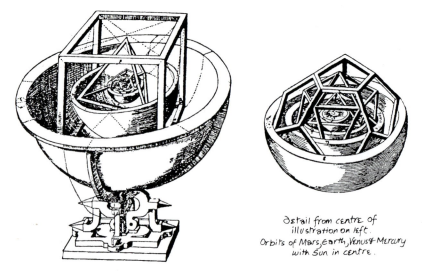

detail from centre of
illustration on left.
Orbits of Mars, Earth, Venus & Mercury
with Sun in centre.

Figure 3.3   Kepler's attempt to fit the Platonic solids within the planetary orbits (assumed spherical).

apparently simple-ratio intervals (such as the fifth, major third and minor third) are mere approximations to the simple Pythagorean ratios, the actual ratios used being governed by the rationality of tempering and the twelfth root of two! Although in Western tonal music the fifth plays a central role (next to the octave), this cannot be put down merely to its Pythagorean simplicity. The well-tempered ratio $((\sqrt[12]{2})^7 \;(= 1.48){:}1)$ is in no sense simple and it is difficult to see in what sense it approximates 'simplicity' — are we to say that it is simpler than the ratio 4:3 because it is closer to 2:3? — in that case, would not $2{:}\pi$ be simpler than 4:3?

     One further point: Pythagoras' theory essentially establishes relationships between simple, stable vibrations. Current (and in fact ancient) musical practice is not solely concerned with such sound phenomena and the advent of computer analysis and synthesis permits us to understand and control much more complex sound phenomena.

Helmholtz, Fourier and Standard Musical Practice

The next major breakthrough in our physical understanding of the nature of sound came with an important discovery by the mathematician Fourier. While attempting to solve various problems relating to the conduction of heat in solids, Fourier discovered that it was possible to represent an arbitrary mathematical function by a sum (possibly infinite) of simpler functions. The simpler functions which he chose for this representation were the elementary sine and cosine functions with which we are all now familiar from work in acoustics or electronic music. It is possible to give an approximate description of the Fourier method without going into mathematical details to anyone familiar with the concept of *vector*.

A vector may be regarded as a line of a particular length and a particular direction. In three-dimensional space we may affix to one end of this line a set of three lines at right angles to one another, a system of coordinates. The point where these lines meet is called the origin. If our vector starts at the origin no matter where its other end point is, it is always possible to reach that end point by proceeding from the origin a certain distance parallel to one axis, a certain distance parallel to the second axis and a certain distance parallel to the third axis (see Figure 3.4). These three new vectors are called the components of the original vector. Roughly speaking the fact that the three components are at right angles to one another means that they are independent of one another (one cannot express any of the components in terms of the others). The components are then said to be *orthogonal*.

If we now take an arbitrary function (see Figure 3.5), this associates with every point along the horizontal axis a point on the vertical axis. We

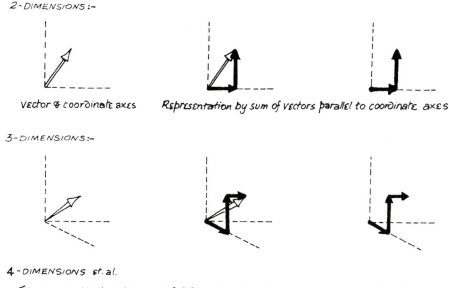

2-DIMENSIONS :-

Vector & coordinate axes   Representation by sum of vectors parallel to coordinate axes

3-DIMENSIONS:-

4-DIMENSIONS et. al.

This cannot be physically drawn or modelled, but the mathematical representation is precisely parallel.

Figure 3.4 Representation of vectors in a coordinate system.

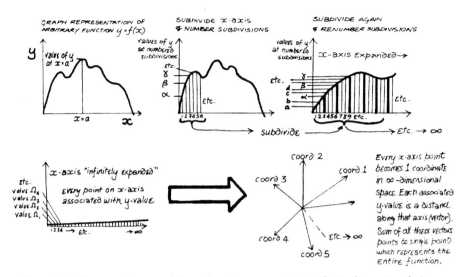

Figure 3.5   Representing an arbitrary function as a point in infinite-dimensional space.

now need to make a leap of the imagination and imagine that every infinitesimally small point along the horizontal axis corresponds to a dimension in an infinite-dimensional space and that the corresponding value on the vertical axis corresponds to a distance along that particular dimension. We can now, at least conceptually, represent the entire function by a single point in this infinite dimensional space. If now, just as in the case of the vector in three-dimensional space, we can set up a system of orthogonal coordinates and define a set of related components in the space (which in this case will turn out to be other mathematical functions) then we can make a representation of the original arbitrary function. The set of sine and cosine functions used by Fourier, can be shown to fulfil the criterion of orthogonality. Hence we have discovered a very powerful mathematical tool. It soon became clear that Fourier's method was especially applicable to the description of sound phenomena. As is now well-known, any sound phenomenon, no matter how complex, is carried by variations of pressure within the air and can be represented as a function of air-pressure against time. Such functions are, at least in principle, directly amenable to Fourier's method of analysis.

Helmholtz and others, working with what they called 'musical' tones, i.e. the sounds of conventional musical instruments, proposed a simple theory of pitch and timbre perception. A sound perceived as a single pitch was found to be made up of various sine wave components (through Fourier analysis). These bore a simple harmonic relationship to one another. The frequency of the higher sine tones were integral multiples of the frequency of the lowest (which for the moment we will assume to be the fundamental) frequency. The pitch of a sound corresponded directly with the frequency of the fundamental, the timbre was the result of the presence (relative amplitude) or absence of the other sine tones (the partials). Before going on to criticise and comment upon this theory, we should note that it seemed to absolutely confirm the ruling musical ideology that pitch was primary and timbre secondary. Pitch could be seen as fundamentally related to frequency and timbre as merely a secondary phenomenon arising from the combination of the frequencies of the constituent sine tones. Timbre appeared to be thus almost a fused chord over a fundamental pitch. However, the fact that Helmholtz's theory appeared to confirm the ruling musical ideology should come as no surprise. It was framed within a culture which took that system of musical thinking for granted. Helmholtz confined himself to the analysis of what he arbitrarily defined to be 'musical' tones, i.e. sounds forced onto the pitch-timbre-duration lattice by preconceptions of the musical and their realisation in instrument technology. Furthermore, the assumptions firstly that timbre was a unitary phenomenon and secondly that pitch and timbre were clearly separable qualities, were taken for granted directly from preconceptions of music tradition.

Walsh functions, indeterminacy and the missing fundamental

The first question we must ask about Fourier analysis is, although it is clearly a very powerful mathematical tool, does it bear any relationship at all to our perception of sonic reality? Is the Fourier analysis of sonic events into sine tones unique, or is there any other alternative analytic breakdown? It turns out that other systems of orthogonal functions can be defined and used to represent arbitrary mathematical functions. One such system is that of *Walsh functions* illustrated in Figure 3.6. With the advent of digital technology some programs have already been developed for the synthesis of sounds using Walsh functions rather than the more usual sine tones. However, whereas the Walsh function analysis of a sound-object seems to bear no clear intuitive relationship to our aural experience, Fourier analysis relates very clearly to what we hear. It has been shown in fact that the human ear is a kind of Fourier analyser so that we may assume that up to a point the mathematics of Fourier analysis has some direct relationship with our perceptual experience.

The result of Fourier analysis is what is called a *Fourier transform*. The mathematics of the Fourier analysis convert information about the variation of amplitude with time (time-domain information) into information about

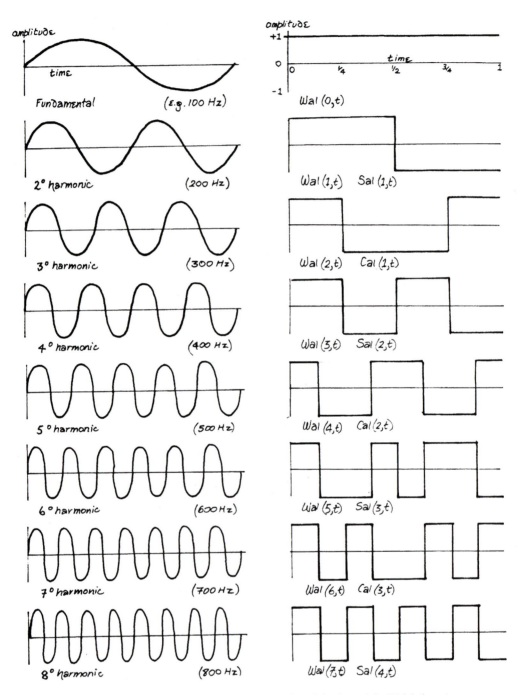

Figure 3.6   The first eight harmonics (sine waves) and the first eight Walsh functions.

the variation of amplitude with frequency (frequency-domain information). Simply put, we start off with a graph of amplitude against time and we end up with a graph of amplitude against frequency (see Figure 3.7). The *inverse Fourier transform* performs the opposite function, turning information about frequency and amplitude into information about amplitude and time.

It must be said immediately that the notion that somehow frequency (periodicity) is more physically real than spectral information is hard to justify. In a simple instrumental tone, periodicity can certainly be more easily seen from a graph of amplitude against time than can any spectral information. However, this is partly the nature of the beast being analysed and when we consider more complex musical objects (see the section on noise below) we will find that the graph of frequency against amplitude (i.e. the spectrum of the sound) is far more lucid than the amplitude against time graph (which may be totally aperiodic). In fact, to be entirely reductionist for a moment, all that really exists is the amplitude of displacement of the air or the ear-drum and its variation in time. Both periodicity and spectral information are higher-level derived entities.

A more important problem is simply that the ear is unable to function as a Fourier analyser above frequencies of around 4,000 Hz

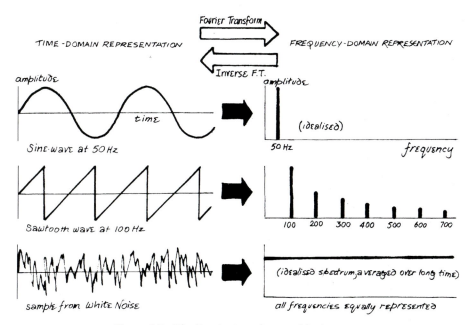

Figure 3.7 The Fourier transform and its inverse.

although frequency information above this threshold can be very important in our perception of timbre. In relation to these I quote from Schouten, Ritsma and Cardozo:

> *[...] there may exist one or more percepts (residues) not corresponding with any individual Fourier component. These do [however] correspond with a group of Fourier components. Such a percept (residue) has an impure, sharp timbre and, if tonal, a pitch corresponding to the periodicity of the time pattern of the unresolved spectral components.*
> (Schouten, Ritsma and Cardozo 1962: 1419, emphasis added)

Put simply, above 4,000 Hz we hear timbre simply as timbre!

A more serious problem with the ideologically natural view which equates sine tones with 'pure pitches' and their combination with timbre is related to the principle of indeterminacy. Towards the end of the nineteenth century a serious problem arose in the theory of the absorption and emission of radiation by heated bodies. Put simply, conventional theories seemed to predict that any body in thermal equilibrium should radiate infinite amounts of energy in the ultraviolet region of the spectrum and this was consequently known as the *ultraviolet catastrophe*. The problem was eventually solved by Planck's introduction of the *quantum of action*. The Quantum Theory is now central to contemporary physics and its central assumption is that energy can only be emitted in small finite packets (known as *quanta*). The size of these energy quanta (E) is directly related to the frequency (f) of the oscillator emitting or absorbing radiation by the formula $E = hf/2\pi$ where h is Planck's constant.

An important cornerstone of quantum mechanics is Heisenberg's *Uncertainty Principle*. This states simply that the position and momentum of a particle cannot both simultaneously be known exactly. In fact, the more accurately one is known the less accurately the other *must* be known. A similar relationship holds between energy and time, i.e. it is possible to know the energy of a particle with great accuracy only if one does not know exactly at what time it has this energy. The Uncertainty Principle is often presented in elementary books about modern physics as a result merely of the interference of the instruments of observation with what is being observed. It is after all more natural for us to assume that the particle does have a definite energy at a particular time and it is merely a problem of getting to know what that is. The conventional view among physicists, however, is that the Uncertainty Principle is intrinsic to the nature of reality rather than a mere accident of experimental design. It can be shown that the mathematics resulting from an assumption of the truth of the Uncertainty Principle has observable physical consequences which would not be expected if the uncertainty were not an intrinsic part of nature (for example, so-called *exchange phenomena* between electrons in chemical bonding).

Energy/time indeterminacy (which has a direct relationship to our discussion of the structure of sounds) can be understood fairly simply. First of all, we must remember that in Quantum Physics the energy of a system is related to its frequency. How can we therefore measure the frequency of a system at a particular instant in time? The answer is simply that *we cannot* because frequency is a property of the system dependent on its actual evolution through time. We can say that a system vibrates five times in a second but we cannot talk about how many vibrations it undergoes at an instant in time. Hence the instantaneous energy of a system is not definable. Fourier analysis of a signal into its spectral components is similarly limited. The mathematics of Fourier analysis assumes that the signal persists for an infinite length of time. If it does not, even if it appears in the time domain to be a pure sine tone, in the frequency domain it will be found to have some spectral colouration. The reader may intuitively grasp why this is so by looking at Figure 3.8. Thus when only a very small part of the curved edge of a sine wave is present we have no way of predicting that this will continue as a sine wave or that it will prove to be the leading edge of

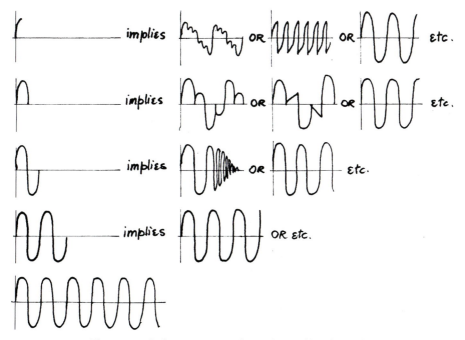

Figure 3.8 Indeterminacy in the analysis of brief signals.

an essentially stepped signal with sinusoidal rounding (for example). Even when we have a complete cycle of a sine wave we do not know that this is one complete cycle of the wave. It may be only the opening formation of a more complex pattern. Even when we have two cycles of a sine wave, though now we can perceive a regularity in the structure, it is still not certain that we have the complete picture. As more and more cycles of the sine wave are taken into our sample, the uncertainty in the nature of the signal reduces rapidly but it only reduces to zero when the sine wave persists to infinity.

The physical consequence of this is that if we produce a single cycle of a sine wave (no matter how 'pure' it may be) what we will in fact hear is a click, a sonic impulse whose frequency is maximally indeterminate. This is not as some of the *Groupe de Recherches Musicales* writings seem to suggest just a limitation of the ear. It is intrinsic to Fourier analysis itself and therefore any physical instrument performing a spectral analysis on the signal would register a similar indeterminate result. Hence a sine tone, no matter how 'pure', if sufficiently brief has no definite pitch! This phenomenon is illustrated in Examples 3.1 and 3.2. The same melody is played in both examples but in the first the individual elements are less than five milliseconds long, whereas in the second example they are ten milliseconds long. In the first example no sensation of pitch is conveyed.

For similar reasons, if we suddenly switch on a pure sine tone and then suddenly switch it off we will experience (and analysis will confirm) a spreading of the spectrum at the start and end of the sound. In this case we are not talking about switching transients in the apparatus which generates the sine tone (which we may assume we have eliminated) but the inevitable results of Fourier analysis of a finite signal. This frequency spreading can be reduced by using a cosinusoidal envelope on the attack and decay of the sample (see Figure 3.9).

It will no doubt have occurred to the reader that no real sounds last for an infinite length of time! Furthermore, few sounds exhibit constant periodicity for any length of time. Also, a sound does not have to be random to have a constantly changing wave-shape. A simple example would be a portamento on any instrument. Any practical Fourier analyser (including the human ear) must do a kind of piece-wise analysis of sound and link up the results in order to gain any reasonable conception of the nature of the complex sound-world surrounding us.

Having discovered that 'pure' sine tones may have no definable pitch, we may also discover that clear pitches may not be associated with the appropriate sine tone! The simplest example of this is illustrated by first recording a low note on the piano (Example 3.3) and then filtering out

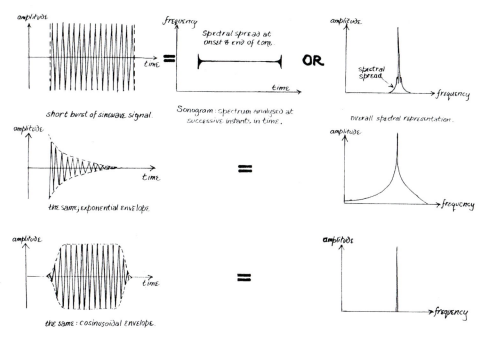

Figure 3.9 Spectral spreading in finite signals.

all frequencies below the second harmonic,[3] i.e. filtering out what we assume to be the fundamental pitch (Example 3.4). Amazingly the filtering has no effect on the sound whatsoever and we are led to conclude that there is no single component in the sound corresponding to what we hear as the fundamental pitch! The fundamental is in fact a mental construct extrapolated from the information contained in the higher partials. This effect is not peculiar to piano tones and can be demonstrated for other types of sound.

Most spectacular of all (Example 3.5), using extremely precise control of the overtone structure of a sound through computer synthesis, we can trade off the increase in perceived 'fundamental frequency' against the weighting of high and low partials in the sound in such a way that the pitch of a sound glissandos upwards at the same time as the sound descends gradually to the lower limit of the perception of pitch! The sound appears to ascend and descend simultaneously. Such experiences lead us inexorably to the conclusion that pitch is an aspect of the perception of

---

[3] Strictly 'second partial' as the piano spectrum is substantially *inharmonic* (*Ed.*).

timbre, and not vice versa. At the very least, we should become aware that the strict separation between pitch and timbre is an artefact of the way we have constructed our musical reality.

The inharmonic and the non-periodic: a dual conception of pitch

So far we have confined ourselves largely to Helmholtz's material, i.e. sounds of stable tessitura in which the partials are integral multiples of the frequency of the real (or imaginary) fundamental. When the relationships between the partials of a sound are not of this kind (i.e. when they are inharmonic) the Fourier analytical attempt to extract a single pitch characteristic from the sound breaks down. The object appears to perception as an aggregate of various pitches, more fused than a typical chord in instrumental music but definitely not a singly-pitched note. Many bell and bell-like sounds are of this type. Composers working in electro-acoustic music seem to be particularly attracted to these kinds of sounds and one speculates whether it is not due to their similarity to chord structures in conventional music. The sounds, in fact, are not radically different from the normal sound-objects found in conventional musical practice. They lend themselves to similar (lattice-based) modes of organisation and do not challenge our conception of what is and is not a musical object (as sounds with dynamic or unstable morphologies will do). At another perceptual extreme we have entirely non-periodic signals. In the architecture of typical analogue synthesisers (and in much discussion of electronic music) such sounds, usually referred to as 'noise', are often treated as entirely separate entities from materials with clearly defined spectra usually generated from simple oscillators. In fact, as we shall discuss, there is no simple dividing line between periodic and non-periodic signals, but in fact a multidimensional array of complex possibilities between the two extremes. Noise is not something to be treated separately from other materials, either compositionally or conceptually, but an alternative way of perceiving and relating to sound phenomena which we shall now discuss.

As discussed earlier, the result of Fourier analysis is to transform information about a sound from the time domain into the frequency domain. The most immediately striking thing about noise-type sounds is that the time domain criteria apparently cease to apply. For example, if we take a recording of a typical periodic pitched sound or even an inharmonic sound and we play back the recording at double speed the time domain information passes us at twice the rate and we hear the sound transposed up an octave. If, however, we try the same experiment with white noise, we experience no change in the frequency domain information (Example 3.6).

More complex signals may yield even more startling results (for instance in Example 3.7 where a complex sound is played first at normal speed and then at double speed. The sound appears to shift by about a third).

The explanation for this lies in the characteristics of noise-type sounds and the way we perceive them. For noise-type sounds the time domain information is essentially random. The amplitude of the signal varies randomly with time and, for example, for Gaussian noise, the probability that the amplitude will have any particular value at any particular time is maximum for zero amplitude and dies away smoothly to a probability of zero as the amplitude increases. A Fourier analysis of a small sample of a noise signal will yield a somewhat arbitrary array of frequencies and amplitudes. Analysis of another similar sample will yield a quite different but equally arbitrary array of frequencies and amplitudes. The only way that we can achieve a coherent analysis of this signal is through a statistical averaging process. We can show the average amplitude of the various frequencies in the signal over a long period of time. For white noise the frequency domain analysis reveals a completely flat spectrum. All frequencies are present with equal probability. This explains the phenomenon illustrated in the example. When the tape is played at double speed, all the frequencies are shifted up an equal amount and those that were lost near the bottom of the spectrum are replaced by even lower frequencies (which, due to the physiology of hearing we might not even have been able to perceive previously).

There are two things we must bear in mind when considering the nature of noise-based signals. First of all by declaring that a typical noise-based signal contains all possible frequencies at random amplitudes distributed randomly in time, the typical text book on acoustics tends to imply that noise is essentially an aggregate of more elementary sounds. This conception is an artefact of our perception of the analysis. As anyone who has switched on a synthesiser will know, noise is a perfectly coherent source, no less coherent than a typical sine wave oscillator and need have no particular granular characteristics. What we are saying here applies particularly to white noise but the noise concept (involving time-averaging of a spectrum) may be applied to a great many sound-objects, and noise-like objects may certainly be produced through the aggregation of simpler objects. For example a dense cluster in the lower register of the piano has a fused noise-like quality quite different from a similar cluster played in the high register. Secondly, and most important, noise involves a different mode of listening. In fact, it might be more accurate to suggest that the noise conception is a property of the way we hear rather than of the object itself. This distinction might seem arbitrary when we consider only oscillators and noise-sources on a typical synthesiser but when we begin to consider sounds with extremely complex evolving and semi-irregular spectra, the distinction comes strongly into play.

With sounds therefore that we describe as noise, or noise-based we appear to respond directly to information in the frequency domain as there is little information to be gained from the time domain. This fact may be illustrated in two ways. In Figure 3.10 we see time domain representations of Gaussian and binary noise. The Gaussian noise has the random amplitude fluctuations we might expect. The binary noise, on the other hand, flips randomly backwards and forwards between two very definite

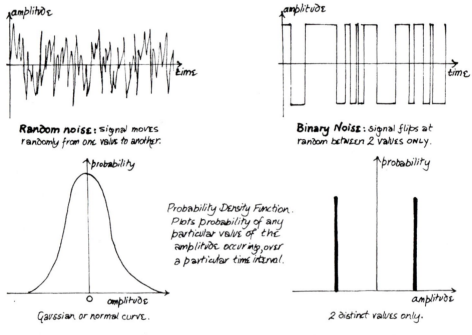

Random noise: signal moves randomly from one value to another.

Binary Noise: signal flips at random between 2 values only.

Probability Density Function. Plots probability of any particular value of the amplitude occurring, over a particular time interval.

Gaussian or normal curve.

2 distinct values only.

HOWEVER, provided the "flip times" in the Binary Noise are entirely randomly distributed both types of noise may have the same spectrum: —

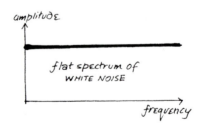

flat spectrum of WHITE NOISE

Figure 3.10 Random and binary noise (independence of frequency-domain representation).

amplitudes. However, the frequency domain information can be the same in both cases and we can perceive both as the familiar 'white' noise. In Examples 3.8 and 3.9 we hear first of all the effect of transposing white noise by an octave (no effect on the frequency domain information) and secondly a 'melody' created by filtering variously the white noise to produce bands of different 'coloured' noises. Again the effect of the latter on the time domain information would be barely perceptible but can be clearly heard in the frequency domain. Perhaps the most striking example of the independence of frequency domain hearing from time domain information in noise perception is the experience of comb-filtering. In this particular case a brief delay is imposed on the noise signal and the result mixed with the original signal. The time domain representation presents us with no perceivable patterning but in the frequency domain we discover that various regular peaks and troughs appear in the spectrum, the spacing of these being related to the duration of the time-delay. Perceptually speaking, a pitch or particular spectral characteristic is imposed upon the previously undifferentiated noise source (see Figure 3.11).

Filtering noise can be used to produce broad bands which can be perceived to be higher or lower than one another but are not perceptibly pitched or to produce narrower bands which are perceived as being more or less clearly pitched. This suggests that there are at least two conceptions of pitch involved in our perception of sound-objects. The first type of pitch is related to periodicity and arises from the real or implied fundamental frequency of vibration of the source (or several of these in the case of an inharmonic sound). The second results from the imposition of a spectral envelope through some sort of filtering or resonance procedure acting on a noise-averaged spectrum. Just as the perceived fundamental pitch may be multiple (in an inharmonic spectrum) the spectral envelope itself may be quite complicated and we will normally refer to this as a *formant structure*. These two conceptions of pitch (in a sense one related more strongly to the time domain and the other more strongly to the spectral domain) meet most strikingly in the sound production of the human voice where the pitch of standard musical practice is defined by the fundamental vibrations of the larynx while the articulation of vowels in speech (and in song) is defined by varying formant structures.

We may now imagine very complex tones in which the two concepts of pitch are traded off against each other. For example, an inharmonic tone in which the various partials are in constant and rapid motion might be given a focused pitch sense by the strong accentuation of a narrow formant band using a filter. Conversely and more commonly heard, the time domain pitch of a sung tone is clearly maintained through the most extreme variations of

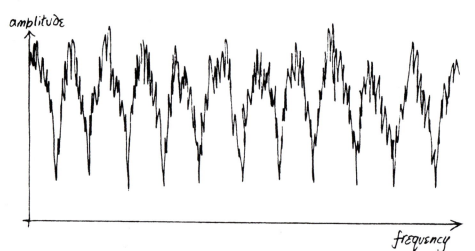

Comb-filtered noise: patterning of spectrum. Amplitude peaks
are in a harmonic relationship to one another. We hear pitch.

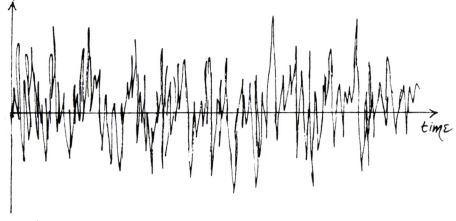

Comb-filtered noise: lack of patterning remains in time-domain.

Figure 3.11   Comb-filtered noise (perception of pitch direct from frequency domain).

formant structure details. The question of what happens when both of these
change at once will be dealt with in the following chapters!

Spectral evolution: harmonic and dynamic timbre

A much more fundamental break with Helmholtz may be made. Simple
experiments with sound-objects demonstrate that timbre is not merely

dependent on spectral information but also upon the way that information evolves through time. The most striking illustration of this fact is given in Examples 3.10 and 3.11. In Example 3.10 we hear first the sound of a piano note whose envelope has been smoothed and flattened. Following this is the sound of a flute playing the same note. The two are virtually identical. In the second example (3.11), we first hear the sound of a flute on which has been imposed the amplitude envelope of a piano note. This is followed by a piano note at the same pitch. Again, the two sounds are indistinguishable. The fact is that in this particular register the spectral content of piano and flute sounds are very similar. What differentiates these sonic objects is the temporal evolution of the amplitude of the event. The flute remaining relatively constant whilst the piano decays linearly[4] from a sharp attack. Thus dynamic aspects of the spectrum enter into our perception of timbre, so we see that timbre is at least a two-dimensional entity contrary to the conventional wisdom.

Furthermore, the characteristics of the evolution of the amplitude envelope are of fundamental importance. If we take a sound of relatively constant envelope and edit away various parts of it, we experience no noticeable change in timbre (Example 3.12). Extending this notion we need not keep the amplitude constant but merely maintain a constancy in its rate of change. (A constant amplitude is simply an amplitude envelope with constancy of change, the rate of change being zero.) With a piano, the sound actually dies away but the rate of this decay is constant (linear decay). If we therefore edit off various amounts of time from the beginning of the piano note, its timbre will not be noticeably changed (Example 3.13). If we try the same experiment with an instrument whose amplitude envelope varies non-linearly, we discover that editing off the beginning of the sound changes the timbre distinctly (for instance, Example 3.14 using a bell). This mode of argument applies equally well to unpitched sound and may be heard by listening to Example 3.15 which uses a cymbal having a linear decay with noise-type material.

To be even more precise we must take into account the evolution of amplitude of each component of the spectrum in our sound. If we repeat the same experiment using a vibraphone (Example 3.16), we will find that when we lose the very start of the sound it is altered significantly, but editing off more of the sound's beginning has no further appreciable effect. This is simply because there is a rapid spectral change during the initiating moment of a vibraphone note, due to the metallic sound of the hammer striking the

---

[4] 'Linearly' in terms of the perception of loudness (roughly speaking dBs); not amplitude which is decaying exponentially with time. *(Ed.)*

key but then the subsequent resonance dies away linearly (as with a piano note) because of the material and design of the instrument.

Even a conventional instrumental sound may contain significant noise components. In Examples 3.17 and 3.18 we first of all hear a flute sound without its initial 50 milliseconds (followed by the original recording) and the same experiment repeated with a trumpet. The effect is very much more marked with the flute because the flute sound is partly characterised by a noise-based breath-sound which initiates the resonance of the tube. Thus, even with conventional instruments, we begin to see a sequential breaking up of the characteristics of the sound-object which we will explore more fully in the section on multiplexing and which is more typically characteristic of speech-streamed sound-objects. The discovery that timbre itself is partly dependent upon the evolution of spectral characteristics is our first real link with sounds of dynamic morphology, i.e. sounds in which the perceived pitch spectrum, amplitude envelope etc., all evolve through time.

Coherence of sound-objects; aural imaging

Having discovered that sound-objects may be exceedingly complex and that our perception of them may involve processes of averaging and attention to spectral evolution, an obvious question presents itself; how are we ever able to differentiate one sound-source from another? As all sounds enter our auditory apparatus via a single complex pressure wave generated in the air why do we not just constantly hear a single source with more or less complex characteristics? We might ask the same question in reverse: how is it that a complex sound does not dissociate into a number of separate aural images? Much research has already been done and much is still being carried out on the problem of *aural imaging*. The following observations are drawn from the work of Steven McAdams at IRCAM in Paris (see McAdams 1982).

To phrase the question a little more technically, once our auditory mechanism has dissociated the incoming sound into its constituent sine wave components, or at least generated some kind of spectral analysis, how can it then group the various components according to the separate sources from which they emanated? There appear to be at least four mechanisms in operation here. These are:

(1) components having the same (or very similar) overall amplitude envelope, and, in particular, components whose onset characteristics coincide will tend to be grouped together;

(2) components having parallel frequency modulation (either regular in the form of vibrato or irregular in the form of jitter) will be grouped together;

(3)   sounds having the same formant characteristics will be grouped together;

(4)   sounds having the same apparent spatial location will be grouped together.

Any or all of these factors may enter into the process of separating one aural image from another. The importance of onset synchrony is demonstrated in Example 3.19 where the various constituents of a sound are separated by increasing time-intervals and then the time-intervals successively reduced until there is again complete synchrony. The sound-image will be heard to split into its component parts and then recohere. The importance of frequency-modulation information has been most eloquently demonstrated in work by Roger Reynolds[5] (Example 3.20). Data from a phase vocoder analysis was used to resynthesize an oboe tone, elongating it as well. The regenerated oboe tone was projected from two loudspeakers, the odd harmonics on one side, the even on the other. These two groups of partials were each coherently, but differently, frequency modulated. Because the even set was modulated at a rate corresponding to vocal vibrato, and the odd necessarily had a clarinet-like sound, the listener experiences a distinctive composite as the amplitude of modulation increases: clarinet on one side, voice on the other at the octave, and the sum, an oboe sound, in the centre. In this way we can contemplate playing with the aural imaging process and not merely destroying the convention of instrumental streaming.

Conversely, we may use these aural imaging factors compositionally to integrate sound materials which might otherwise not cohere into objects. Thus, by imposing artificial attack and amplitude characteristics on a complex of sounds (e.g. a small group of people laughing), by artificially synchronising the onset of two or more normally quite separate sound-objects, by artificially synchronising the vibrato and jitter on two or more normally quite separate sound-objects we may create coherent composite sound-objects. A recently popular example of this approach is the use of the vocoder where the evolution of the formant characteristics of a speaking voice is imposed on an otherwise non-coherent source (e.g. the sounds of a large group of people speaking before a concert as in Michael McNabb's *Dreamsong*). This further opens up our conception of what might be considered a coherent musical object.

With all these potential sound-materials at our disposal a further problem arises. Music is normally concerned with establishing relationships

---

[5] Working with Steven McAdams and Thierry Lancino at IRCAM. This example is based on band 2e on the IRCAM LP 0001 which is described somewhat differently on the sleeve note. It is from his work *Archipelago*. (*Ed.*)

between various kinds of material. The question is what determines whether we perceive a particular piece of sound-material as related to another. Speaking of sound organisation in the broadest possible sense, the answer to this question will clearly depend partly on context (upon which aspects of sonic organisation are being focused upon — pitch, spectral type, formant streaming etc.). But whichever approach we take there will be a point beyond which the manipulated sound-material will cease to have any audible relation to its source. This can already be perceived in conventional music where in some types of complex serial organisation, the concept of the derivation of material from a source set becomes meaningless. In the studio it is seductive to assume that a sound derived from another by some technical process is hence derived from the original in a *musical* sense. A simple example of this may be given as follows. Suppose that we start with a sustained orchestral sound, the sound of a large crowd and the sound of a stable sine tone. Let us now take each sound, put it on a tape recorder and switch the tape recorder onto fast wind so that the sound accelerates from speed zero to very fast and as the tape recorder reaches its maximum speed fade out the sound to nothing.[6] Having done this with all the sounds, let us now speed them up to at least sixteen times their original speed. In what sense are the resultant sounds related to the originals? What we perceive in each case is a brief, high frequency glissando. Furthermore, and most striking, all three sounds now appear very closely related whereas the sounds from which they originated have no relationship whatsoever. At this distance of derivation it is the overall morphology of the sound-structures which predominates. We may learn two lessons from this. First of all, with sound-objects having a dynamic morphology, it is this morphology that dominates our perception of relatedness- unrelatedness, rather than spectral or even more general timbral considerations. Secondly, if the organisation of our music is to be based on the audible reality of the listening experience, the music must be organised according to *perceived* relationships of materials or *perceived* processes of derivation of materials. In order to accomplish the former we need an analysis of sound-materials based upon their perceived properties, a phenomenological analysis of sounds.

The phenomenology of sound-objects

The pioneering work on the development of a phenomenological description of sound-objects and an aesthetic based upon it was done by Pierre Schaeffer and the *Groupe de Recherches Musicales*. Certain aurally-

---

[6] Unedited from 1983, this phenomenon may be simulated in digital systems (*Ed.*).

perceived characteristics of sound-objects have already been discussed above and this section is intended to complement what has already been said. It draws largely upon the GRM research incorporating ideas drawn from the writings of Robert Erickson and Iannis Xenakis. Perhaps the most important concept advanced by Pierre Schaeffer was that of the *acousmatic*. This term was originally applied to initiates in the Pythagorean cult who spent five years listening to lectures from the master, delivered from behind a screen (so that the lecturer could not be seen) while sitting in total silence. Acousmatic listening may therefore be defined as the apprehension or appreciation of a sound-object independent of, and detached from, a knowledge or appreciation of its source. This means not only that we will ignore the social or environmental origins or intention of the sound (from a bird, from a car, from a musical instrument, as language, as distress signal, as music, as accident) but also its instrumental origin (voice, musical instrument, metal sheet, machine, animal, larynx, stretched string, air column etc.). The idea of acousmatic listening is easily appreciated by anyone who has worked with recorded sound-materials in the electro-acoustic music studio. When working with large numbers of sounds from different sources and particularly when this material has been transformed, if only slightly, it becomes difficult to remember from where the various sounds originated and from a compositional point of view such origins need have no special significance. The transformation of the flute tone into the sound of a piano (above) illustrated this thesis, though a truly acousmatic approach would demand that we forget not merely that the sound derived from a flute but also that after its transformation it appeared to derive from a piano! We should concern ourselves solely with its objective characteristics as a sound-object. Example 3.21 illustrates the need for the separation of sound-object description from any reference to the source. The various sounds here are all derived from the same source-object (a tam-tam excited by a variety of objects).

From our discussion in the previous section we became aware of a distinction between sounds which are transposed by a change of replay-speed (time-domain transformation) and sounds (like white noise) which do not change their pitch, or change pitch in some unpredictable way under the same transformation. We also discovered that various properties of a sound may be altered by filtering. With certain sounds, however, though qualitative changes can be perceived as a result of filtering, we do not feel that the underlying sound-object has been fundamentally altered. The instrumental tones of conventional musical practice are typical examples of sounds which can be transposed by time-domain transformation and are resistant to filtering. They are not the only ones, however, and it is necessary to define a more general characteristic of sound-objects having this property. Following the French terminology, we will refer to this as *mass*. An example of a complex sound having a definite mass and illustration of its resistance to filtering and its transposition are given in Example 3.22. In actual practice, of course, there will be a large, grey area where time-domain-based perception of complex timbres and spectral perception of formants (see previous section) meet.

A second perceived characteristic of sound-objects is *grain*. If we take a slowly repeating pulse and gradually speed it up beyond about 20 Hz, we begin to hear a definite pitch and as the speed increases further we begin to lose any sense of the original individual impulses. In between the extremes of impulse perception and pitch perception we perceive a pitched object with a certain amount of 'grittiness' as the individual impulses are still apparent in some sense to our perception of the sound-object. This internal 'grittiness' is the *grain* of the sound-object and is illustrated for an electronic impulse (Example 3.23) and for a bassoon note (Example 3.24) in the sound examples. In this particular case we are talking about a regular, periodic grain, but it is possible to define grain in a more general manner. If we have a sound made up of a large aggregate of brief impulses occurring in a random or semi-random manner, we can talk about the statistical average rate of occurrence of these impulses and this particular parameter will have an effect on the perceived characteristic of a sound. Erickson (1975)) refers to this characteristic as *rustle time* and might also be thought of as *aperiodic grain*. It has an important role in our perception of particular types of percussion sounds. For example, we may note the perceptual difference between sounds of types of rattles filled variously with sand, seeds and shot. Note, however, that the spectral characteristics of the individual impulses in all these cases will also contribute (probably in a statistically averaged way) to the perceived character of the resulting sound. Aperiodic grain also has a bearing on the particular sonority of sizzle-cymbals, snare-drums, drum-rolls, the lion's roar, and even the quality of string sound through the influence of different weights and widths of bows and different types of hair and rosin on the nature of bowed excitation.

It is important to realise that there is a perceptual threshold at which we cease to perceive individual events as individual events and begin to experience them as contributing to the grain of a larger event. As a result, at sufficiently high speed, any sequence of sound-objects may become fused into a larger object with grain. Example 3.25 illustrates this first for a descending scale and then for an irregular melodic pattern. Incidentally, if we applied the same process to a string of speech sounds (Example 3.26) we approach the conception of a *multiplex* to be discussed in the next chapter.

Combining the concept of rapid rustle-time with multiplicities of brief sound-objects of various spectra we begin to define another huge class of possible sound-objects (e.g. the sound of rain, of poured pebbles, etc.) hinted at in Xenakis (1971/1992). This book is a very interesting early analysis of a generalised notion of sound-objects as evolving groupings of

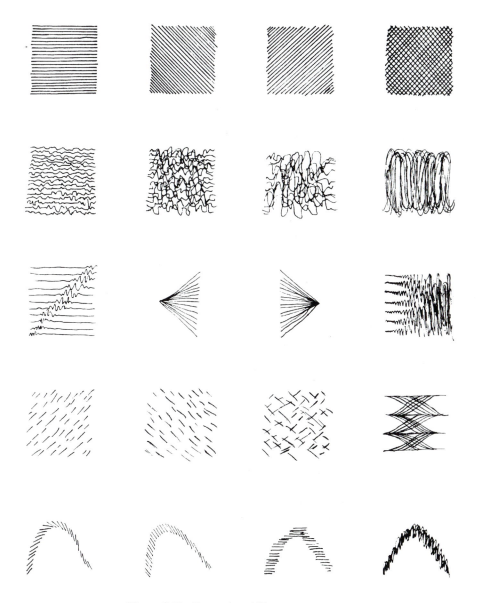

Figure 3.12 Examples of filament structure.

elementary particulate sounds. Unfortunately, the musico-descriptive potential of the approach gets rather lost in Xenakis' absorption in the particular mathematical methodology (stochastic processes and Markov chains) leading the composer off in a rather specialised aesthetic direction. In the book, however, Xenakis does deal with the *grain structure* and *filament structure* of dense sound-objects. Just as grain structure may be thought to apply to sounds made up of elementary impulses, filament structure applies to sounds made up of elementary sustained units. Figure 3.12 expanding on Xenakis' descriptions, illustrates various possible filament structures. If we now begin to discuss the temporal evolution of such concepts as aperiodic grain and filament structure a whole new world of complex sound-objects begins to open up before us. The GRM classification goes on to discuss the concepts of *complex-note*, *web* and *eccentric* sounds but I will discuss sounds of this and related types in a somewhat different manner in the following chapters. A more complete description of the GRM methodology can be found in the *Solfège de l'objet sonore* (Schaeffer, Reibel and Ferreyra (1983)[7]).

---

[7] The *Solfège* is still available on three cassettes from the INA/GRM (Paris) at time of press but the trilingual printout of the recorded French commentary which accompanied the LP version appears to have been discontinued (*Ed.*).

Chapter 4

THE NATURE OF SONIC SPACE

Structure of pitch-space; harmonicity and adjacency

It might be assumed, wrongly, from Chapter 3 that one only runs into new, non-lattice-based, conceptions of musical ordering when dealing with sounds having complex mass or noise characteristics. This is not the case, as we shall explain in the next chapter, but we must begin exploration with a closer analysis of the Pythagorean concept of consonance or harmonicity. A simple reading of Pythagoras' theory would seem to imply that an interval is more consonant the simpler the ratio of the frequencies of its components. In fact, we can define a measure for this simplicity as follows: calculate the ratio of the frequencies, reducing it to the simplest fractional representation (thus 600/350 becomes 12/7) now add together the numerator and denominator of the fraction (for this example, 19). Confining ourselves to intervals contained within a single octave this procedure gives us a reasonable measure of the simplicity of a given frequency ratio.

It might now seem merely a simple matter to plot the simplicity of the ratio (corresponding to the degree of consonance) against the interval. However, anyone familiar with the difference between rational and irrational numbers will be immediately aware of the following paradox. If, for example, we take the interval of a fifth with the Pythagorean ratio 3:2 and hence a consonance value of 5 and we shift the upper tone by an infinitesimal amount either upwards or downwards in frequency, the ratio of the two frequencies making up the new interval immediately becomes non-simple. In fact, in general, the ratio of the two frequencies will not be expressible as the ratio of two finite integers. The simplicity value will in fact be infinite. If we confine ourselves merely to ratios along the line which are expressible with non-infinite integers, we will discover that the simplicity-value leaps around in an extremely erratic fashion as we proceed along the interval axis. This behaviour is illustrated for a limited number of points in Figure 4.1. Both the rigorous and the approximate description of the situation lead us to the bewildering conclusion that if we play a constant tone and make an upward portamento on a second simultaneous

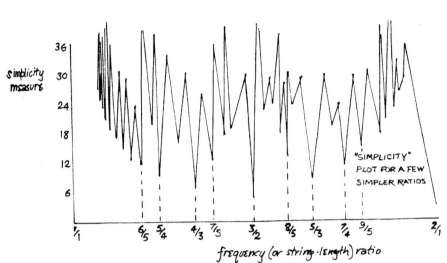

simplicity
measure

36
30
24
18
12
6

"SIMPLICITY"
PLOT FOR A FEW
SIMPLER RATIOS

1/1   6/5 5/4   4/3 7/5   3/2   8/5 5/3 7/4 9/5   2/1

frequency (or string-length) ratio

Plot of "simplicity" of intervals as predicted by Pythagorean theory.
It is always possible to generate a less simple ratio that lies between 2
existing ratios on the graph. This procedure may be followed ad infinitum

i.e. to generate a less simple ratio than 10/9 & 9/8, but lying between them

Take the bigger fraction (9/8), multiply numerator & denominator by 2 (18/16)
& add one to each (19/17). Then 10/9 < 19/17 < 9/8, but 19/17 is less
simple than 9/8 & 10/9 (simplicity measure 9/8 → 17 10/9 → 19 19/17 → 36).

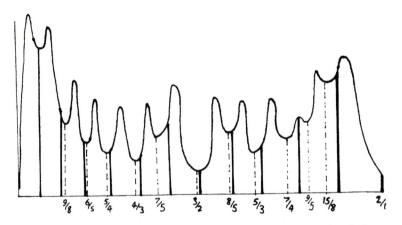

9/8   6/5 5/4   4/3 7/5   3/2   8/5 5/3 7/4 9/5 15/8   2/1

A schematic plot of our actual perception of "harmonicity". The solid black
vertical lines correspond to tempered-scale intervals. On the previous graph
these lines (if plotted) would all extend well beyond the top of the page (in
fact, to infinity !!).

Figure 4.1   Harmonic 'simplicity' of intervals as predicted from Pythagorean theory and as
perceived.

tone starting at the precise interval of a fifth from the first tone we should experience a sense of very rapid shifts in consonance between the two tones no matter how slow the portamento is made. This prediction is, of course, only true if we stick rigorously to the Pythagorean view.

Clearly, our actual aural experience is quite different. The ear is aware that a particular interval is at, or close to, the fifth (ratio 3:2), that it is moving away from the area of this ratio, and soon that it is approaching another recognisably different simple ratio (e.g. 8/5, a 'natural' minor sixth). We must therefore conclude that a second principle of relatedness enters our perception of pitch. We will refer to the Pythagorean criteria as the principle of *harmonicity*. The new criteria we shall refer to as the principle of *adjacency*. This new principle states merely that two pitches which are sufficiently close together will be heard as being related.

We can now give a new analysis of the original experiment of the portamento of a tone against a fixed tone which corresponds more closely to our aural experience. Whenever the frequency ratio between the two tones approaches one of the simple (Pythagorean) ratios, we perceive a harmonic relation between the two tones. As the sliding tone moves away from this tone we perceive the interval between the two tones as being closely related to the previously perceived interval. A sense of distance from the interval increases until we experience moving close to a new simple frequency ratio. Otherwise our experience of any continuous pitch motion would be hopelessly atomised and incoherent.

The principle of adjacency helps to explain how it is possible to construct systems of scales which do not use the precise Pythagorean ratios and yet function as if they do! For example, the interval of a fifth in the tempered scale does not correspond to the simple ratio 3:2, yet the whole system of tonality founded upon this scale system assumes that this approximate fifth is one of the simplest, most consonant, intervals in the system, thus establishing the dominant-tonic relationship (though other factors, particularly the overlap of membership of the asymmetric sets of pitches which make up the scales in this system, play an important role here). The principle of adjacency can also be seen to be of paramount importance in all those articulatory and gestural characteristics of musical practice which fall outside the lattice-based description which we have discussed at length earlier. Melodic practice, especially outside the modern Western tradition, is heavily dependent on the co-existence of the two principles of harmonicity and adjacency. What we have discovered is that in the continuum of intervals between the unison and the octave, the ear is attracted towards certain nodes of perception, defined somewhat loosely by the Pythagorean ratios and otherwise perceives adjacent intervals as being

closely related. But we may ask, when is a frequency ratio perceived as a
node and when is it not? How simple does the frequency ratio have to be
for us to perceive that ratio as a node within the system? Or more simply,
how many nodes are there within the octave? Here, culture takes over
from nature. It is clearly a matter of cultural practice how many intervals
within the octave are perceived as being harmonically distinct. In many
cultures only five nodes are recognised, the pentatonic scale resulting. In a
pentatonic culture intervals not falling on the pentatonic nodes are still
used as ornament or portamento decoration but are related by the listener
to the pentatonic nodes through the principle of adjacency and not heard
as separate harmonic entities in themselves. Seven, eight or nine nodes are
common in many musical cultures and these may arise from an underlying
theoretical framework positing an even greater number of nodes (twelve in
the Western chromatic scale or the twenty-two or more *srutis* of Indian
music).

It is interesting to ask just how rational the Western tempered
scale is. Why should it have twelve equal intervals rather than seven or
twenty-three? If we plot various possible equal-tempered scales against
the simple Pythagorean ratios (see Figure 4.2) we will see that a scale of

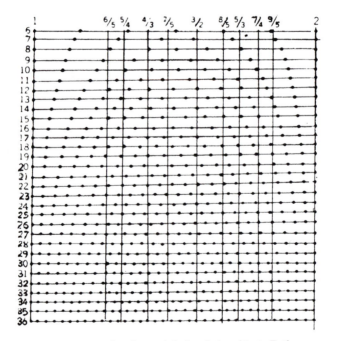

Figure 4.2   Various tempered scales and their relationship to Pythagorean ratios.

nineteen equally-spaced elements would have generated a set of intervals more closely approximating the Pythagorean ideal. Having made these observations we may now plot a graph of consonance against interval which corresponds more clearly to our aural experience. In the graph I have chosen a set of nodes which perhaps corresponds most closely to what the typical Western listener might experience. An experienced Indian musician might want to include several more nodal points in such a graph.

Metric structure of the Pitch-Continuum

The most important result of the perceived nodal structure of the pitch continuum is in giving us a means of measuring distance in the dimension of pitch. We will say that the pitch dimension has an audible metric. To explain what this means let us consider two separate sound-systems. In the first we deal with pairs of stable pitches. If we put the first pitch on a fixed note and then vary the register of the other pitch, it is always possible to say of the interval between these two pitches that it is smaller or larger than another interval. If we now repeat this experiment with two noise-band sources filtered so as to be of particular colours, but sufficiently wide so as not to present any aural experience of a definite pitch, we can produce the same result. Keeping one band fixed, while changing the register of the second band we can always judge whether the interval between the two bands is smaller or larger than another interval. If, however, we now change the register of both sounds in the two sets, our experience is quite different. First of all, we play two different pitch-sounds; and then we move both pitches to different registers and listen again. In this case, we can still say which interval is larger or smaller. Repeating the experiment with the noise-bands, however — here it is very important that the noise-bands are sufficiently wide not to present any pitch characteristic — there is no way in which we can judge which 'interval' is larger because we have no frame against which to measure the distance between the bands.

It should be stressed here that we are talking about our aural experience. It would of course be possible to make physical measurements with appropriate instruments and establish the frequency separation between the central frequencies of the bands of noise and from this establish a ratio of these frequencies which we could then compare between different experiences. The problem is that aurally we are not able to do this. The reason for this we can now see is simply that the dimension of pitch has a nodal structure. Given two pitches sounding together we do not have to rely merely on the linear separation of the two sound-objects along the dimension of pitch (the criterion of adjacency) but we can relate them to adjacent nodes and thus, via the principle of harmonicity, establish their intervallic distance. In the case of the noise-bands, the dimension of 'noise colouration' has no perceivable nodal structure and therefore we can only have a sense of linear distance (principle of adjacency) between the objects. This does not suffice for comparing intervals originating from different base lines. We will express this difference between the two systems by saying, at least in our aural experience, the dimension of 'noise colouration' has no metric.

It is the existence of this underlying nodal structure and the resultant ability to define an audible metric on the dimension of pitch which permits us to establish subtly different nodal scales (as, for example, in Indian music). It might at first seem that a mode might be exhaustively described in terms of the intervallic distance between successive notes as one ascends the scale. The question is, however, how does one know that a particular interval is larger or smaller than another, especially on a very small-scale? What accounts for our ability to perceive the subtle intervallic differences between different modes in Indian music? The answer is that we do not relate merely to the frequency distance between the notes but to the underlying nodal structure of the pitch dimension. We are able to tell where the individual notes of the mode are in relation to the nodes in the pitch dimension. We can tell with a fair degree of subtlety whether a particular note is very close or not quite so close to a particular nodal point. It is this which gives us a sense of measure and enables us to distinguish subtle differences between modal structures.

We might now consider the question, is it possible to establish nodal structures in 'noise-colouration' space? Can we have modes made up out of (unpitched) bands of coloured noise? We can, of course, artificially define such a mode; but if we define two such modes, each with very slight differences between the placement of certain bands, can we distinguish the two as different musical entities? The answer to the question is probably in most cases no, and that even where we can we will experience no qualitative difference in the nature of the music based upon the two different modes. This is because, as there is no underlying nodal structure to the dimension of 'noise colouration' then there is no qualitative point of reference enabling us to experience the two structures in a musically different way. It should be said that in the world of serialist permutationalism where the nodal structure of the pitch dimension is often ignored and pitch levels treated as abstract permutatable entities (like sizes of shoes, having no intrinsic relationships among themselves, only the extrinsic relationship of ordering in a set), then this distinction may be difficult to comprehend. We are assuming, however, that formalists will have abandoned this book after reading Chapter 1.

Two other features are of great importance in the conception of music on the lattice. The first is that the set of nodes is finite and closed.[1] In the sense that once we reach the octave the set of nodal values is in a clearly definable sense reproduced over the ensuing octaves. Music based exclusively on the lattice is thus a finite closed system with a metric. This is a more precise exposition of Boulez's conception of a music of hierarchic relationships upon a finite set of possibilities.

This conception can be extended to the harmonic system of Western tonal music. First of all let us note that one feature we have not discussed in the definition of a mode is the ability to recognise the root (or dominant tone). Where we have an entirely symmetrical intervallic structure (such as in a chromatic scale or the whole-tone scale) a root can only be defined by emphasis. Normally, however, the scales used in typical musical systems are asymmetrical in intervallic structure. This allows us to define where we are in the scale in relation to any particular note. If a root has been established we can therefore relate where we are in the scale to that root, even if the root itself has not been sounded for a very long time. The asymmetry allows us to tell where we are in relation to an absolute point of reference.

If our asymmetric scales are selected from an underlying symmetric set (for example the chromatic scale) then we can define scales having identical asymmetric structures (for example the major scale, T T S T T T S, where T is the interval of a tone and S of a semi-tone) but with different roots. If we now compare the members of these various scales, we will find that the scales on certain roots will have more notes in common with the scale on a particular root than others. This again allows us to define a concept of *harmonic* distance between *keys*. Note that the major scale is chosen so as to establish the closest relationship between scales whose roots are a fifth apart. Experimentation with modal structures will reveal that it is possible to construct scale systems where the closest relationship between roots, as defined by numbers of notes in the scale in common, is the interval of, for example, a minor third.

We can measure harmonic distance in relation to the cycle of fifths (in fact the cycle of approximate fifths used in the tempered scale system) and we can aurally perceive the measure of distance between two keys. It is interesting to note that in the relationship between major keys we

---

[1] We are assuming here that nodal structures reproduce themselves at the octave as is assumed in tonal music theory. If objections are raised to this conceptualisation then we will say merely that the set of nodes is countable and therefore has a structure unlike the continuum which is mathematically described as an uncountable infinity. The distinction between countable and uncountable infinities is clearly established in the mathematical literature.

might presuppose that the simple Pythagorean relationship of a fifth between the roots of the scales of keys was the predominant factor but when we look at relationships between major keys and their relative minor keys, we see that in fact common set membership is the predominant perceptual force. There are twelve notes in the cycle of fifths, which, being a cycle, is of course closed, hence we can see that the Western harmonic system is also a finite closed system with a metric (see Figure 4.3).

Structure of timbre-space; multi-dimensionality and non-metricity

Can we expand any of the insights we have gained from our analysis of the structure of the pitch dimension to an understanding of the world of timbre? Some crude attempts have of course been made to expand the ideology of lattice-based music to the organisation of timbre but this is, I feel, merely an *a priori* imposition upon the object of musical study. We can, in fact, draw upon the insights we have already gained but the conclusions we will reach will be radically different from the formalists. The area of timbre will be seen to have a radically different structure from the dimension of pitch. This does not mean that we should abandon it or regard it as essentially secondary in musical practice, but merely that we should investigate what criteria of sonic organisation would be appropriate to this particular area. The first obvious remark we should make about timbre is that it does not have one single dimension, as does the pitch continuum. This finding often surprises musicians brought up exclusively in the tradition of Western instrumental music where timbre has been streamed in specially acoustically-refined instruments and adapted to the logic of pitch/duration lattice architecture. It is obvious, however, from our discussion in the previous section that timbre is a multi-dimensional phenomenon.

David Wessel conducted some preliminary psycho-acoustic experiments to establish whether any structure exists in this timbre space. In one experiment timbre has been plotted in a two-dimensional space in which one dimension relates to the quality of the 'bite' in the attack, the other the placement of energy in the spectrum of the sound (its 'brightness') (Wessel 1979: 49). By this means Wessel has demonstrated that there is in fact a continuum of values existing within this space which can be perceived by the listener (Example 4.1).[2] I also recall a brief discussion at IRCAM

---

[2] Wessel's examples consist of the same melody articulated in two ways: in the first successive notes are constructed from timbres remote from each other in his two-dimensional timbre space ('quality of attack', 'brilliance') while in the second the timbres are close forming a continuous path. The first is perceived as a number of counterpointed lines, the second to a much greater extent as a single *gestalt*.

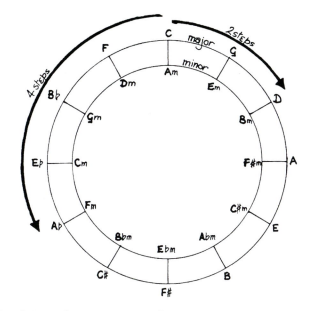

Cycle of 5ths: The cycle is closed (moving from C clockwise, or anticlockwise, we return to C). Distance between keys is measured by smallest number of 5th-steps around the cycle.
Thus C to D is 2 steps (clockwise), and C to Ab is 4 steps (anticlockwise).

C = set of notes in key of C
G = set of notes in key of G
Am = set of notes in key of A minor

C∩G = Set of notes occuring in *both* **C** & **G**.
C∪G = set of notes occuring in *either* **C** or **G**.

(**C∪G**) - (**C∩G**) ⇒ key "distance" measure

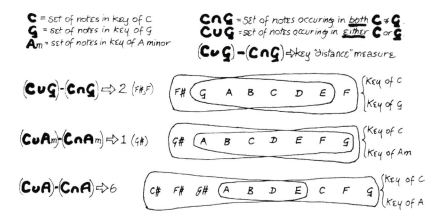

(**C∪G**)-(**C∩G**) ⇒ 2 (F#, F)

(**C∪Am**)-(**C∩Am**) ⇒ 1 (G#)

(**C∪A**)-(**C∩A**) ⇒ 6

Set membership measure: distance between keys can also be measured by comparing the notes used in each key, as above. This gives the same relative distances between keys as the cycle-of-5ths measure, & also includes the minor keys. The set model is also closed because the notes used in all 24 keys are selected from a (small) finite set of 12 (the chromatic scale).

Figure 4.3 Representation of Western harmonic system as finite and closed in which harmonic distance can be measured.

(undocumented) on this topic between David Wessel and Tod Machover in which two contrary views were expressed: roughly speaking that, on the one hand, there is the possibility that the timbre domain will be discovered to have a structure which we can relate in some way to the structure of the pitch dimension, and on the other that the timbre domain is quite distinct in its structure from the pitch dimension. My musical experience leads me to favour the latter conclusion. But not, therefore, to come to the Boulezian conclusion that timbre is essentially secondary, of necessity, in any conceivable musical practice.

As we have already remarked, timbre is multi-dimensional. In fact, the two dimensions of Wessel's experimental model need to be expanded to include factors such as grain, noise characteristics, inharmonicity and various morphological characteristics. Given this, even assuming that we are able to discover nodes in the space, it is difficult to see how these might be ordered in any way similarly to the one-dimensional and finite set of nodes in the pitch dimension. If we could separate out each of these dimensions and discover a nodal structure in each then there might be some hope of success in this direction. It would seem, however, that, just as with 'noise colouration', there are no perceivable nodes in any (or at least most) of the independent dimensions of timbre space.

But if we look at timbre space as a whole it is true that we can recognise or define particular sub-sets which we might define analogically as 'plucked', 'struck', 'sustained', or even 'scraped', 'broken' etc.. I will return to such (morphological) descriptions in later chapters but for the moment it is merely important to note that these sub-sets are not orderable in the sense that the nodes of the pitch continuum form an ordered (and also closed) set. On the other hand, the existence of clearly-distinguishable timbre archetypes does mean that we can apply the concept of a *field* — as in the usage *harmonic field* — to groups of timbres and work with a *timbre field*. I will return to this idea in a later chapter. The important factor about the Wessel examples is that although we can certainly define a concept of *distance* in the two dimensions which he demonstrates, we cannot, however, define a *metric*; there are no nodes in the particular dimensions illustrated. In fact, we will now declare that timbral space as well as being multi-dimensional is also not finite, not closed and does not have a metric. Does this mean, therefore, that it has no structure and that we cannot organise it in any way?

Referring back to our analysis of the structure of the pitch continuum we remember that we uncovered two complementary principles, those of harmonicity and adjacency. The structure of timbre space means that the principle of harmonicity is not applicable and therefore simply that all the principal assumptions of lattice-based musical practice cannot be applied to our thinking about timbre (except in an entirely formalist, *a priori* pre-conception). The principle of adjacency, however, remains. As demonstrated by the Wessel example, timbral objects which are close to each other in their multi-dimensional space of timbre are perceived as being related. It is therefore conceivable to establish a feeling of progression through timbre space moving via the principle of adjacency from one distinguishable timbre area to another. This type of progression may be thought of as in some ways similar to tonal progression in Western harmonic music and I have in fact used it as the basis for compositional work (as in for example the piece *Anticredos*). It does, however, differ from tonal progression in very important respects. In particular, the system is not closed and has no metric so, if we make a progression, this will involve a different sense of distance from that experienced in tonal music. As we progress, we will be able to sense that we have moved a noticeable distance from the previous timbral area. We will not, however, be able to measure how far we are from a different timbral area occurring earlier in the piece. In this way, our sense of causality or necessity in the musical progression is confined to the short term but breaks down when we attempt to refer it to longer stretches of time. This need not be a disadvantage and, depending on one's philosophical viewpoint, may be considered a distinct advantage![3] Modulation (in the sense of clear progression from one field of sound-objects to another field) can be clearly demonstrated and utilised in timbre-space. Modulation between different timbral sets could clearly be used as a basis for the large-scale architecture of a work, though this does not define how or why we should work on the small scale. I will discuss this problem in a later chapter.

Does the continuum have any structure?

If we accept that timbral space is a multi-dimensional continuum, does this mean that it can have no structure, or that there are no existing structural models which we can apply to it? Once one becomes locked into lattice-based or permutational thinking, the apparently natural way to deal with any quality is to chop it up into a number of distinct and distinguishable steps and then apply various well-established criteria for the organisation of a countable set of objects. If, however, we are to deal with the continuum as the continuum we must break this habit of thought.

---

[3] Contrary to the commonly-held conception of a deterministic, if not determinable, world, I hold the view that the world cannot be shown to be, and therefore is not, deterministic and that it is determinable in the short run but not in the long run. The type of musical architecture in timbre space described above corresponds very happily with my own philosophical viewpoint!

We must ask whether this multi-dimensional continuum can have any structure of its own. Our natural habit of thinking from the parameterisation of lattice-based music is to assume that all parameters extend indefinitely in all directions (or at least to the limits of audibility) and that the space is hence somehow entirely uniform. Continuous space will then be seen as some kind of endless fog extending in every direction. Continua do, however, exhibit different structures and this is the subject of the mathematical discipline of topology. Topology studies the properties of objects (or spaces) which are not changed by continuous deformations. Roughly speaking, what properties of a rubber object are retained if it is stretched in any conceivable way but not broken, torn or pierced? If we look at Figure 4.4 we see that, topologically speaking, the blob is equivalent to the sphere and to the cube as one may be deformed into the other by suitable stretching. None of these, however, is equivalent to the objects with a hole in them (as it will be necessary to pierce the former objects in order to obtain this hole), whereas all the objects with a single hole (including the cube with a handle) are topologically equivalent to one another. Similarly, objects with two holes are topologically equivalent to one another and topologically distinct from the other objects we have discussed.

Does timbral space have a topology? When working with existing musical instruments we may construct a map of the timbral possibilities of the instrument. To do this, rather than merely listing all the possible sound-types which an instrument such as a violin might produce, we would attempt to place these on a map (which might be multi-dimensional) on which similar sound-objects would be placed close to each other and sound-objects which are quite different from one another would be placed at a greater distance. A rough map of the sounds available from the string section of an orchestra is illustrated in Figure 4.5. An examination of this map shows that, due to the physical limitations of the instrument itself (and sometimes of the player), the space does, in fact, have a distinct topology. At least it is relatively easy to get from normal arco sounds to multiphonics played arco sul ponticello by infinitesimal motion in the timbre space (adjacency) but relatively difficult to get from normal arco to percussive effects on the wooden body of the instrument. In fact, to make a 'modulation' in the timbre space from arco sounds to percussion on the wooden body sounds, it is almost essential to go through col legno production or through pizzicato production. This means that timbral space viewed as a space in which timbral progressions (modulations) will be made has a distinct structure which, although neither closed nor having a metric, imposes specific limitations on our musical options.

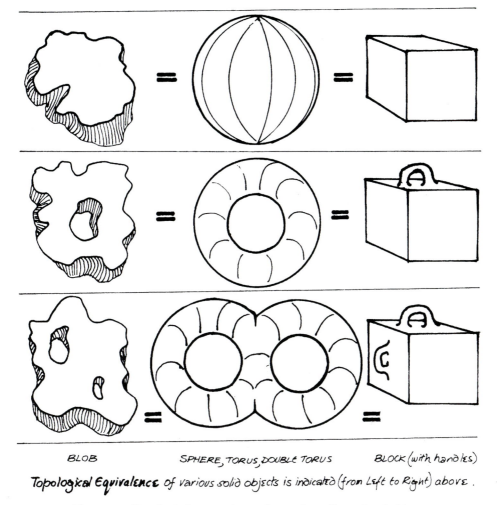

BLOB   SPHERE, TORUS, DOUBLE TORUS   BLOCK (with handles)

Topological Equivalence of various solid objects is indicated (from Left to Right) above.

Figure 4.4 Topological comparisons of some three-dimensional objects.

It will be interesting to see if the flexibility of the computer will allow us to overcome all such topological restrictions in timbre space (in some ways this would be a pity) or will we discover that timbre space has an intrinsic and insurmountable topological structure quite different from the infinite-coloured fog it is usually taken to be. A second and related question is, can there be any qualitative distinctions between the ways we move through this multi-dimensional continuum? Can motion itself in the continuum have any structure? Let us say first of all that the study of motion

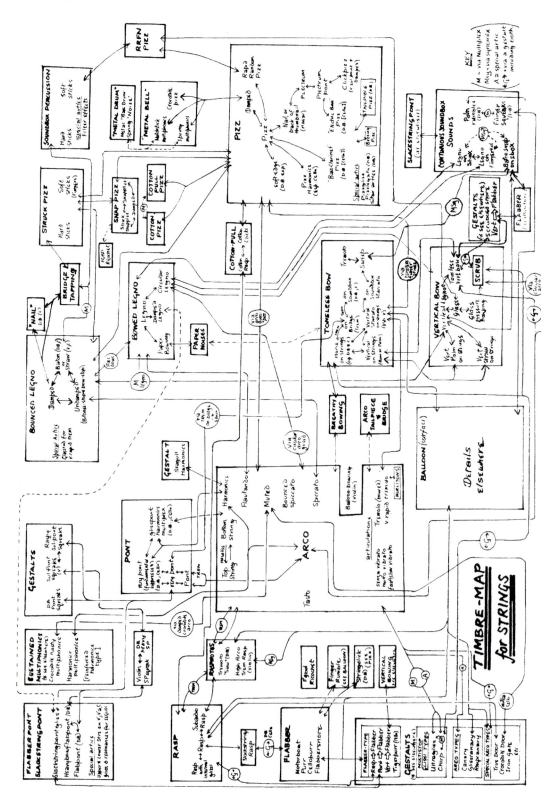

Figure 4.5   Timbre map for strings.

in the continuum has been a central topic of study in science since the days of Galileo and Newton. Motion in the continuum is usually described in terms of differential equations. The principal concern of physical science has been with systems which are structurally stable; for example, if we are studying the motion of a ball down some sort of incline we must assume that a small variation in the starting position of the ball will result in a small variation in its finishing position. If this were not the case, then the slightest error in the measurement of the initial position of the ball would lead to totally false results about its final position. As there is always some degree of error involved in physical measurements, the idea of physical prediction would become untenable if the system were not stable in this sense. Stable systems may have different kinds of structures. For example, see Figure 4.6; in the diagram on the left the ball rolls down a slope onto a concave surface and wherever we start the ball from at the top of the slope it will always end up at the bottom of the cup. In the system on the right, however, the ball rolls down the slope onto a convex surface. There are now two possible final positions for the ball. It will arrive either to the left or to the right. Both systems are entirely predictable yet different. Let us now study what happens when we gradually deform the lower surface from a concave shape into a convex shape. At a certain point (a point of catastrophe) the system slips over from having one stable state to having two stable states and at the exactly intermediate state where the lower surface is completely flat there are an infinite number of possible finishing positions for the ball.

Let us consider a wind instrument in this light. If we have a column of air and we excite it with a breath, a stable resonance will be set up, the

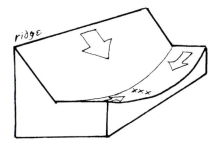 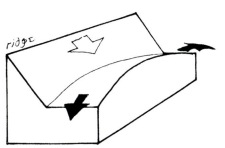

System 1: a ball placed anywhere on the ridge will eventually roll down to the depression xxx. There is only one possible outcome.

System 2: a ball placed anywhere on the ridge will now roll off the block either to the left, or to the right (see black arrows). There are now (only) 2 possible outcomes.

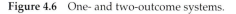

Figure 4.6   One- and two-outcome systems.

water surface (see Figure 4.9) or to the breaking of waves. One of its most significant scientific applications seems to be in the study of the structure of the form of organisms. Organic structures may be looked upon as the end product of continuous growth processes. The form of an organism may be viewed as the various instants of a process of continuous evolution successively frozen in time to create a structure existing in space. Studies of such phenomena were conducted by D'Arcy Thompson (1961) and Figure 4.10 illustrates Thompson's view of the parallel between the formation of a 'crown' when a droplet falls into water and the shape of various cup-like structures in many minute organisms. Thompson's work also illustrates how various rates of growth influence the final form of various organic structures from the shells of sea-living creatures to the skulls of primates and men (see Figure 4.11).

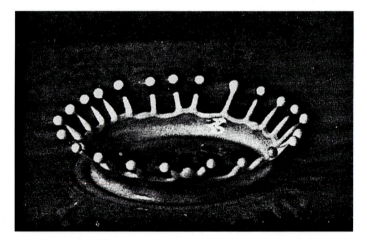

Figure 4.9   Instantaneous photograph of a splash of milk.

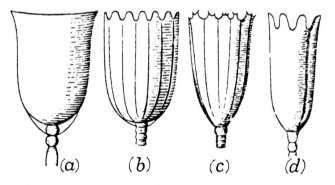

Figure 4.10   Calycles of Campanularia (after D'Arcy Thompson (1961)).

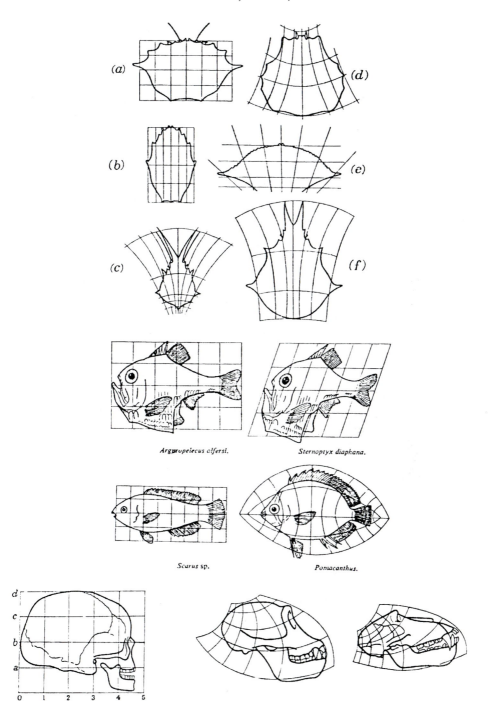

Figure 4.11 Patterns of growth compared: carapaces of crabs; shapes of fish; skulls of human, chimpanzee and baboon (after D'Arcy Thompson (1961))

The theoretical study of such forms of evolution in the continuum (see Thom 1975) suggested that there were only seven fundamentally different structures of evolution, or catastrophes in three-dimensional space and time. Two of these, the 'swallow-tail' and 'butterfly' are illustrated in Figure 4.12. More recent research shows that it may not be possible to generalise this conclusion to high numbers of dimensions. The important

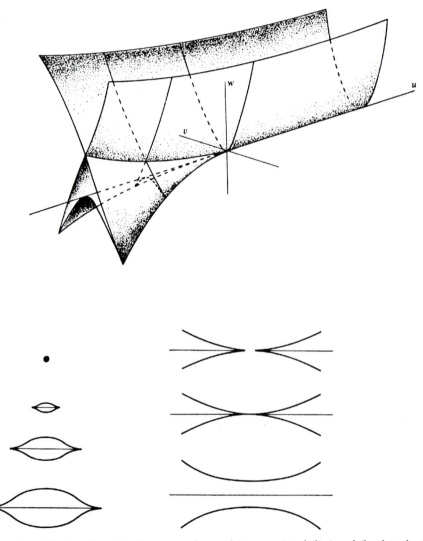

Figure 4.12a   The 'swallow's tail catastrophe' and its associated 'lip' and 'beak-to-beak' singularities (after Thom (1975)).

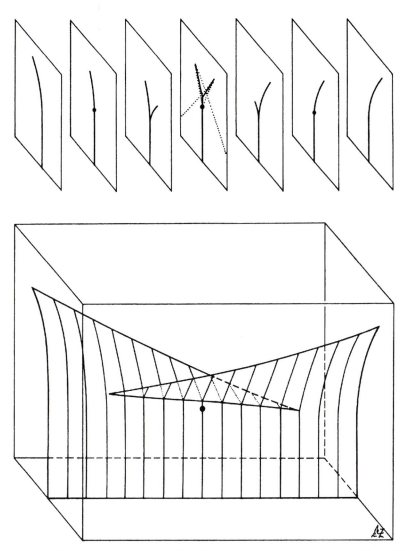

Figure 4.12b   The 'butterfly catastrophe' and its associated shock wave (after Thom (1975)).

point, however, for anyone concerned with structures evolving in the continuum (for example, musicians working in timbre-space) is that there are clearly definable and distinct structures. As Catastrophe Theory is generally applicable to both the behaviour of physical objects through time (for example, instruments, electronic sources, the voice or musculature) and to the description of time-based phenomena (such as acoustic phenomena) we may reasonably assume that a perceptually valid categorisation of time-varying acoustic phenomena (either the structure of sound-objects with dynamic morphologies or the description of the formal properties of sound-structures evolving through the continuum) is a feasible proposition. It also strongly suggests why there might be a link between the morphology of sound-objects or streams of sound, even where these are not intentionally produced by human gesture, and the quality of human response to these events.

I shall not, however, succumb to the formalist temptation to categorise all sound structures in the continuum in advance with reference to existing catastrophe theory but will, in later chapters, point to some perceptible and differentiable archetypes of sound morphology. The important point to be made here is that the continuum is not an undifferentiated seamless fog, opaque to human intellectual control but rather a wonderful new area for exploration provided we have the tools to control the phenomenon (the computer) and the right conceptual categories to approach the material.

Chapter 5

SOUND STRUCTURES IN THE CONTINUUM

Lattice-free objects; dynamic morphologies

A first reading of Chapter 3 may have seemed to imply that we only run into the area of non-metric adjacency-based organisation when we leave sounds with simple stable harmonic spectra and deal with sounds of complex mass or significant noise structure. This would be a misreading. Although we can define a metric on the dimension of pitch, we do not have to do so. Let us define some sound-objects based on elementary spectra which are not amenable to the pitch-lattice description. The simplest object will be a sine tone with portamento. In lattice-based music such portamento events are perceived to centre on the pitch of the start or the end of the portamento. However, we can design a glissando in such a way that it is very smooth and has such an envelope that the beginning and end do not significantly stand out from the rest. A music made up entirely of such sound-objects would fail to draw our attention to the nodal structure of the pitch-dimension because, without imposing some very special means of organisation upon the music, nothing in the musical structure would lead us to focus our attention upon a point of reference which would enable us to define nodes in the pitch dimension and hence relate sound-events to these. Continuing with the same material we may imagine a dense texture of such portamentoed sine tones constructed with such an average density that no particular pitch centre was predominant. Finally, we may imagine sweeping a filter across this texture in an arch form (see Figure 5.1). This final object has a clearly-defined structure of pitch motion imposed upon the texture of elementary pitches-in-motion but nowhere can we define the sense of a pitch in its traditional lattice-based sense.

Let us now define the concept of *dynamic morphology*. An object will be said to have a dynamic morphology if all, or most, of its properties are in a state of change — I use the word properties rather than parameters here, because I feel at this stage that it is important to view sound-objects as totalities, or *gestalts*, with various properties, rather than as collections of parameters. The concept of a musical event as a concatenation of parameters

Pitchfree glissando   Music of multiple glissandi   Dense glissandi   ditto with filter sweep

Figure 5.1   Assembling a non-classical pitch-motion structure.

arises directly from lattice-based musical thought and is singularly inappropriate to the musical structures we are about to discuss. In general, sound-objects with dynamic morphology can only be comprehended in their totality and the qualities of the processes of change will predominate in our perception over the nature of individual properties.

In his book *Sound Structures in Music*, (1975), Robert Erickson discusses the concept of *spectral glide*, essentially the evolution of spectral characteristics over a sustained pitch while Pierre Schaeffer (1966) discusses the concept of *allure*, subtle variations in dynamic and spectral envelope over a sound of otherwise constant mass. Here these will both be regarded as special restricted-case examples of dynamic morphology. A more typical sound will be one in which the spectrum, dynamic and pitch level all change through the continuum in the course of the sound. This kind of transition is illustrated on a more expanded time-scale in the two Examples 5.1 and 5.2. The first (5.1), synthesised using the *Chant* programme at IRCAM moves from pure bell-like sonorities into a vocal sound through a combination of an acceleration of the individual impulses and simultaneous widening of the formant structures involved. The second example (5.2), taken from my work *Red Bird*, uses a combination of vocal performance and classical studio techniques to transform the syllable 'sss' of "Lis(ten)" into birdsong. We may imagine similar total transformational processes taking place within sound-objects of much shorter duration and distinctive sound-objects of this type can be found both in the natural world and in the realm of speech phonemes and animal sounds.

We may illustrate the relation of these sound-objects to the classical lattice by attempting to draw them in the three-dimensional pitch-duration-timbre space of conventional musical thought.[1] In Figure 5.2 we see on the

_____

[1] It should be said that in order to represent timbre accurately we will need a number of dimensions for timbre alone so that our representation should be in at least four, if not six, dimensions. We maintain the fiction that timbre has only a single dimension here merely in order to be able to draw a diagram.

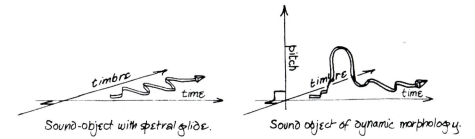

Figure 5.2   Schematic representations of spectral glide and dynamic morphology.

left a representation of a sound-object with spectral glide and on the right a sound-object of dynamic morphology. The difference between the two is immediately apparent from the figure. The spectral glide object remaining within a simple two-dimensional plane, whereas the object of dynamic morphology winds around freely in all dimensions.

Unstable morphologies: recognition by morphology

From here onwards we will assume that sounds with spectral glide are a special sub-category of sounds with dynamic morphology. There is, however, a further class of sounds to be considered: sounds of unstable morphology. These may be conceived of as sounds which flip rapidly back and forth between a number of distinct states. In my own writing I often refer to these as *multiplexes*. Such sounds are coherent in the sense that the overall field of possibilities remains constant but the immediate state of the object is constantly changing in a discontinuous fashion. Example 5.3 illustrates a typical vocally-produced multiplex. To complicate matters further, multiplexes themselves may have a dynamic morphology! In this case, the nature of the individual components of the multiplex undergo a process of gradual change through the timbre space so that the general field characteristic of the multiplex changes with time. This is illustrated in Example 5.4.

At this stage, anyone thoroughly enmeshed in the lattice-based mode of musical thinking may feel that such objects are essentially formless and incapable of any coherent musical organisation. In fact, however, the morphology of such objects is a significant recognition indicator in our everyday experience. To take two simple examples: first of all the sound of ducks which is normally imitated in the English language by the word "quack"; the most striking feature of the duck call and the only real feature which is paralleled in the word "quack" is the spectral glide characteristic as the formant structure moves from a stressing of the lower formants to a stressing of the higher formants (caused in the human, and presumably also in the duck, by the gradual but rapid opening of the vocal cavity).

More significantly, morphology appears to be an essential characteristic of recognition for certain consonant sounds in speech discourse. In the *Chant* programme, developed by Xavier Rodet and colleagues at IRCAM (See Rodet, Potard and Barrière 1984), vowels have been successfully modelled by defining their spectral (formant) characteristics. These models can be used without great difficulty to model strings of vowels which imitate vocal production very precisely. The attempt to model consonants has however met with difficulty as consonant structures have turned out to be extremely context-dependent. Although spectral characteristics (including noise-based aspects) are important in our recognition of consonants, they are not sufficient. What does appear to be preserved, however, from case to case is the shape of the motion, or the morphology of the consonantal sound-object.

Notation procedures for the continuum

In my work with extended vocal technique and the extended use of instruments, I have developed a number of notation conventions which are particularly useful for dealing with continuum phenomena and unstable acoustic objects. These notation conventions may be applied both to long-term transitions in the timbre (or in fact in any) field and also to the detailed, inner articulation of brief sound-objects. The illustrations in Figure 5.3 are taken from *Tuba Mirum* (1979).

The basic convention for this notation is that objects and processes are separated. Objects may be thought of as referring to specific delimited sound-objects or to specifically definable qualities of a sound-object at any particular time. Thus for example on the tuba we might define a normally produced tuba note to be one type of sound-object and a tongue-slap resonance through the instrument to be another. Similarly, various types of vocal production projected through the tuba may be described as objects. These objects may then become the material of multiplexes or enter into transformation procedures (see below). Alternatively, the object notation may be used merely to define particular states of a system which is in fact changing continuously. The simplest example of this would be the use of the standard phonetic symbols for the various noise-based consonants (s, f, h, and ʃ etc.) to indicate various aspects of a field which is in fact changing in a noise-spectrum continuum which might pass through any of these points (see below and also Figure 5.4).

We may now apply to these objects the process notation illustrated in Figure 5.3. A symbol with three arrows emanating from a point indicates that

PROCESS NOTATION

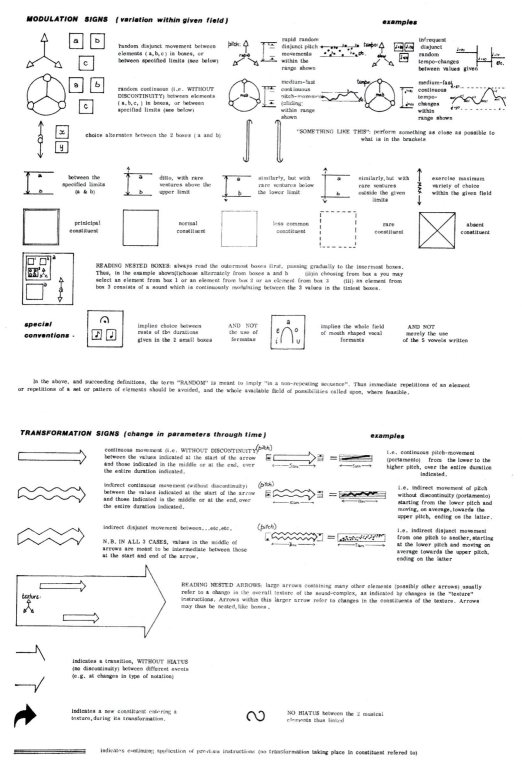

Figure 5.3   Process notation (from Introduction to *Tuba Mirum*).

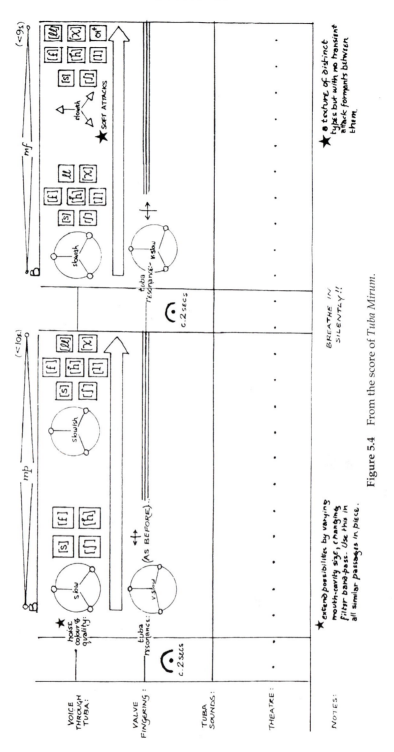

Figure 5.4   From the score of *Tuba Mirum*.

the performer is to move in a rapid disjunct fashion between the various elements indicated in the boxes (the sound-objects). This notation is particularly useful for describing sounds of unstable morphology (multiplexes). The symbol with three small circles on a larger circle works in a similar fashion, except that we are to move in a continuous fashion (i.e. through the continuum, without discontinuity) between the elements in the boxes. Looking again at Figure 5.4 we see the use of this sign in combination with various noise-phonetics. The sound intended here is thus a seamlessly-evolving noise-band approaching and passing through the various indicated states, and not a disjunct motion between these states. Further symbols help us to refine the description of these complex or unstable sound-objects, for example, we may give the various constituents different weightings (see various types of boxes in Figure 5.3).

The transformation signs indicate changes in the quality of the complex sound-objects through time. In the example from *Tuba Mirum* (see Figure 5.4) these symbols are used in an elementary fashion to indicate slow changes of emphasis over extended sound-objects. In Figure 5.5 they are used to describe global evolution in the structure of a multiplex stream and a series of transformations (with qualifications, the equivalent in timbre space of modulation in the space of tonal harmony) within a sound-object.[2] In the final example, see Figure 5.6, a complex series of transitions in texture, spectrum, pitch-stability, articulation etc. is defined by a set of nested transformations.

Incidentally, in all these examples the expanded vocabulary of sound-objects presented by extended vocal techniques is presented through a set of special symbols extending certain standard phonetic notations to incorporate features more appropriate to musical development than to simple linguistic description of phonemic characteristics. Similarly, a fairly detailed graphic symbolism for notating the timbre/pitch continuum is used in the example from the vocal pieces, the expanded phonetic and transformational vocabulary being employed in parallel as a detailed commentary upon the evolution of the graphic symbols. Once a work of this type has been learnt it is possible to perform it simply from the graphic stream. This '2-stave' procedure appears to be a satisfactory reconciliation of the needs of clear timbral and morphological description of sound-events with performance legibility. The simple convention of the (horizontal) transformation arrows has made possible the development

---

[2] Note that the three voices involved in the latter process form a single stream to the listener, as they are projected via a loudspeaker system as emanating from a single, moving point in space — see the comments on aural imaging in Chapter 3 — the rests in the three parts are therefore not intended to break up the perceived stream.

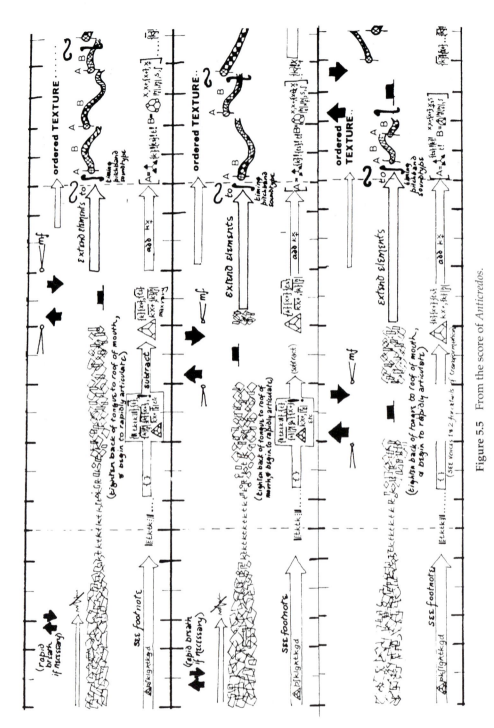

Figure 5.5 From the score of *Anticredos*.

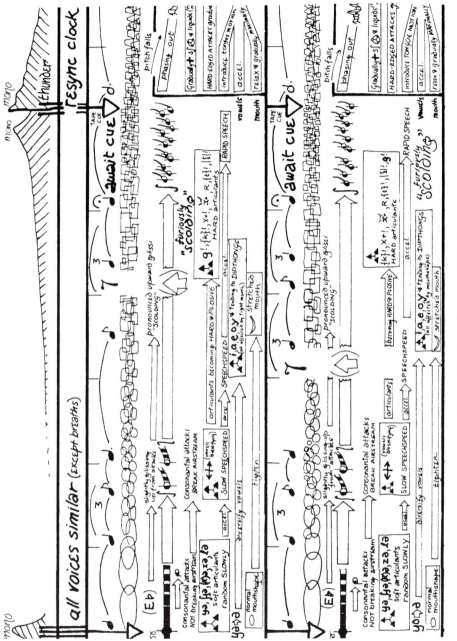

Figure 5.6   From the score of *Vox-1*.

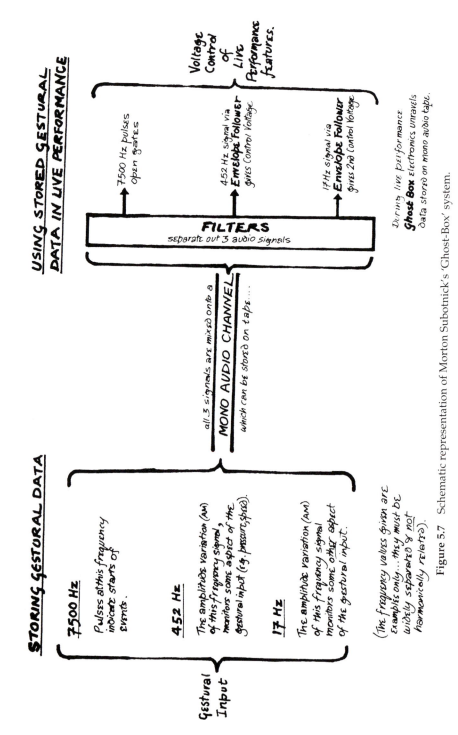

Figure 5.7   Schematic representation of Morton Subotnick's 'Ghost-Box' system.

performance practice. Aurally speaking, — I am now speaking of my aural experience of the music and not of the composer's theories — Ferneyhough's music stands at an interesting meeting-point of gesturally conceived musical practice and more traditional serialist thought. To my ear, a work such as his *Second String Quartet* presents an interesting approach to the counterpoint of musical gestures, which I will be discussing in the next chapter, whereas some of his works for larger ensemble appear to bury the articulation of gesture in the density and complexity of their serial architecture; the music ceases to breathe gesturally.

Postscript: the integration of pitched and unpitched architectures

The principal problem facing music which focuses upon sound-objects of dynamic morphology — and here I am talking particularly of objects whose pitch is not stable — is how one achieves some kind of coherent connection with more traditional pitch architecture. Much music, of course, starts out from the basis of traditional pitch architecture and articulations of the continuum are conceived within this framework. Music adopting a more radical approach to the use of sound-material, however, has to find a solution to this problem. When the musical objects used in an architecture do not in themselves imply any particular lattice structure it becomes difficult to justify any steady-state pitch material which enters into the musical discourse. Often a pitch or pitch lattice may be introduced as a drone, either on a single pitch or over a harmonic field emerging out of a noise-based structure in which pitch is not clearly differentiable. This process takes a certain time to unfold convincingly, hence the appearance of such drones.

There are clearly three principal approaches to this problem. The first lies in relating harmonic field structures to the internal structures of inharmonic spectra. This approach of course only applies where there are stable spectra present in the music already. The second approach depends on defining a harmonic field (or a series of such fields) such that any occurrences of stable or temporarily stable pitch objects fall on the lattice defined by the field. In this way a lattice-based architecture may coexist with an architecture of dynamic morphologies. This approach is in fact similar to the idea of music hung on a lattice (see Chapter 2). It may be thought of as a lattice hung on a morphological music, a change in emphasis. Finally, the imposition of stable resonant structures on complex (and noise-based) objects through, for example, filtering techniques may be a way of achieving a mediation between a morphologically-based and a lattice-based architecture in the musical structure.

It is interesting to note in this respect that musicians schooled entirely in lattice-based musical thinking will tend to latch on to aspects of stable pitch or resonance in any object (unfortunately, in many cases, they will see this as carrying the primary musical substance of the object). The way one relates to a complex object having some degree of resonance or time-domain pitch-structure depends entirely on the contextualising mode of organisation of the materials. At least in our culture it seems extremely difficult to achieve a balance between morphological and lattice-based architecture. For many musicians, lattice structure is what differentiates music from non-music and morphological architecture will be perceived as either chaos and no architecture at all or at least of no concern to the musician. Hopefully as we approach the end of the twentieth century we are growing out of this culturally ingrained habit.

Chapter 6

GESTURE AND COUNTERPOINT

Gesture and pitch-structure

Up until now it seemed reasonable to assume that the gestural characteristics of a musical performance were conveyed by dimensions of sound-space other than pitch. This, however, need not be the case. In lattice-based musical practice, pitch is constrained to manifest itself on the steps of the lattice defined by the system. In natural processes, however, this need not be the case. Thus, in a simple instrument such as a siren, the sense of pitch is generated by the rotation of a physical system, itself set in motion by the flow of breath. Due to the natural inertia of the system, when we blow hard into a siren the pitch rises initially from zero cycles to its maximum level in a rapid portamento and when blowing ceases it falls slowly back to zero. Pitch here is a measure of the degree of motion or activity of the system which is itself related to the gesture of blowing. The gesture of blowing (see Figure 6.1) may have an almost square envelope, but the physical inertia of the siren system will smooth this out into the shape shown which also expresses the pitch-contour experienced. Hence we obtain a somewhat fluid mapping of the energy input of the gesture of blowing.

Pitch-contour can also be an indication of energy input in such natural phenomena as the whistling of wind through telegraph wires, higher pitch being associated with greater wind velocity and therefore more energy. Similarly, the vocalisations of terror of most creatures are emitted with great energy and are of high pitch (more will be said on this subject in Chapter 11). Inversely energy contours may be suggested by pitch contours. In Example 6.1 from my work *Anna's Magic Garden* the vibration of a piece of elastic is used as a sound-source. When the piece of elastic is physically vibrated with more energy, the perceived pitch rises. In addition, due to the inertia of the system, when a switch-on, switch-off gesture is inputted to the system (like the blowing gesture through the siren) it is smoothed to give the characteristic pitch-contour perceived in the case of the siren, though in this case the decay time is much shorter. If this sound is recorded and speeded up one senses that there is more energy in the system. This is partly to do with the

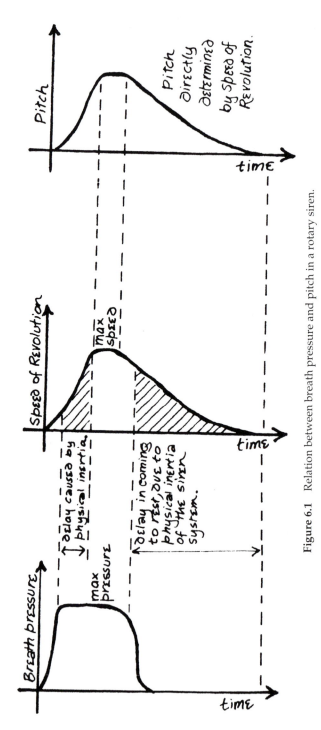

Figure 6.1 Relation between breath pressure and pitch in a rotary siren.

physical characteristics of the sounding object. Note that in the case of the voice a speeding up above a certain point moves the characteristic formant bands and the voice begins to appear unvoice-like (typically, a real voice may change its time-domain pitch but its spectral domain pitch or formants remain fixed for a given vowel). The vibrating piece of elastic clearly has no fixed formant spectrum and thus we accept its speeding up on playback as if it were a physically realisable phenomenon. Due to other characteristics of the sound (particularly its internal motion and its spatial movement) an aural metaphor of flying is suggested or, at least to the less poetically inclined, an intensification of energy and perhaps a sense that this energy is 'thrown' to a high point and falls back as the pitch falls towards the end of the signal.

In the next example (Example 6.2) a related effect is achieved with material from a quite different source. In this segment from Parmegiani, it might be that the sound-objects are made by fast-winding a continuous texture past the heads of a tape-recorder (though clearly many other processes are involved). Again, however, the formant structure permits us to link pitch with energy input and the sense of short gestures rising to a plateau and rapidly falling away helps to produce a sense of something being thrown and returning. This segment is in fact from a piece entitled *Etude élastique*. In both these cases I am not seeking to poetically elaborate the sound experience, but merely to attempt to offer some coherent explanation of our response to the sound in terms of the physical characteristics of the real world and our own experience of gesture.

We may now extend such considerations to melody itself. Although musical practice constrains melodic gestalts to notation on lattice pitches, performance practice (particularly the articulation of sustains with, possibly variable, vibrato and the closing of leaps by portamenti in some cases) would suggest that melodic contour has something to do with the expression of gestural energy through pitch-motion. Obviously in a musical practice dominated by lattice-based notation, considerations deriving from harmonic structures and motivic development will play an important part — in some cases an exclusive part — in the structuring of melody. However, I would suggest that in many cases we can perceive some gestural core to the structure of melodies. One observation in favour of this proposition is the tendency of melodies to cohere into a single object of perception, a structure essentially destroyed by dissection and permutation. This point of view will, of course, seem strange in the twentieth century climate of motivic or serial thinking. But in music where melodic thinking (as opposed to motivic thinking) is still of primary importance, this statement will be clearly understood. In modern Western practice, of course, the dominance of the notation system and the associated system of theory has permitted a gradual breakdown of the concept of melody, first into that of motif and latterly its complete atomisation into the concept of the (contour-independent) series. Productive though these may be, I would suggest that the perception of a true melody as a coherent whole has something to do with its relationship to a coherently articulated gesture — the codification of motivic practice, starting first with neumic notation, is part of a certain puritan thrust apparent in Western Christian civilisation!

Taking a simple example, the melody illustrated in Figure 6.2 is based on a motivic device with clear gestural import. The excitement generated by the melody is to a large extent generated by the sense of sudden accelerated energy as a pitch is thrown upwards and then falls back slightly in this gesture. I am not suggesting for one moment that melody is reducible purely to a gestural description but mean merely to indicate that gestural thinking is not confined solely to aspects of sound experience which are not normally notated. The important thing about gesture or dynamic morphology in general, is that it is essentially a time-varying property of a whole sonic object and cannot be atomised in the same way that pitch-lattice components can be separated through their discrete notation. Conversely, this property of gesture is one reason why it can be applied to the analysis or control of sound-objects which are varying in a continuous manner in many dimensions of the continuum. It does not need to be atomised or broken into dimensions, though of course, gestures articulated in independent ways in several different dimensions can carry more information than a gesture whose evolution takes place in the same way in all dimensions. In the same way, gesture is not reversible. To take an elementary example, becoming more intense is in no sense a close relation of becoming less intense! (Except of course if we insist on perceiving gesture out of time, a habit ingrained in Western art music practice through centuries of using spatialised time in notation.)

Figure 6.2   Gestural contour in a melodic shape.

Gesture in language, popular music, dance

As we have remarked earlier, language utterances do not consist exclusively of a combination of phonemes. Many other components (tone of voice, state of breathing, intonation, use of stress etc.) enter into the conveying of meaning through language. Some of these factors are in fact culturally based, particularly, for example, the stress patterning in particular languages, and are correctly termed paralanguage, needing some structural explanation in terms of linguistic categories. Other aspects of language (intonation, voice quality in relation to sex recognition, loudness etc.) appear to inhabit an expressive sphere independent of language itself. These matters will be discussed more fully in the sections on animal communication and human communication in Chapter 11. Here we may note that a piece like Berio's *Visage* depends on the existence of translinguistic expressive components in vocal utterances for its effect (Example 6.3). Berio describes *Visage* as —

> *Based on the sound symbolism of vocal gestures and inflections with their accompanying 'shadow of meanings' and their associative tendencies, [...] [including] [...] vocal events from inarticulated or articulated 'speech', [...] from patterns of inflections modelled on specific languages [...].*
> (Berio 1967)

The languages which Berio mentions include Hebrew, Neapolitan, Armenian, English and French (Emmerson 1976: 28). In many cases in this piece the phoneme-like components merely act as carriers of vocal gestural articulation which is carried through articulation of pitch, dynamics, timbre inflection within and over different sound-objects, rhythmic grouping and especially the integrated articulation of all these dimensions of gesture. It might also be suggested that the observed stress-patterns and patterns of inflection of specific languages have some more primordial source and that some remnants of this quality remain despite the evolution of culturally specific stress patterns in particular languages. It may also be the case that when conversing within a language we interpret articulations of stress and inflection as conventional but in listening to a language we do not understand we tend to interpret these in a more direct gestural manner. Language use therefore suppresses the gestural implications of the stress and inflection patterns used. A very typical gestural structure, 'pushing to a stable articulated position', the archetypal expressive gesture of the ballad singer in popular Western music, is the sustained note which is attacked very slightly flat and then portamentoed towards the standard pitch while gradually bringing in vibrato. This gesture is, loosely speaking, a parallel, in the domain of the continuum, of harmonic resolution.

Gestural analysis may in fact be extended to realms of human activity which do not involve the production of sound. Many aspects of dance are self-evidently gestural. A fairly complex analytic notation for dance movement was developed by Rudolf Laban. Laban himself attempted to notate the stress patterns of movements and more recent developments of the notation have attempted to describe the internal flow of 'strength' in a movement (see Figure 6.3 in which black commas indicate particularly strong movements, white commas particularly light movements). These and some other aspects of Laban notation may be seen as relating to the articulation of gesture in sonic utterance. It might be argued in fact that the very attempt to establish a relationship between dance movements and music (apart from timing of movements and rhythmic pulse) relies on the unwritten assumption of a common gestural substrate at some level. This

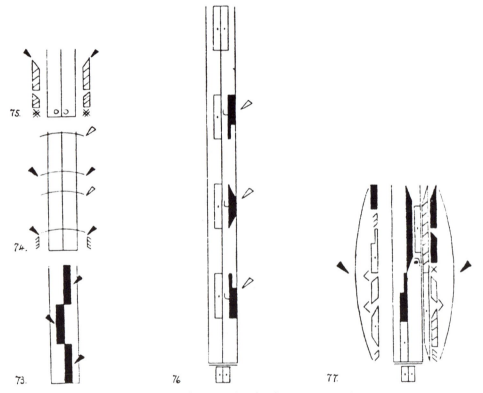

Figure 6.3 Laban notation for dance movements.

does not preclude dance (like music) having other concerns, such as the use of mime-imagery in disco dancing.

Contrapuntal structure

Can we establish a truly contrapuntal method of working in the continuum? To answer this question we will need to analyse the concept of counterpoint in lattice-based music and attempt to generalise the conception so that it is no longer dependent on the existence of a lattice structure. We should also examine some existing approaches to contrapuntal structure in the continuum.

The example from *Pithoprakta* by Xenakis, quoted in Chapter 2, illustrates a form of rudimentary counterpoint. The three lines of string sounds, none of which is based on the pitch lattice (glissandi of glissandi), are in fact streamed in terms of a timbre lattice. We differentiate the three streams because of their different and consistent timbral qualities. The three lines certainly coexist in the same musical space and are heard as distinct entities, but we can hardly describe them as contrapuntal as there is no real interaction between the parts except in their coming together in the high register before the sustained chord material is revealed.

In my own piece, *Anticredos*, for six voices using extended vocal technique, (listen to Example 6.4), a simple example of stream-divergence is set up. When we are dealing with continuously evolving streams, we can imagine that a single stream evolves through the continuum into two distinctly separated streams. These may be separated in pitch or pitch area, timbral characteristics or space (in the example given, all three). The important point is that this division of one stream into two may take place quite seamlessly, an effect which would be, to say the least, extremely difficult to achieve in lattice-based instrumentally streamed music. Also, in this particular example, the two independent streams are themselves undergoing continuous timbral transformation as they independently circle the audience (the live work is projected on four loudspeakers surrounding the audience). In this case, therefore, we have streaming without instrumental streaming of timbre. However, stream divergence is the only 'interaction' between the two existing musical threads.

A more complex and highly-articulated development of the concept of seamless divergence and merging of sonic streams may be imagined (see Figure 5.2) and this would certainly be an entirely new realm of musical development dependent on our acceptance of the multi-dimensional *continuum* as a valid substrate for physical composition. The gradual separation or reintegration of the streams might be emphasised by the imaginative use of spatial movement (another continuum parameter).

We may, however, develop a conception of counterpoint closer to what we understand by that term in lattice-based music theory. Let us first of all attempt to make a generalisable analysis of the substance of the contrapuntal experience. For us to describe the musical experience as contrapuntal in a more conventional sense, it is not sufficient for us to experience the mere coexistence of a number of musical streams. These streams must be felt to relate to one another or interact in some way during the course of their separate development. In lattice-based counterpoint this will involve the ebb and flow of rhythmic co-ordination and harmonic consonance (or 'normality' defined in some other sense) in the relationship between the parts. Ideally, in tonal counterpoint, we should expect to feel that the overall musical texture is 'going somewhere'.

Thus, in addition to the streaming of individual parts, we can establish two criteria for our recognition of a contrapuntal structure. First of all, an *architectural principle* which supplies points of reference in the overall progression of the musical material. This corresponds to the key structure in tonal counterpoint. Secondly, a *dynamic principle* which determines the nature of the motion. In tonal note-against-note counterpoint this is related to the ebb and flow of rhythmic co-ordination and the ebb and flow of harmonic consonance-dissonance that we have discussed previously, both of which arise from the way in which notes in individual parts are placed relative to notes in other parts. The lattice structure of tonal music allows us to develop a detailed and elaborate sense of contrapuntal development.

Few explicit attempts have been made to achieve the same contrapuntal results when working in the continuum. An interesting exception is the relational notation used by Stockhausen in *Mikrophonie I* (see Figure 6.4). Here the development and interaction of the individual parts is organised according to a simple set of relational and transformational symbols. This notation, however, seems to be essentially enabling and tells us

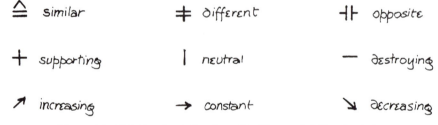

Figure 6.4   Relational notation from Stockhausen's *Mikrophonie I*.

little about the details of interaction between the internal structures of sonic objects which occur in the actual performance. In fact, the experience of the counterpoint of the performance is quite separate from the rationale of the score, an approach we would like to leave behind.

I would therefore like to suggest a more detailed model for counterpoint in the continuum, deriving from my generalised analysis of counterpoint above. In the architectural dimension we will replace the progression from one key to another, which is the architectural base-line of tonal counterpoint, by the concept of transformation from one timbral or sound-morphological area to another (this is discussed in Chapter 5). In the dynamic dimension, we will replace the interplay of consonance-dissonance in harmonic progressions by the idea of gestural evolution and interaction between the separate streams.

A fundamental characteristic of our original analysis of tonal counterpoint is that the two dimensions, the architectural and the dynamic, are independent of one another. Thus the tonal contrapuntal development is articulated upon the key structure and is not a mechanical manifestation of the tonal progression implied by the architecture. The problem with our earlier example from *Anticredos* is that there was no separation between the architectural and the dynamic. The two streams of sound evolved timbrally, but their content was entirely determined by this timbral evolution. There was no separate dimension in which a dynamic could be developed. What we are now suggesting is that the evolving stream may be gesturally articulated and we may coordinate (or not) the gestures between the various parts in such a way as to create a viable contrapuntal structure. I will attempt to illustrate how this approach might be realised with reference to the piece *Vox I*.

In *Vox I*, four vocalists, using extended vocal techniques, perform against an 'orchestra' of natural-event sounds on four-channel tape. The principal timbral progression of the piece is from pitch-free, unarticulated multiplexes towards pitched language-like unison utterance. The line of development is not direct (the piece 'modulates' back to unarticulated multiplexes in its central section) and passes through a number of distinct timbral-morphological areas. Although the piece uses four voices as its sound-sources, these are not necessarily projected as four independent streams. Using mixing and spatial motion facilities the listener may be presented with a single stream, two equally-weighted, or unequally-weighted streams, three unequally-weighted streams or four streams of sound, and in any of these cases, the perceived streams may move around the quadraphonic space in the auditorium. The timbral-morphological progression in the piece can be partly analysed in terms of standard (spectral and dynamic) timbral properties, but another important feature is the mode of articulation (an aspect of gestural structure) itself. Roughly speaking, this develops from continuous unarticulated multiplexing through continuous articulated multiplexing,[1] distinct articulated multiplex units to distinct speech-articulated units.[2]

As mentioned before, this progression is not a simple motion from A to D. Furthermore, the development of 'articulateness' is further complicated by the division (and sometimes merging) of the sound-streams. For example, at the commencement of the piece, the continuous, unarticulated multiplex we hear is produced by a mixing of all four voices. This slowly evolves (as in the *Anticredos* example) into two distinct continuous streams which then begin to be articulated and at this point the articulations begin to interact. At a later point, this stream divides again, this time into four distinct vocal streams. Conversely, towards the end of the piece, four distinct and separately-articulated vocal streams gradually converge both in content and articulation to form the unison stream of coordinated, speech-like articulation which ends the piece. The tape part, which forms another layer in the composition, is also related to this development. The initial stream of the four voices emerges seamlessly out of the tape material whilst, at the end, the tape for the first time settles on fixed pitches (as do the voices) and through vocoding procedures slowly begins to parallel the articulation of the unison speech-like material in the voices. There is thus a clear, architectural sense of progression through the piece.

Once, however, more than one vocal stream appears, it is necessary to develop a contrapuntal articulation between the streams. This becomes particularly significant towards the end of the piece, where the four voices, clearly separated on the four separate loudspeakers, each perform highly complex sound-objects gradually evolving the material of the speech-like utterances. I will give here a simplified description of the procedure employed to develop a contrapuntal feeling in the music. I should stress, in line with my comments earlier in the book, that in the end I am governed by my aural experience of what actually functions as counterpoint. I am not attempting to set up a formal procedure which can be followed blindly (or rather deafly, notationally) by anyone else. However, this particular problem is hardly likely to arise as, to be explained below, the gestural procedures do not appear explicitly in the notation.

---

[1] This articulation is achieved partly through using the cupped hands as a variable filter on the continuous vocal source.

[2] It should be emphasised that the speech is speech-like articulation, the language is imaginary.

My approach to defining a gestural structure would be simplified, not because, as some may think, gesture itself is a simplistic parameter, but quite the opposite. To make a short digression, let us consider the gestural articulation of a standard, stable musical note. In fact, let us consider just one single dimension of this, the use of vibrato (that is the iterative fluctuation of frequency around the mean). First of all, note that vibrato has two different dimensions, at least: the rate of iteration and the depth of the frequency variation (we might also have considered iterative spectral variations). For the purposes of this discussion, we will define a number of morphological archetypes for the gestural articulation of vibrato, bearing in mind that these are merely poles in a continuum of possibilities. Referring to Figure 6.5, we might classify the possible gestures in three ways:

(1)   According to *magnitude*. Hence the depth of the vibrato might be shallow, medium or deep (note also that the speed of the vibrato may also be sluggish, normal or rapid). We consider here only three levels for the sake of simplicity. In the case of vibrato which changes, we should consider the three ranges narrow-to-normal, normal-to-wide and narrow-to-wide.

(2)   The *morphology* of the vibrato. In fact this is really only the first-order morphology, as we will explain below. Let us choose just eight distinguishable archetypes: stable, increasing, decreasing, increasing-decreasing, decreasing- increasing, unstable, stable-becoming unstable,

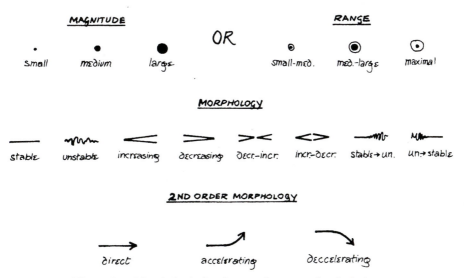

Figure 6.5   Morphological archetypes for gestural articulation.

unstable-becoming stable. Unstable should be understood to mean non-periodic or semi-random fluctuation in frequency widths (or iteration-rate) of the vibrato. Clearly this list might be extended, but these seem to me to be eight perceptually quite distinct gestural morphologies.

(3) *Second-order morphology.* In the case of changing morphologies, such as an increase or a decrease in the depth of the vibrato or a change in its stability of range, it is clearly possible to perceive a second-order structure. Thus a change may be quite smooth or it may accelerate as it gathers momentum, or begin quickly and slacken in pace. Thus we might imagine a note which, from the moment it is attacked, begins to vibrato minutely and this vibrato grows wider, smoothly with time. Alternatively, the note is attacked and appears to remain stable in tessitura for a short time after which shallow vibrato becomes apparent but, as soon as we become aware of the vibrato, it rapidly increases to a maximum. Alternatively, a note may be attacked and very rapidly increase its depth of vibrato, reaching a stable plateau of wide vibrato for its end portion. With the increasing-decreasing morphology, these second-order effects would alter the temporal position of the maximum point. With a steady rate of change the maximum point would be reached at the centre of the note. With an accelerating change, the maximum point would be reached towards the end of the note, followed by a more rapid decrease and with the slowing shape the vibrato would increase to a maximum quite rapidly and then die away in range slowly. These three second-order morphologies may be referred to as direct, accelerating and decelerating.

Each of the second order morphologies may be associated with the first-order morphologies which exhibit change. This gives us twenty-two perceptible different morphologies and each of these may be associated with the three magnitudes, giving a total of sixty-six gestural archetypes. If we now remember that these articulations may be applied to both the frequency width and the rate of iteration of the vibrato, we now have 3,756 ways of articulating vibrato! We may now apply the same gestural criteria to the overall dynamic envelope of the note and the tremolo characteristics. We can hence describe 14,106,536 possible articulations for a standard musical note. If we now enter the field of the true continuum and consider portamento motions of the pitch and timbral transformation of the pitch through time, we discover 50,000,000,000 perceptible distinguishable sound-objects. At this point, serial methodology loses its charm.

Let us therefore assume for the moment that there are only four distinguishable gestural types which we shall apply to the gross characterisation of a sound-event (we are making no attempt at parametric separation). We will describe these as stable, unstable, leading-to and leading-from; each of our four lines of counterpoint will consist of musical gestures which we will describe in terms of these four archetypes. (Note here that the description is a convenient fiction, in practice we will articulate each musical object with greater subtlety. The four-pole characterisation merely enables us to get a handle on the gestural structure.) The sequencing of gestures in a single line will be strongly determined by the particular type of expressive coherence (or lack of it) in that line. This will determine both the type of gesture used, the sequence of individual gestures and the average rate of gestural activity.

We may now look at this structure 'vertically'. From this point of view, the overall rate of occurrence of gestures from moment to moment will be an important parameter. This may be defined, for example, by marking off blocks of time in which equal numbers of gestures occur, counting all four parts at once — although clearly from a perceptual point of view if the gestures in two parts move exactly synchronously the overall rate of gestural activity will appear to be half that we would obtain by counting up the gestures separately in each part. We now have a matrix in which horizontal and vertical considerations of the timing of gestures interact.

We may go a stage further, however. We may consider the gestures in the various parts over a short period of time and consider (a) if the gestures in different parts are similar to one another (homogeneous) or different from one another (heterogeneous) — note that this is independent of whether the gestures in an individual part are homogeneous, or heterogeneous — and (b) whether the gestures appear to interact with one another or appear to behave independently of one another. The first criterion requires no qualification, the second, however relies on musical judgement in the act of composition (in the act of listening the distinction is quite clear).

From this analysis, we may derive six archetypes for the vertical ordering of gestures (see Figure 6.6). Gestures which are the same in all parts may be organised completely in *parallel*,[3] semi-parallel (in which the parts follow the same gestural logic, but not in a synchronous way) and *homogeneous independence* (where the parts appear to be behaving independently of one another). When the vertical organisation of gestures is heterogeneous these may also be independent (*heterogeneous independence*),

---

[3] Akin to *tutti* so long as we bear in mind that we are talking here about gestural structure and not spectral type.

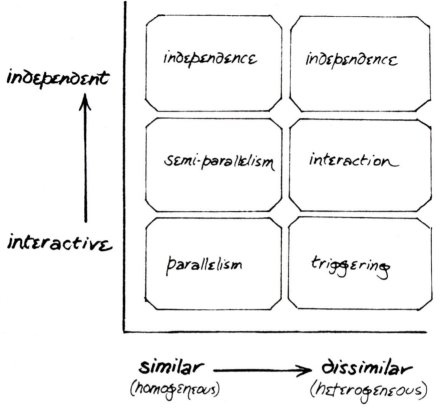

Figure 6.6   Six archetypes for the vertical ordering of gesture.

they may appear to be *interactive* (for example through the relative placement of stress accents between parts which may suggest causal or imitative links between events in different parts) or *triggering*, in which a gesture in one part appears to initiate an event or change in another part quite clearly. For example, one part sustains some material, a second part enters quietly and becomes louder in an accelerating fashion, cutting off at the point of maximum loudness. At that same instant the other part begins to articulate rapidly. The event in the second part appears to trigger the change in the first one.

The independent sets of horizontal and vertical criteria for the organisation of gesture allow one to develop a subtle architecture for the contrapuntal development of the music. At the same time it is important to realise that gestural structure is independent of the timbral characteristics of the sound-objects themselves. In *Vox I*, therefore, the evolution from multiplexes towards speech-articulated, stable-pitched sound-objects is articulated through the counterpoint of gestures of the individual sound-objects in the vocal streams (see Figures 6.7 and 6.8). Although, of course, it would be possible to set up a serial net of possibilities and thereby permute the various conceivable gestures, this would seem to me to defeat the object of contrapuntal development. Hence the articulation of gesture must underline the sense of timbral transformation and help carry it forward. In actual practice, therefore, various *nodal points* in the musical architecture are established where, for example, crucial sound transformations materialise or a particular gestural structure (for example, complete parallelism or a strong, trigger device) is decided upon. I would then decide on the positioning of other minor nodes and construct the remaining architecture of the music, both horizontally and vertically, in such a way as to move the music towards and away from these points with a sense of purposive development. Nodal and sub-nodal points are also provided by the evolution of the materials on tape, all of which have a gestural structure which can be related to the gestural counterpoint in the voices themselves. Spatial placement and movement is also used to articulate the material and I will discuss this aspect in Chapter 10.

I found this approach to be a powerful heuristic tool for composing with this kind of material. It was possible to lay out the structure of the overall density of events on the score, then compose the gestural structure of a section using elementary symbols like those in Figure 6.7 and then, working from the overall plan of timbral and articulatory development, score in the details of the individual sound-events in each voice. (In practice, of course, the general nature of the sound-events in any section is already in one's mind when the gestural structure is being composed.) This means, however, that the underlying gestural structure does not appear explicitly in the score (for example, it is not a simple correlate of any specific parameter notated in the final score) and could only be teased out by a sympathetic music analyst, prepared to listen to the music itself. Finally, it should be said that I have only been able to attempt a theoretical description of gestural counterpoint given here, because of my attempt to write down music using complex sonic objects. When working entirely in the electro-acoustic music studio, gestural structure can be finely tuned by the experience of aural feedback and *need* not involve any separate process of conceptualisation. Having initially rejected the medium of music notation some years ago and after working in the electro-acoustic music studio had brought me face-to-face with its implicit musical ideology and intrinsic limitations, I have found the attempt to evolve new and appropriate notational procedures to be very fruitful. I would still insist, however, on the

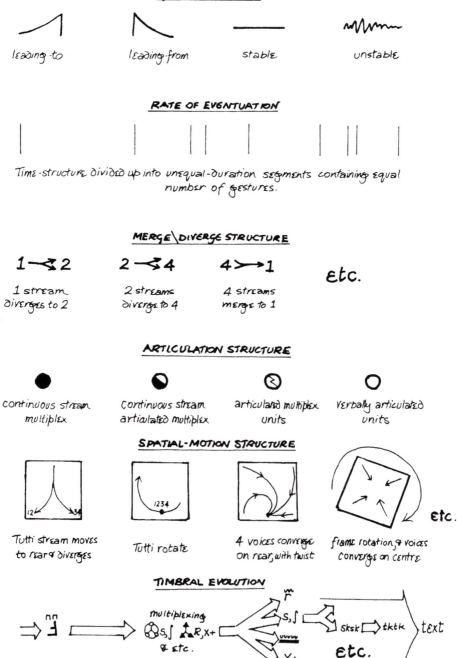

Figure 6.7   Some working parameters for the composition of *Vox-I*.

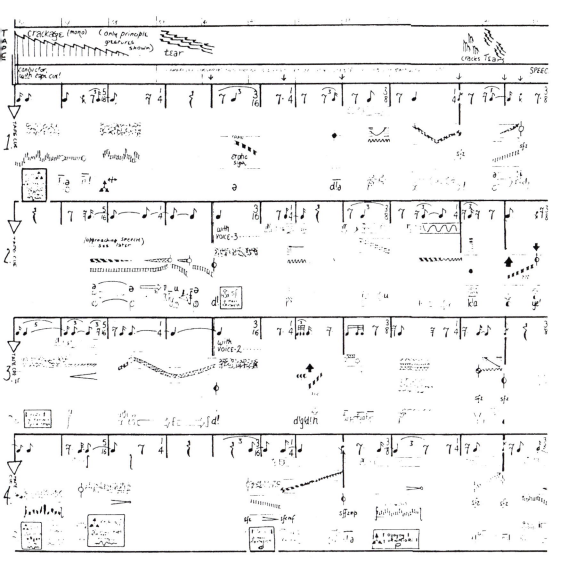

Figure 6.8 Section of four-part gestural counterpoint from *Vox-I*.

ultimate validation of any musical procedure through the unmediated and unprejudiced listening experience. No notational *logos* can in itself justify a musical procedure. A rationale based on listening to and working with acoustic materials — whether or not it is rigorous or elegant (and if it is either of these we should already be suspicious) — will be needed when we approach the multi-dimensional continuum opened up by digital sonics.

Part 2

Landscape

Chapter 7

SOUND LANDSCAPE

Any sound which has too evident an affinity with the noises of everyday life, [...] any sound of this kind, with its anecdotal connotations, becomes completely isolated from its context; it could never be integrated, [...] Any allusive element breaks up the dialectic of form and morphology and its unyielding incompatibility makes the relating of partial to global structures a problematical task.
(Boulez 1971: 22–23)

I thought it had to be possible to retain absolutely the structural qualities of the old musique concrète without throwing away the content of reality of the material which it had originally. It had to be possible to make music and to bring into relation together the shreds of reality in order to tell stories.
(Luc Ferrari interviewed in Pauli 1971: 41)

Chapter 4 of Pierre Schaeffer's *Traité des Objets Musicaux* (Schaeffer 1966) is entitled *The Acousmatic*. According to the definition in Larousse, the Acousmatics were initiates in the Pythagorean brotherhood, who were required to listen, in silence, to lectures delivered from behind a curtain such that the lecturer could not be seen. The adjective *acousmatic* thus refers to the apprehension of a sound without relation to its source. It is important in Schaeffer's development of the concept of the sound-object that it be detached from any association with its source or cause. The sound-object is to be analysed for its intrinsic acoustic properties and not in relation to the instrument or physical cause which brought it into being. However, in our common experience, we are more often aware of the source of a sound than not and studies of behaviour and aural physiology would suggest that our mental apparatus is predisposed to allocate sounds to their source. We can see in a very crude way how this ability was essential for our survival in the period before our species came to dominate the entire planet. One needed to be able to differentiate between harmless herbivores and dangerous carnivores, predator and prey, friend and foe. Even in the cultured detachment of today's world, however, when we are listening to a concert of instrumental music, except where the texture is very dense or produced in a way which is novel to our ears, we are always very aware of the instrumental source of the sounds we hear. We might, in fact, go a stage further and notice that in the tradition of virtuoso performance our awareness of the source and the performer's physiological, balletic and dramatic relation to the source can become part and parcel of our aesthetic reaction to the concert experience.

The formalisation of musical parameters, the lattice of the tempered scale, the rhythmic co-ordination required by harmonic structuration, the subordination of timbre to pitch and its streaming in separate instrumental layers, is in many ways an attempt to negate the impact of the recognition of the source (human beings articulating mechanical sound-sources) and focus our attention upon the lattice logic of the music. Part of our enjoyment of the music, however, remains an appreciation of the human source of the sounds themselves (this is in a sense distinct from the articulation of non-notated parameters of the sound through performance gesture which we have commented on in earlier chapters).

In some contemporary instrumental music it has been possible for a composer to specify a type of architecture and a mode of sound production which limits the possible impact of gestural characteristics upon the acoustic result, and when such music is heard on loudspeakers a large degree of detachment from recognition of the source may be achieved for some listeners. With music for voice, however, it is doubtful if we can ever banish from our apprehension of the sound the recognition of a human source for those sounds. Furthermore. that recognition often plays a significant role in our perception of the music itself. For example, in the *Trois Poèmes d'Henri Michaux* of Lutoslawski, our perception of a mass of human 'utterers' is important in itself and becomes especially so in the crowd-like sequence, the recognition of 'crowd' or 'mob' contributes significantly to our aesthetic appreciation of the work (Example 7.1).

At this stage, let us place these various characteristics of the sound experience related to our recognition of the source of the sounds under the general heading of *landscape*. It is important at this stage to differentiate the idea of landscape from that of *association* as it is frequently used in reference to programmatic music. Thus in our listening to the final movement of Tchaikovsky's *Manfred* symphony we may be led (by the programme note or otherwise) to associate the acoustic events with the idea or image of the distraught Manfred wandering through the forest. It may in fact be that there is some analogical relationship between our supposed experience of the events described in the programme and our experience of the acoustic events, perhaps related to the structure of musical gestures and their relation to more universal human gestural experience (I would not like to press this point too far!). The landscape of Tchaikovsky's *Manfred* is however musicians playing instruments. Landscape, at least at this level, is then a reasonably objective criterion, related to our recognition of the source of the sounds. However, in the traditional Western repertoire there are instances more difficult to classify. Generally speaking, these are situations in which some degree of mimicry of non-instrumental or non-human vocal sounds is attempted by the musical instrument or voice. In the first example, from Janequin's *Le Chant des Oyseaulx*, human voices are used to mimic the sounds of birds. This mimicry is however confined within very specific limitations (Example 7.2 and Figure 7.1). In particular the typical pitch ordering of Renaissance counterpoint is not contravened and hence the typical pitch architecture of birdsong is not represented. Rather an attempt is made to mimic the perceived articulation of bird calls through the morphology of the syllables used for vocalisation. To the modern ear, apart from the cuckoo, the effect is more like the setting of sound-poetry to music than of an imitation of nature.

In the second example (Example 7.3 and Figure 7.2) from Beethoven's *Pastorale* symphony, the same kind of bird imitation is attempted on woodwind instruments. Here at least the spectral and attack characteristics of the acoustic sources are more strongly related to the vocal emissions of birds themselves. However, the mimicry is formalised to meet the constraints of the rhythmic and pitch structures of the musical idiom. We do not really hear birds. At this point the limitations of the concept of association become apparent. We are aware that the landscape of these sounds is musicians playing instruments, but we are also aware that there is some attempt being made to mimic the natural sounds of birdsong. Do we then 'associate' these instrumental sounds with birdsong, and if so in what sense is this similar to the association of a progression of purely orchestral sonorities with the programme note of the *Manfred* symphony discussed above?

As a third example, let us consider Respighi's *The Pines of Rome*. In this otherwise purely orchestral work, the composer overcomes the problems inherent in attempting to imitate birdsong on traditional instruments by introducing instead a gramophone recording of a bird into the orchestral texture. In this case, then, there can be no confusion between the source of the sound as instrument and the source of the sound the instrument is attempting to mimic. We recognise the sound as coming from a bird (it can of course be argued that the sound comes from a gramophone record; this point will be discussed more fully below). Here, in fact, an interaction of associationism with landscape takes place. The harmonic melodic structures developed in the orchestra are meant to suggest, through association, some kind of natural scene. The birdsong, however, presents it quite directly.

Figure 7.1   Vocal bird imitations in Janequin's *Chant des Oyseaulx*.

Figure 7.2 Instrumental bird imitations in Beethoven's *Pastorale* Symphony.

In our final example from Stockhausen's *Trans*, the orchestra is used to suggest an alternative landscape (to that merely of people playing instruments) in a different manner (Example 7.4). In his comments upon the piece, Stockhausen has talked of a dream in which he perceived various animated events as if through a veil or curtain. The piece begins with the gradual unfolding of a cluster on the stringed instruments quietly from the high register to a broad band cluster filling the entire range and played loud. This sound persists almost without change throughout the entire piece and 'rises' again at the end in an approximate retrograde of the opening sequence. In some senses, this composite sound-object may be considered as an aural metaphor for 'curtain'. Aurally speaking the effect is heightened by the fact that the animated melodic material on wind instruments is heard 'through' — or at least 'against' — this wall of sound and the attempted detachment from the typical apprehension of the orchestral landscape is heightened by the use of a pre-recorded loom-shuttle which passes back and forth across the acoustic space. This type of aural metaphor relates more strongly to our notion of a natural morphology of musical objects (which is to be discussed below) than to the more conventional idea of association. In fact, Stockhausen attempts to distance the audience from the normal perception of the orchestral landscape through the orchestral staging of the piece. The metaphor of the curtain is paralleled by the use of an actual curtain on stage and through the physical disposition of the string players who are seated in a line across the stage, hiding the wind instruments, who thus play 'through' the curtain, and they are instructed to bow exactly in parallel with one another so that the individuality of the players is subordinated to the theatrical (and sonic) image (see Figure 7.3[1]).

Despite, then, its general playing-down in the discussion of musical structure, the figurative has played a part in the traditional Western instrumental and vocal repertoire. Furthermore, the relationship between the figurative and the so-called *abstract* is not a simple one. A glance at the development of painting would lead us to a similar conclusion. Up until this century painting was generally thought of as essentially figurative. It is interesting to note that the impact of technology on music and painting has been in opposite directions: the tape recorder has introduced the representational more easily into music, while the camera has tended to replace the figurative role of painting and allow painting to pursue the non-figurative domain.[2]

Virtual acoustic space: redefinition of landscape

With the arrival of sound recording the question of source-identification of sounds became of great importance. On the one hand, it allowed the electro-acoustic musician to isolate a sound physically from its producing medium by recording it and hence enabled Schaeffer's conceptualisation of the acousmatic. At the same time the reproduction of sound on loudspeakers caused the question "what is the source of the sound?" to become problematic.

Whereas previously we have defined the landscape of a sound to be the perceived physical source of the sound, what are we to make of a recording of Beethoven's *Pastorale* symphony played on loudspeakers? In this case the physical source of the sounds is the vibration of the cones of the loudspeakers. But, of course, the loudspeaker is able to *re*-produce sounds from any other source so that noting that a sound originates from loudspeakers tells us almost nothing about that sound, except that it has been recorded. We must therefore seek a redefinition of the term *landscape*.

---

[1] There is a further pair of loudspeakers behind the audience.

[2] The complicated relationships between representation, association, visual metaphor, visual gesture and 'abstraction' can be intimated by comparing four paintings of Paul Klee: *Polyphony* (1932), *Gate in the Garden* (1926), *The Future Man* (1933), *Around the Fish* (1926) (Hall 1992: (plate 33 (:97); plate 21 (:73); plate 35 (:101); plate 23 (:77)).

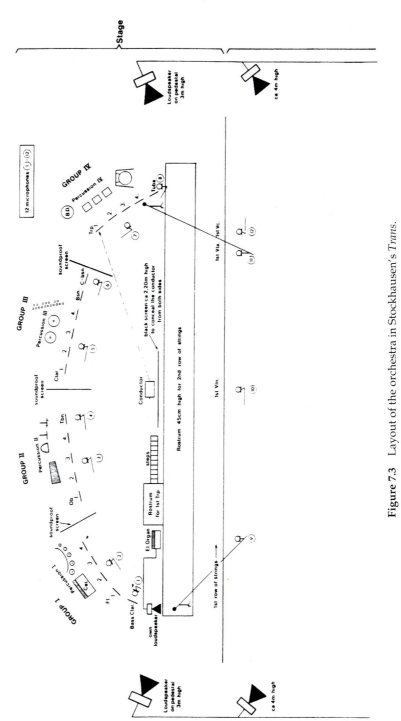

Figure 7.3 Layout of the orchestra in Stockhausen's *Trans*.

If the term is to have any significance in electro-acoustic music, we must define it as the source from which we *imagine* the sounds to come.

Thus, when we are sitting in the concert hall listening to the Beethoven symphony the landscape of the sounds is the orchestra. When we are sitting in our living room listening to a recording of the Beethoven symphony the landscape of the sounds remains the orchestra. The loudspeaker has in effect allowed us to set up a virtual acoustic space into which we may project an image of any real existing acoustic space such as that of the concert hall or, for example, in the case of a wildlife recording, that of a wood at night.

The existence of this virtual acoustic space, however, presents us with new creative possibilities. The acoustic space which we represent need not be real and we may in fact play with the listener's perception of landscape. This aspect of sonic architecture was not an aspect of the traditional craft of the musician because, before the invention of sound recording, it was not open to the composer or performer to control. It is therefore easy to dismiss it by linking it with the somewhat cruder and culturally circumscribed procedures of associationism (programme music) and mimicry which exist as a somewhat marginal aspect of the central vocal and instrumental tradition of Western art music. This, however, would be foolish. Not only does the control and composition of landscape open up large new areas of artistic exploration and expression, in the sphere of electro-acoustic music it will enter into the listener's perception of a work regardless of the composer's indifference to it.

One of the first composers to seize upon this new compositional possibility was Luc Ferrari, whose comments were quoted at the opening of this chapter. He described his approach as 'anecdotal'. *Presque Rien Nr.1*, from the vantage point of the musician the most radical work in this genre, takes a recording of several hours of activity on a beach and compresses (by selective choice) this material into twenty minutes, without in any way attempting to negate or transform (other than enhance by concentration) the perceived landscape of the beach. Alternatively, in the work *Music Promenade* four independent linear montages of recognisable material (including military music and marches, crowd sounds, conversations etc.) are presented simultaneously and articulated by the occasional heightening of sound-events through the use of echo or focus (for example, isolating a single breath or a single phrase).

Parmegiani, on the other hand, developed a kind of surrealistic approach to recognisable sources, lying more easily within the frame of reference of musique concrète. As Simon Emmerson (1982: 125–126) has noted, Parmegiani has used such devices as duality (recognisable/abstract), perspective (near/far), and the juxta- or superposition of unrelated images to achieve an effect similar to that of certain surrealist paintings (those of Max Ernst, for example) — the intimation of real landscape without its actually being present (Example 7.5 is the transition from *Matières induites* to *Ondes croisées* from *De Natura Sonorum*). Duality refers to the use of recognisable sounds which have then been reordered in such a way as to appear almost abstract, for example as sound-objects with scintillating overtones etc.. Changes in aural perspective on an object can be obtained by recording it at a normal listening distance and then close-miking it. These produce quite different acoustic results and when they are juxtaposed in the aural landscape our sense of aural perspective is transformed. Finally, unrelated images (e.g. water/fire or electronic/concrete) may be brought into close proximity and by the use of similar musical gestures or the creation of similar overtone structures made to have a very strong aural interrelationship.

Even earlier, however, a similar concern with aural landscape developed in the radiophonic departments of radio stations broadcasting drama. Whereas Parmegiani was concerned to hint at possible landscapes in an essentially acousmatic approach to sound-materials, radiophonics was, at least initially, concerned exclusively with the suggestion of real landscapes in the virtual acoustic space of the radio receiver which were not physically present in the recording studio. In most cases these landscapes were associated with spoken text or dialogue which itself might suggest a landscape context. Often simple devices such as distance from the microphone, the use of echo, or the sound of a door opening or closing might be sufficient to 'set the scene' but as time went on more elaborate scenarios were developed through seventeenth century battles to the purely imaginary landscape of alien spacecraft.

These so-called 'sound-effects' fall largely into the category of what I would call contextualising cues which permit us to identify a particular landscape. Technically they may be divided into four categories: *actuality*, *staged*, *studio* and *mixed*. *Actuality* involves, as its name suggests, an actual recording of the event which is to be represented, such as a football match, a crowded street, a clock striking and so on. Similarly, *staged* involves the real staging of an event which could not be otherwise recorded for practical reasons (a rare event, an event involving obsolete vocabulary or technology such as a seventeenth century battle and so on). *Studio* sound-effects on the other hand were simulations of actual sounds using materials far removed from the original sound-sources. Thus in staging a medieval dual we would involve two actors and actual swords of the period; this would be staged. To generate the sound of horses' hooves, however, it was typical to use a pair of coconut shells in a tray of sand. For most listeners, and with the added cue of human speech (possibly modified to suggest that the speakers were being jogged up and down by horses), this was an acceptable acoustic analogue of the sound of horses' hooves. In some cases indeed studio-produced sound-effects proved to be more acceptable than the real thing! In the case of the horses' hooves it may be largely a matter of getting a clear recording of the type of horse movement that we want (how do we get away from the sounds of modern traffic, how do we get the horse to behave in exactly the way we want and so on). In the case of, for example, fire we have a different problem. Even with an excellent digital recording, the sounds of fire seem somehow less impressive when we hear them from a recording than when we hear them in real life. This is something to do with the fact that a fire is a multi-media experience. The impact of the visual movement of flame and the heat from the fire are much more intense than the impact of the fire sounds and the whole adds up to a very powerful sensory experience. The recreation of the effect 'fire' by purely auditory means, can simply fail to evoke the power of the multi-media image of fire. In this particular case, where we are restricted to the medium of sound, the use of studio fabrication (such as the recording of crinkled cellophane and its subsequent speed-changing, filtering and mixing with other sources) provides an aural image which is more acceptable than the real thing. This apparent paradox is explained by the fact that in this case the aural image has to partly replace our visual and tactile experience. It also points out that the concept of aural landscape is far from straightforward!

Generally speaking, sound-effects have been used in this fairly straightforward manner but on some occasions their use has been extended. In 1978 the BBC presented a play whose dramatic and narrative content was carried exclusively by sound-effects as there was no text present.[3] Although the play demonstrated the inherent power of sound-effects techniques, it appeared, however, as a poor substitute for a real text-based narrative rather than the development of an entirely new art-form based on the subtle composition of aural landscape. The only really creative use of sound-effects seems to have been in the sphere of radio comedy where absurd structures and events (such as endless staircases, maps as large as cathedrals, and so on) were suggested by the simple transformation of aural landscapes (Example 7.6). The appearance of science fiction drama permitted the development of less obvious landscape devices but radiophonics largely confined itself to simply exploiting the unusualness or novelty of a sound-object (which very rapidly became clichéd and predictable). Before the very

---

[3] 'The Revenge' by Andrew Sachs, first broadcast on BBC Radio 3 on the 1st of June 1978.

particular quality of aural landscape manipulation could be explored and developed (see below), the concreteness of the television image took over and radiophonics declined to an even more marginal position. The use of landscape concepts in radiophonics is, however, very important in our attempt to conceptualise the area of aural landscape for the purposes of sonic composition.

Finally, we should also mention that the landscape technique of mimicry has much wider application than its use in music would imply. Mimicry is often used in everyday conversation and in formal presentations, for example by comedians or sound-poets, as a means to indicate an alternative source for the information than the actual speaker or mimic. Thus the imitations of accents, age and sex characteristics of vocalisation, or even the imitation of birds (by whistling) or dogs may be catalogued. Mimicry is not, as one might suspect, an entirely human occupation. It has been observed in the behaviour of birds, both in imitating humans (human whistling) and in the imitation of other species of birds (usually predators, which suggests some kind of denotative function).

Defining characteristics of landscape

To briefly recapitulate, we have defined the landscape of a sound-image as the imagined source of the perceived sounds. The landscape of the sounds heard at an orchestral concert is 'musicians-playing-instruments'. The landscape of the same concert heard over loudspeakers is also 'musicians playing instruments'. In some cases it is difficult to identify the source of the sounds. This fact is particularly pertinent to music designed for projection over loudspeakers. When listeners who are accustomed to listening to music at concerts where instrumentalists perform attend concerts of electro-acoustic music projected on loudspeakers they often express a sense of disorientation. This is usually attributed to the lack of any visual focus at the concert. However, it seems clear that this reaction is prompted by an inability to define an imaginable source, in the sense of a landscape, for the sounds perceived. This sense of disorientation produced in some listeners by the impact of electronic sounds was the basis of the early use of electronic sound-materials for science fiction productions. The inability of the listener to locate the landscape of the sounds provided the disorientation and sense of strangeness which the producer wished to instil in the listener. The development of the concept of the acousmatic and the general tendency in mainstream musique concrète to destroy clues as to the source or origins of the sounds can be seen as a specific reaction to the problem of landscape in electro-acoustic music.

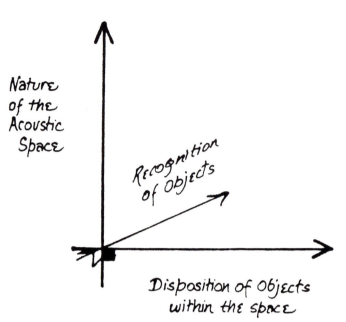

Figure 7.4 Defining characteristics of *landscape*.

What aspects of our perception of an aural image enter into our definition of landscape for the sounds we hear? We may effectively break down our perception of landscape into three components (see Figure 7.4) which are not, however entirely independent from one another. These are:

(1)   the nature of the perceived acoustic space;
(2)   the disposition of sound-objects within the space;
(3)   the recognition of individual sound-objects.

We will discuss each of these in turn.

In practice the nature of the perceived acoustic space cannot be separated from our perception of the sound-objects within it. We obtain our information about, for example, the reverberant properties of the space, by hearing out the temporal evolution of the sound-objects within the space and, for example, the different reverberation times of different objects within the space may give us further clues as to the overall acoustic quality of the implied sound-environment. Furthermore, the acoustic of the space may change and in some works such changes may be organised in such a way as to prevent us building up any overall acoustic image. Although this 'destruction' of landscape has been an aim of certain kinds of electro-acoustic music composition, we will here put it on one side, as a very special case, and deal with landscape as normally experienced.

Landscape: the nature of the acoustic space

Usually, any sort of live recording will carry with it information about the overall acoustic properties of the environment in which it is recorded. These might include the particular resonances or reverberation time of a specifically designed auditorium or the differences between moorland (lack of echo or reverberation, sense of great distance indicated by sounds of very low amplitude with loss of high frequency components etc.), valleys (similar to moorlands, but lacking distance cues and possibly including some specific image echoes) and forests (typified by increasing reverberation with distance of the source from the listener). Such real, or apparently real, acoustic spaces may be recreated in the studio. For example, using the stereo projection of sounds on two loudspeakers we may separate sound-sources along a left-right axis, creating a sense of spatial width. We may also create a sense of spatial depth by simultaneously using signals of smaller amplitude, with their high frequencies rolled off. Depending on which type of acoustic space we wish to recreate, we might also add increasing amounts of reverberation to these sources, the more distant they appear to be. In this way, depth is added to the image and we create an effective illusion of two-dimensional space. This illusion is enhanced if sound-objects are made to move through the virtual space (see Figure 7.5). (A detailed discussion of the control of spatial motion will be found Chapter 10.)

The digital technique known as convolution allows us to impose in a very precise manner the acoustic characteristics of any preanalysed sound-environment upon a given sound-object. Ideally, the sound-object itself would be recorded in an anechoic environment. To implement the process of convolution we begin by measuring the impulse response of the acoustic environment we wish to recreate. This involves playing a single very brief impulse (Figure 7.6a1) with a very broad and flat spectrum (see Chapter 3), e.g. a gunshot, into the natural acoustic environment and recording the result; this is represented in Figure 7.6a2 as a series of 'instantaneous' digital samples - the impulse response of the environment. Provided all audible frequencies are equally represented in the initial impulse, the resulting recorded signal should indicate the overall resonance characteristics of the environment. (If the impulse is specifically pitched we will be measuring only the resonance characteristics of the environment at some particular frequency.) Let us now assume that we have a digital recording of our sound-object. Because digital recording involves a sampling process, the

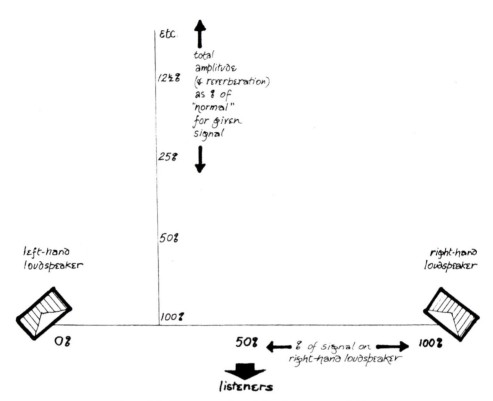

Figure 7.5   Representation of depth in a stereo field.

sound-object may be regarded as a collection of instantaneous impulses which taken together define the overall waveform of the sound-object. If we now replace each individual sample in the digital representation by the graph of its impulse-response (which will be magnified or reduced according to the amplitude of each impulse) and then sum at each sampling instant the resultant values (see Figure 7.6b[4]) we obtain a waveform corresponding to the sound perceived as if the sound-object had been recorded in the sound-environment which we analysed.

Sound recording and the presentation of recorded material has, however, brought with it a number of other acoustic spaces which are conventions of a mode of presentation. We shall refer to these as *formalised* acoustic spaces to distinguish them from the real acoustic spaces we have previously been discussing. There is, of course, not a clear dividing line

---

[4] In addition, we need to apply a so-called 'normalisation' procedure to ensure the final signal does not go 'out of range' of the digital system.

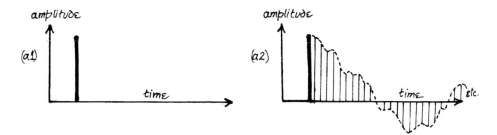

Figure 7.6a Generating the *impulse response* of an environment.

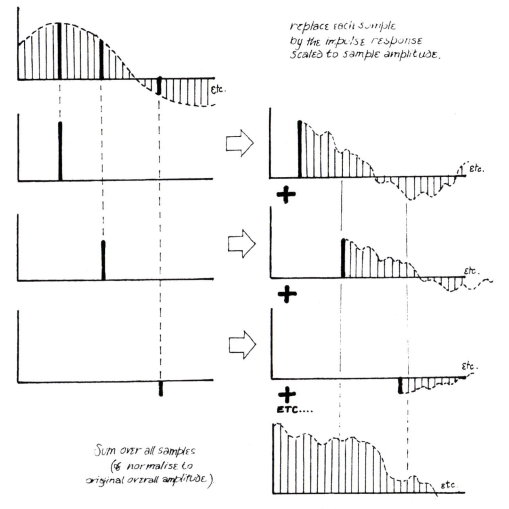

Figure 7.6b The process of *convolution*.

between these two categories because, as broadcast sound becomes an ever more present part of our real sound-environment, it becomes possible to question, for example, whether we hear orchestral music, the sounds of a radio (playing orchestral music) or the sounds of a person walking in the street (carrying a radio (playing orchestral music))! These questions are not trivial when we come to discuss electro-acoustic music, such as Stockhausen's *Hymnen*, which attempts to integrate existing recorded music into its sonic architecture. And in fact some sounds which have been modified by the technological means of reproduction might almost be accepted into the category of real acoustic space, for example, the sound of a voice heard over a telephone or the sound of a voice heard over a distant distorting channel as with the sounds of voices transmitted from space.

The formalisation of acoustic space is found in all kinds of contemporary music production. The negation of any consistent landscape in some kinds of electro-acoustic music has been mentioned previously. In the studio recording of rock music albums, various formal manipulations of the acoustic space are taken for granted. The most obvious is the rebalancing of instruments by means of differential amplification. A soft-spoken singing voice or a flute may become much louder than a whole brass section. A piano, initially heard in close perspective, may 'duck' to a lower dynamic level at the instant at which a singing voice enters. Popular music is also very much concerned with the sense of intimacy or distancing involved in the recording of the voice. Electrical amplification permitted 'crooners' to sing at a very low level, and hence adopt the vocal characteristics of intimacy only available at low vocal amplitudes, yet still be heard against a large orchestra. At the other extreme, singers commonly use effects of reverberation, echo (often in a self-consciously clearly non-natural way) and phasing (an effect that is confined in the natural world almost exclusively to our perception of aeroplanes passing overhead!) to distance themselves from the listener or appear larger than life. Such techniques have parallels in certain pre-literate cultures. However, as these techniques are usually applied on an all-or-nothing basis in a particular song and are used extremely commonly, they begin to cease to have any landscape ramifications and become conventions of a formalised musical landscape. We begin to perceive these things as new timbres in a formalised acoustic space; they become no more unusual than the rebalancing of instruments. At this stage in the development of these devices, they can only become useful tools for the elucidation and elaboration of landscape properties of our perception of sonic art if we abandon the all-or-nothing usages and investigate the effects of transformations between different representations of the voice, having at the same time a sensitivity to the concept of aural space.

This kind of formalisation of acoustic space does not apply merely to music. It is an aspect of the formatting of productions for radio (or TV) broadcasts. A typical formalised landscape might be that of the disc jockey presentation of rock music. We are not meant here to recreate an image of a person sitting in a studio speaking into a microphone and putting records on turntables (in fact in many Californian rock stations this has now been entirely replaced by automated synchronised tape recordings). We have merely a formalised conventional structure. The record ends or draws to a close, the voice of the disc jockey enters and speaks. This is often mixed with special snippets of music or sound-effects; a kind of logo in sound, or pure linkage material — 'keep the music playing' — until the next song begins. This controlling voice floating in a sea of musical snippets has now become a broadcasting convention and has no special landscape implications. It is interesting, however, to speculate what one might do by using this conventionalised format and beginning to break down the underlying conventions. This would be simple to do in the direction of the abstract (in the sense of a space which is neither universally accepted as a convention nor real) but might be more interesting if moved in the direction of the real or the surreal (see below).

Finally, we might consider the case of electro-acoustic compositions such as Stockhausen's *Telemusik* or *Hymnen* which use elements of recognisable recorded music within a sonic architecture using a wider sound-palette. In both pieces the absorption of finite portions of recognisable recorded musical forms within an ongoing stream of electronically generated sound-materials tends to suggest a particular sort of relationship to the pre-existing music i.e. their absorption in a larger process and hence a view from outside or above the cultural substratum from which the musics come. We are here in a sort of 'cosmic' media space which, generally speaking, has no real-world reference. This 'distancing' or detachment from the real (no recognisable acoustic space, no recognisable real-world referents, although some kinds of natural processes are suggested in *Hymnen*) predisposes us to perceive the pre-recorded musics (themselves often heavily distorted) in a distanced way. As, however, they are the only elements which refer directly to our experience of real acoustic spaces, we are viewing the real world as if at a distance. Such generalised use of landscape phenomena (i.e. the sense of detachment underlined by the lack of real-world referents) tends to become accepted as convention as time goes by and this aspect of Stockhausen's aural metaphor may not survive (it may be perceived merely in formal terms) as our familiarity with electronic sound-sources increases. Already in our discussion of *Hymnen* we are touching on the areas of sound-source recognition and the vantage point of the listener which we will deal with more fully below.

Landscape: the disposition of sound-objects in space

Given that we have established a coherent aural image of a real acoustic space, we may then begin to position sound-objects within the space. Imagine for a moment that we have established the acoustic space of a forest (width represented by the spread across a pair of stereo speakers, depth represented by decreasing amplitude and high-frequency components and increasing reverberation) then position the sounds of various birds and animals within this space. These sound-sources may be static, individual sound-sources may move laterally or in and out of 'depth' or the entire group of sound-sources may move through the acoustic space. All of these are at least capable of perception as real landscapes. If we now choose a group of animals and birds which do not, or cannot, coexist in close proximity to one another, and use these in the environment, the landscape would be, ecologically speaking, unrealistic but for most listeners it would remain a 'real' landscape.

Let us now begin to replace the animal and bird songs by arbitrary sonic objects. We might accomplish this by a gradual process of substitution or even by a gradual transformation of each component of the landscape. At some stage in this process we begin to perceive a different kind of landscape. The disposition of the objects remains realistic (in the sense that we retain the image of the acoustic space of a 'forest') yet the sound-sources are not real in any sense of the word. Here we have the first example of an imaginary landscape of the type *unreal-objects/real-space*.

If we now take the original sound-objects (the animal and bird sounds) and arbitrarily assign different amplitudes and degrees of reverberation or filtering to each occurrence, we achieve a second but quite different kind of imaginary landscape of the type *real-objects /unreal-space*.

If we now imagine a more extreme example of the ecologically unacceptable environment (!) described earlier, we arrive at a third type of landscape. For example, imagine that, by appropriate editing and mixing procedures, we are able to animate a duet between a howler monkey and a budgerigar or a whale and a wolf, we have a landscape in which the sound-sources are real and the perceived space is real, yet the relationship of the sound-images is impossible. This bringing together of normally unrelated objects in the virtual space created by loudspeakers is closely parallel to the technique of bringing together unrelated visual objects in the space defined by a painting, a technique known as surrealism and I therefore propose to call this type of imaginary landscape (*real-objects /real-space*) *surrealist.*[5]

Example 7.7 from the television soundtrack of my *Automusic* illustrates one of these landscape genres. Earlier in the same piece, we have heard the sound of traffic which is characterised both by the typical spectra type of motorised traffic and the typical rise and fall in amplitude with the intervening Doppler pitch shift which is a feature of the movement of the sources through space.[6] Here at the end of the piece the amplitude envelope and Doppler shift attributes of the motion of traffic are retained but the sounds themselves are not clearly recognisable (they are in fact aggregates of vocally-derived sounds). This, then, is an example of unreal sounds/real space landscape. (Note that the 'reality' of the aural space has been established by its earlier presentation in an entirely real context.)

Motion in space may also be used to alter the perceived characteristic of a landscape. In Chapter 3 we discussed some aspects of aural imaging and described a sound which began life as an oboe situated in the centre of the stereo space but then apparently diverged into a 'cello and a voice-like sonority which moved off towards the two separate speakers. Such imaging phenomena as this do not occur in our everyday aural experience, but can be generated by precise computer control of sound-materials. Even the rapid contrary motion of several voices in a quadraphonic (sound-surround) or three-dimensional space (without the accompanying sound of running feet!) defies our everyday intuition. As has been mentioned previously such devices, if used indiscriminately and in an all-or-nothing fashion, become accepted as mere conventions of electro-acoustic art. If, however, we can learn to control with subtlety the transition from one type of acoustic space and one type of spatial disposition of sound-objects to another, control of landscape and spatial motion can become an important structural and expressive ingredient in sonic art. Once more than one sound is set into motion in the same virtual acoustic space, we may begin to consider the

---

[5] In the original text the author does not discuss the fourth possible combination of his 'real/unreal' categories. Presumably *unreal-objects/unreal-space* is formed when we "begin to replace the animal and bird songs by arbitrary sonic objects" (unreal objects) *and* "arbitrarily assign different amplitudes and degrees of reverberation or filtering to each occurrence" [of them] (*Ed.*).

[6] Raised pitch as a source approaches the listener, lowered as it moves away.

interaction of different kinds of spatial motion. The topic will be dealt with more fully in Chapter 10.

The change in the apparent disposition of sonic objects in the acoustic space may alter the perspective of the listener. For example, where various sound-objects move in different directions, or a single sound spins around the listener's position (in a quadraphonic space), the listener may reasonably assume himself to be at a point of rest. If, however, a number of sound-objects are spaced at various points of the compass around a quadraphonic space, and the entire frame of reference made to rotate, we might suggest to the listener that he himself is spinning in the opposite direction whilst the frame of reference remains still. At a simpler level, differences in amplitude and also in timbral qualities caused by the closeness or distance of the microphone to the recorded object alter not only the listener's perceived physical distance from the source but also the psychological or social distance. With vocal sounds, depending on the type of material used, closeness may imply intimacy or threatening dominance, distance a sense of 'eavesdropping' or of detachment and at various stages in between a sense of interpersonal communication or more formalised social communication. A similar kind of psychological distancing which parallels the social distancing may be experienced even in the case of inanimate sound-sources. To hear sounds in our normal acoustic experience in the same perspective that close-miking provides we would usually need to be purposefully directing our aural attention to the sounds (by, for example, bringing our ear very close to the sounding object). Listening to sounds recorded in this way can thus produce the effect of perception through an aural 'magnifying glass' and is quite different from our experience of normal acoustic perspective. Changes in aural perspective in the course of an event or extended composition are of significance to the listener and need not be approached in a purely formalist manner.

The sense of perspective or distancing we are discussing here is quite different from that discussed earlier in relation to Stockhausen's *Hymnen*. Here we are referring to perceptible acoustic properties of our aural experience which relate to the distance of the sounding object, not merely to a general sense of mental detachment caused by a landscape with no perceptible referents. Let us speculate on another landscape device whereby Stockhausen's sense of distancing from the real might be achieved which uses true aural perspective. Imagine that we create a two-dimensional stereo image (using stereo width with amplitude and equalisation for depth) of a group of people which we project as a narrow image in the centre of a stereo pair of loudspeakers in front of the listener (see Figure 7.7). We now increase the loudness and high frequency response of the four signals and move them

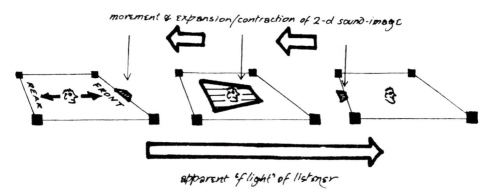

Figure 7.7   The illusion of 'flying through space'.

in such a way that at their maximal point they are distributed over the four loudspeakers of the (sound-surround) quadraphonic space. The transformation continues until the image (now reversed in depth) is situated in a narrow band in the middle of the rear stereo pair. Here we have created the illusion of flying through space, either of the aural image of the group of people (front to rear) or of the observer (flying forwards) and graphically underlined his detachment from the group of people who remain fixed in their position in relation to each other.

Landscape: the recognition of sources

The final element in our definition of landscape is our ability to recognise (or not recognise) the sound-objects themselves. With sound-objects specifically generated by electronic synthesis or musique concrète techniques, the concept of recognition may be extremely problematic, but with sound-sources recorded directly from the acoustic environment, recognition would seem to be a fairly straightforward matter. Even with superb digital recording, however, this is not necessarily the case.

In our normal working lives our experience of the environment is a multi-media one. In particular we rely very heavily on the visual medium to assist in our recognition of objects and events. This recognition may be direct in the sense that we see the object or event which emits the sound, or indirect in the sense that a physical location (e.g. a railway station or a particular type of terrain) or a social occasion (e.g. a concert performance) may enable us to identify a, perhaps indistinctly heard, sound-source. Once we remove the visual and other clues to sound recognition, we must rely entirely on our aural perspicacity. In the virtual acoustic space of an electro-acoustic work

same affective qualities as time processes taking place in the domain of sound. Landscape composition, therefore, has a quite different 'emotional' feel to the sphere of visual animation.

The intrinsic ambiguity of aural space also means that certain kinds of transformations may be effected in aural space which it is very difficult to relate in any way to a visual analogue. In the piece *I am sitting in a room* by Alvin Lucier (Example 7.11) the initial sound-image is that of a voice speaking in a room with a given acoustic (at this stage our attention is not drawn to the room acoustics). The voice is then recorded and the recording played back into the room. This process is repeated over and over again. As this process proceeds the recording becomes increasingly coloured by the room acoustic until finally at the end of the piece we hear essentially the room resonance vaguely articulated by the amplitude fluctuations of the voice. In this case our perception of what is the sound-object and what is the acoustic space in which it is projected have been conflated. At the beginning of the piece we would unreservedly state that the sound-object is the voice. At the end of the piece the sound-object is clearly a more 'abstract' entity whose characteristics derive from the room acoustic. Somewhere in between these extremes our perception passes over from one interpretation to the other. Not only, therefore, can we control the dimensions of, on the one hand, simple recognition/non-recognition and on the other hand recognition-as-A/recognition-as-B, but also the dimension acoustic-space/'sound-object within an acoustic space'.

From what has been said so far about the intrinsic ambiguity of aural space, it might seem unlikely to be able to generate an aural image which is specifically ambiguous, i.e. which has two very specific interpretations. This, however, can be quite simply achieved in certain cases, particularly where one of the sound-sources is the human voice. Thus we may use the vocoder to impose the articulatory structure of unvoiced speech onto, for example, the sound of the sea. The two recognisable aural images remain simultaneously perceptible in the resulting aural stream. Similarly the digital technique of cross-synthesis allows us to transfer certain characteristics (e.g. the changing formant structure) of one recognisable sound-source onto another recognisable source, creating sound-images which demand two simultaneous landscape interpretations.

One final comment on ambiguity and recognisability: we might ask the question, what enables us to recognise a sound as 'like' another? What is the aural basis of mimicry? If we are capable of perceiving that certain sounds, even so-called abstract sounds, are similar to other, possibly concrete, sounds, does this not then affect our perception of all sonic structures? Is there any kind of relationship between our perception of the morphological properties of the natural sonic landscape and our appreciation of composed sound-events and sound-structures? This point will be discussed more fully in the following chapter.

Landscape in music: some sketches

Landscape concepts have now been used extensively by composers of electro-acoustic music. In Luc Ferrari's *Presque Rien Nr.1* (Example 7.12) an existing landscape is simply recorded on tape and concentrated in intensity by compressing the events of a morning into the space of twenty minutes. The landscape itself remains entirely realistic, except that our attention to it is concentrated by the condensation of materials already mentioned and also by its being brought into the concert hall or living room as an independent sonic landscape. In Larry Wendt's *From Frogs* we hear a landscape consisting of the songs of many frogs but in this case these songs are slowed down and hence the rich content of the spectrum becomes more apparent to our ears (Example 7.13). The effect is similar to that of close perspective (recording sounds with the microphone placed extremely close to the source). We have a sense of entering into the inner details of the sound-world. The landscape itself remains 'natural', except for the effect of magnification resulting from the slowing and lowering of the frog sounds. We appear to be in a landscape of giant frogs! A similar effect can be achieved by slowing down birdsong. Roughly speaking the pitch range of a bird is related to the length of its windpipe which is similarly related to its overall size. There seems also to be a relationship between size and the speed of articulation. Hence, slowing down the song of a small bird, we hear what appears to be the song of a large bird. This process can be extended a long way. I have in fact used birdsong at a sixteenth of its original speed, yet without destroying the source-image "bird". Human beings, on the other hand, do not come in such a vast assortment of sizes and even at double or half speed we are no longer prepared to accept vocal sounds as naturalistic.

In Alvin Lucier' s *I am sitting in a room* (discussed above), on the other hand, the acoustic characteristics of the physical space in which the sound-object is first presented are brought to the centre of our attention by the process of natural resonant feedback. Lucier's approach to acoustic space is literal and objective. He is concerned with drawing our attention to, and utilising, the acoustic characteristics of existing spaces, rather than establishing a virtual space through the medium of the loudspeaker. His work also tends to objectively demonstrate or elucidate these characteristics rather than attempting to utilise them for some other expressive purpose.

In Michael McNabb's *Dreamsong* (Example 7.14), however, we are concerned with the transformations of virtual acoustic space. The transformations are neither simply relatable to existing acoustic spaces nor do they relate to any conceivable or visualisable events in the real world. As its title suggests, therefore, we find ourselves travelling in a dream landscape which has its own logic. The further elucidation of this 'dreamlike' virtual landscape is the basis of the piece *Red Bird* which we have mentioned previously and will be discussed at length in the next chapter.

The conventions or idiosyncrasies of media landscapes may become the basis of compositional structures. Two light-hearted examples of this are suggested (Examples 7.15 and 7.16). In the first the defects in an old gramophone record cause the needle to jump about randomly on the disc surface. This effectively arbitrary editing or looping of short segments becomes the basis of the organisation of the material in *Musical Box* (from my *Menagerie*). In the second example the music-plays in a typical disc jockey sequence are replaced by quite different sounds (part of *Still Life* from *Menagerie*).

In Stockhausen's *Hymnen* (discussed above) we encountered the use of a formalised media landscape to produce a general impression of detachment from real world musical objects (the national anthems used in the piece). In the earlier piece *Gesang der Jünglinge* (Example 7.17), landscape considerations enter into our perceptions of the piece (though it is difficult to know to what extent Stockhausen was aware of, or intended this, when he originally composed the piece). Thus, the appearance of the boy's voice in different acoustic perspectives (with different amplitude levels and with different degrees of reverberation) disembodies the singer. The voice is floating in a strange and unreal space. At the same time Stockhausen attempts to set up a kind of serial mediation between the sound of the boy's singing voice and pure electronic tones with various degrees of vocal recognisability or electronic abstractness in between. Here is perhaps the first use of the metaphorical in landscape composition (this will be discussed in the following chapter). There is a sense in which the boy's pure voice appears as the utterance of the individual singer, whilst the pure electronic tones have no such sense of utterance; they are altogether more distanced in our perception. The mediation between these two sound-types suggests some kind of mediation between individual human expression and something much more abstract and distant from human expression, a sonic metaphor for Stockhausen's continuing religious preoccupation. In case this may seem far-fetched to a reader schooled in musical formalism, consider what effect it would have upon our perception of the piece if the transformation between the vocal and the pure electronic were replaced by, for example, a transformation between violin sound and trumpet sound (such as those so effectively executed at Stanford using the new digital technology). The piece might have been composed with effectively the same structure but our landscape interpretation of it would have been entirely different. It is the sense of mediation between the personal (represented by the recognisable human voice) and the more general and abstract which carries a metaphorical content beyond the mere use of serial interpolation between sound-objects.

Finally, in the extract from Berio's *Visage* (Example 7.18), we hear an aural landscape in which a clearly-recognisable source, the human voice, interacts with a more 'abstract' set of (electronically-generated) sound-objects. Just as in typical radiophonic drama work, the human voice provides a contextualising cue for the other sounds. However, instead of words being used to outline the action, we are provided with paralinguistic utterances of fear, pain or suffering. However, it is not merely the vocal context which makes us perceive the more 'abstract' sounds as 'violent' or doing violence to the actress. We could not replace these sounds with arbitrarily different sounds, even if they were equally loud and produced the same impact of violent action. Something in the internal characteristics of the sounds themselves points to a violent origin or gesture. Here, then, we have a quite different use of the sound-object. In the case of metaphor, recognisable sounds or their relationships point outside themselves to ideas and relationships which do not reside essentially in the aural landscape. In the present case, however, the sonic objects point inside themselves towards some kind of characteristic of their morphology which we read as indicative of violence or violent action. Is there a natural morphology of sound-objects? This question will be taken up in the next chapter.

Chapter 8

SOUND-IMAGE AS METAPHOR:
MUSIC AND MYTH

The true answer is to be found, I think, in the characteristic that myth and music share of both being languages which, in their different ways, transcend articulate expression, while at the same time — like articulate speech, but unlike painting — requiring a temporal dimension in which to unfold.
(Lévi-Strauss 1970: 15)

Music and myth

Having established that landscape considerations enter into our perception of sonic art and that representational sound-images are potential working material, what special implications does this have for the sonic artist? In particular, what forms may we develop based on our sensitivity to sound-images. The pieces by McNabb and Stockhausen, which we have already discussed, point towards some new and interesting possibilities. In *Dreamsong* the transmutation of aural landscape is suggestive of the scenarios of dreams, whilst the mediation between the human voice and the 'pure', 'abstract' electronic sounds in *Gesang der Jünglinge* points towards a metaphorical interpretation. *Gesang* takes this single metaphorical opposition and embeds it in a complex musical structure. Although it continues to contribute to our perception of the work, it is not further elaborated as *metaphor*. What would happen if we were to establish a whole system of relationships between sound-images, each having strong metaphorical implications. By articulating the relationships between the sound-images we could develop not only sonic structures (as in the McNabb) but a whole area of metaphorical discourse.

    In 1973, having worked for some time on electro-acoustic compositions which utilised sound-images within an otherwise musical mainstream conception of sonic structure, I decided to attempt to set up a sonic architecture based on the relationship between the sound-images themselves which would however remain compatible with my feelings about musical structure. What I discovered through working on the piece *Red Bird* was that the twin concepts of transformation and gesture, discussed earlier in relation to non-representational sound-objects, may also be applied to the sound-image. On the one hand, sound-images of the voice, or animal and bird cries, have an intrinsic gestural content. More distanced sound-materials, for example, textures developed out of vocal syllables, may be gesturally articulated by appropriate studio techniques. Transformation now becomes the gradual changing of one sound-image into another with its associated metaphorical implications, and a landscape can be seen as a particular kind of timbre-field applying to the space of sound-images (see Figure 8.1). These parallels are not, of course, precise, but they do form the basis of a meeting ground between musical thinking and a discourse using sound-images as concrete metaphor.

In his book *The Raw and the Cooked*, Lévi-Strauss (1970) draws certain interesting parallels between the structure of music and the structure of myth. At one level, in adopting a structural approach to the analysis of myth, Lévi-Strauss calls upon structural categories from the tradition of Western music (such as 'sonata form' and 'double inverted counterpoint'). However, he also implies a deeper relationship between music and myth. Using people, objects and wild animals having a particular significance to the group, the myth illuminates more abstract relationships and categories of thought. At the same time the myth gains its power from its unfolding in time. The way the myth is told is of great importance. The parallels with conventional musical structures are obvious and in fact Lévi-Strauss points to Wagner as the first person to attempt a structural analysis of myth. The fact that he used music as a medium for this is, to Lévi-Strauss, no coincidence.

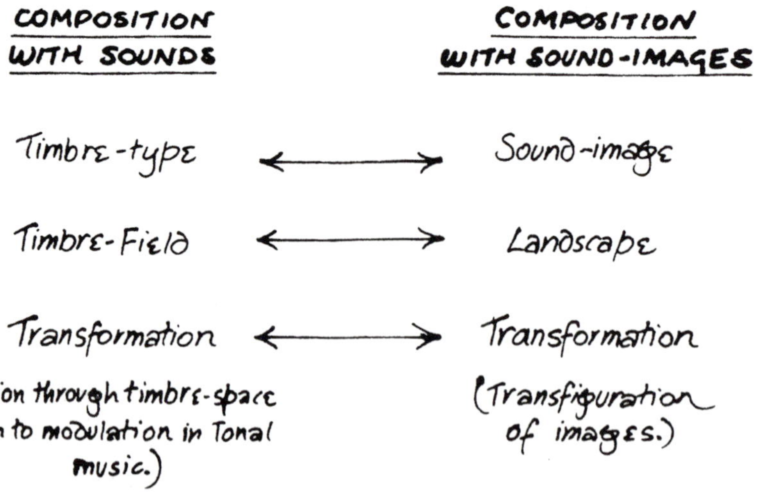

COMPOSITION WITH SOUNDS   **COMPOSITION WITH SOUND-IMAGES**

Timbre-type ←——→ Sound-image

Timbre-Field ←——→ Landscape

Transformation ←——→ Transformation
(motion through timbre-space akin to modulation in Tonal music.)   (Transfiguration of images.)

Figure 8.1 Comparison of sound composition with sound-image composition.

Wagner's methodology establishes a relationship between delimited musical structures (*leitmotifs*) and people, objects or ideas, primarily through association — at some stage musical object and its referent are juxtaposed. By then developing these musical objects and interrelating them, he is able to carry on a discourse which is not subject to the spatial and temporal limitations of the opera stage. This discourse is partly to do with unspoken 'emotions' and partly with metaphor. Using sound-images in the virtual space of the loudspeakers, we can create a world somewhere in between the concreteness of the opera staging and the world of musical relationships. We do not need to associate a musical object with, for example, a bird and thence with a metaphorical meaning, we may use the sound of a bird directly. And the concreteness of theatrical staging is replaced by a dreamlike landscape hovering between musical articulation and 'real-world' events (see Figure 8.2). Having drawn these parallels, however, from this point on there will be little in common between our perception and conception of sound-image composition and that of Wagnerian opera!

Sound-image as metaphor

In looking at Stockhausen's *Gesang* we have already noted that sound-images may be used metaphorically, although in this particular case this use may not strike us immediately as other features of the sonic architecture are more strongly articulated and apparent to our perceptions. It is interesting to note, however, that even in this case the metaphorical interpretation depends on the existence of a transformation. It is the mediation between the sound of a voice and the electronic sound which gives rise to a metaphorical interpretation which would not arise if no mediation were established between the two. In a similar way, we might consider using the aural image 'bird' (as in *Red Bird*) as a metaphor of flight (and hence, perhaps freedom or imagination). In itself, however, the sound of a bird need conjure up no such metaphorical association. If, however, we now make the sonic transformation

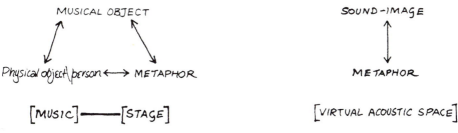

Figure 8.2   Comparison of music-drama with electroacoustic sound-image composition.

"lisss"->birdsong (see the previous chapter[1]), the voice 'takes flight' so to speak; the metaphorical link with the concept 'imagination' is suggested. If this transformation is set within a whole matrix of related and transforming images the metaphorical implications become increasingly refined and ramified. Similarly, the sound of a mechanically repetitive machine has no implicit metaphorical implications, but a *word-machine* made out of syllables of the phrase 'listen to reason' and the relationship between the normally spoken sentence and the word-machine begins to establish a metaphorical dimension in our perception of the sound-image. We may gradually establish a network of such relationships, defining a rich metaphorical field of discourse and just as a change of contextual cues may alter our interpretation of a sound-image (see the previous chapter), it may also have metaphorical import. The sound-image 'bellows/water-pump' (Example 8.1) may be interpreted as the functioning of the machine or the functioning of a human body and when our perception of it changes from one to the other, a metaphor is implied. (These relatively crude attempts to describe the aural image are not intended to be taken absolutely literally, as the aural landscape is always much more ambiguous than the visual). The listener may of course deny or blank out the metaphorical implications but this is possible with all other art forms which use metaphor.

In putting together a sonic architecture which uses sound-images as metaphors, we are faced with a dual problem. We must use sound transformations and formal structures with both sonic impact and metaphorical import. We must be both sonically and metaphorically articulate. Using concrete metaphors (rather than text) we are not 'telling a story' in the usual sense, but unfolding structures and relationships in time — ideally we should not think of the two aspects of the sound-landscape (the sonic and the metaphorical) as different things but as complementary aspects of the unfolding structure. This fusion of conception took place slowly and unnoticed in my mind during the composition of *Red Bird*. The new approach has immediate practical implications. Achieving a convincing transformation between two sounds is a practical problem of sonic art. Computer technology, allowing us to examine the internal structure of sounds, is beginning to make this task easier. The transformations between the sounds of different instruments playing the same note (e.g. oboe-flute — listen to examples in IRCAM (1983)) are very convincing as sonic transformations but unfortunately totally uninteresting as metaphors. The

---

[1] The syllable 'lisss' is understood to be from the phrase 'listen to reason'; in *Red Bird* this is established by context.

transformation voice->bird-sounds is metaphorically quite interesting but much more difficult to generate.[2]

A second, related problem presents itself. In conventional musical practice, we may conceive of a sonic architecture which we notate in a score, partly because the sound-objects we use are universally known and fixed in the culture. With *musique concrète*, on the other hand, we work from a specific sound-object and can thus continually aurally monitor the sound-structures we develop. If, however, we conceive of an exciting metaphorical structure involving the transformation of sound-images, we still have to find or generate specific sound-objects which meet the necessary recognition criteria and are capable of undergoing the transformations. The computer, together with a detailed personal knowledge of the internal architecture of sound, may make it easier for the composer actually to construct any sound which he can conceive of. At the moment, however, we are some way from this ideal and in fact *Red Bird* was made without the intervention of computers at all. The only available procedure was to amass a very large number of samples (of birdsong, articulations of particular syllables etc.), catalogue these according to perceptible (rather than *a priori*) criteria and then institute a search through the material when a specific transformation was to be realised.

Deep structure — surface structure

Lévi-Strauss, in his analysis of myths moves from a description of the surface structure to an elucidation of the deep structure of the myths concerned. In this case the deep structures are seen to be various oppositions and transformations which constitute basic elements of human thinking. In consciously constructing a myth-structure (an activity which I imagine Lévi-Strauss would profoundly disagree with), we must somehow move in the opposite direction. As Lévi-Strauss has pointed out himself, however, myths are not ultimately about what can easily be said, otherwise we would just say it. However, in order to explain what I think is going on in *Red Bird* it is necessary to give some indication of what I perceive to be the underlying 'model'. (Incidentally I do not wish that the listener hear *Red Bird* within any framework suggested verbally by myself. Sonic structures either work or do not work in themselves. If you have not yet heard the piece in its

---

[2] In fact, the programme *Chant* now makes this transformation quite straightforward and we may anticipate that problems of sound-transformation will become increasingly transigent as our experience with computer synthesis and analysis increases.

entirety, either listen to it now or skip the next few paragraphs!). Some things are expressed much better through metaphor and the dynamics of sound architecture. Verbal explications may sound unwieldy or pretentious. With these qualifications, let us continue.

At the deepest level, *Red Bird* is about the opposition between *open* and *closed* conceptions of the world. This opposition can be defined in relation to specific and different areas of thought. In relation to our conception of knowledge (epistemology), a closed view of the world would regard science as an institution enabling us to proceed from relative ignorance towards an absolute knowledge of the nature of the world, thus giving us greater and greater, and finally complete, control over our environment. The aim is a world in which we may rationally control every aspect of our existence. An open view would regard science as a powerful heuristic tool which allows us to gain some control over our environment. It does not, however, tend towards completeness and its preconceptions need to be regularly overhauled. Furthermore, there is no conception that there is a final end to scientific endeavour. The focus is upon the search, the breaking of new ground and not upon consolidation and security.

In social and political terms a closed view sees human society as a functional totality in which each person has, or should have, an assigned role. Society can be entirely rationally organised and ultimately the control of human affairs is to be left to experts. Those who cannot accept this state of affairs are either insane, heretical or criminal. An open view regards human society as rationally orderable only up to a point. There are, however, always ideas and ways of doing things which no-one has yet thought of. These do not arise out of rational discourse because this normally takes place within established frameworks. It is therefore necessary to allow different and often conflicting ideas and modes of organisation to co-exist within the same environment because even those which appear most ridiculous under present circumstances may turn out to be extremely efficacious. We simply cannot know.

A closed view of language (linguistics) would regard meaning as residing entirely within the sphere of semantics as defined by the permutation of various grammatical units. Questions which could not be clearly formulated within this framework would therefore have no meaning (the view of linguistic philosophy of a certain type). An open view of language would regard semantics as merely a vehicle for the approximation of a person's meaning (see Chapter 2). Linguistic communication may involve paralanguage or the poetic use of assonance, alliteration or even song and none of these is arbitrary. Meaning can in fact be conveyed where the words cannot be found to express it. A closed view of natural philosophy would see the world as ultimately reducible to a set of 'natural laws'. Such concepts as free will and imagination are mere chimera. An open view would regard the world as well-ordered but not deterministic. Free will and imagination are real, not merely in the sense that we experience them to be real but in the absolute sense that their consequences are not predetermined.

I am not suggesting that *Red Bird* is about all these things (!), but about the difficult-to-verbalise opposition 'open/closed'. People's reactions to it, however, are usually expressed in a political, linguistic or other frame of reference. Furthermore, in the long run, *Red Bird*, like any other myth or work of art, means what people take it to mean, regardless of what I have to say on the matter!

Establishing a sound-image structure

In order to build up a complex metaphoric network we have to begin somewhere. We need to establish a set of metaphoric primitives which the listener might reasonably be expected to recognise and relate to. Just as in the structure of a myth, we need to use symbols which are reasonably unambiguous to a large number of people. The metaphoric primitives chosen for *Red Bird* may seem crassly obvious. However, these are only the basis upon which the metaphoric structure is to be built. The use of intrinsically esoteric referents (in the manner of T. S. Eliot) would not be appropriate in this context, apart from any other objections we might raise to it. The four basic sound-types used in *Red Bird* are (see Figure 8.3) *Words* (especially 'Listen to reason'), *Birds, Animal/Body* and *Machines*. Although in certain cases these categories are quite clearly distinguishable, ambiguities may arise (and are used intentionally). For example, non-linguistic vocal utterances (from a human or animal voice) may approach linguistic forms and vice versa. A repeated high-frequency glissando may be taken to be of ornithological or mechanical origin. Articulated mid-range pitched material may be both bird-like and animal-like. Each symbolic type is chosen because it either has a conventional symbolic interpretation (birds: flight, freedom, imagination; machine: factory, industrial society, mechanism) or such an interpretation can be easily established (the phrase 'listen to reason' points to itself).

The situation is already, however, more complicated than this might suggest. For example, the phrase 'listen to reason' is open to fragmentation and permutation and many different kinds of gestural articulation (see Figure 8.4) which means that its semantic surface may be utterly transformed or even negated (listen to Example 8.2). More importantly,

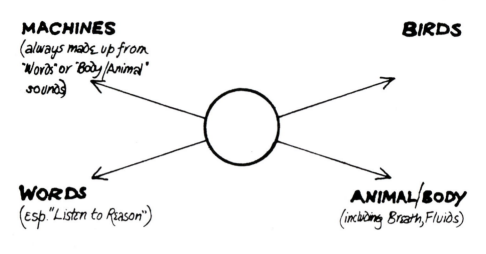

MACHINES
(always made up from
"Words" or "Body/Animal"
sounds)

BIRDS

WORDS
(Esp."Listen to Reason")

ANIMAL/BODY
(including Breath, Fluids)

& large-scale-textural opposition

FACTORY
(integrated around
simple rhythm-cycles)

GARDEN
(co-existing gestalts
in an arhythmic frame)

Figure 8.3   Basic sound-image classification in *Red Bird*.

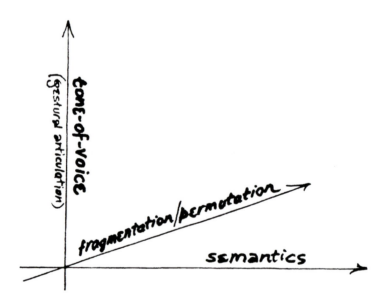

tone-of-voice
(gestural articulation)

fragmentation/permutation

semantics

Figure 8.4   Space of possible transformations of the phrase "listen to reason".

there are two particular kinds of landscape in which the sound-images of the piece may be placed. These may be described as the 'garden' landscape and the 'reason' landscape. Apart from the sound-images involved, the former is characterised by a sense of coexistence of the sound-images in acoustic space and time (listen to Example 8.3), the latter by a sense of spatial and temporal regimentation, the individual images being subordinated to a rigid, rhythmic structure (listen to Example 8.4). In fact, the machines which inhabit this landscape are made up either from phonemes or bodylike visceral sounds, whilst the squeaks and squeals of the machinery's operation are vocal, animal or bird noises.

In both cases the landscape as a whole may be transformed. In a previous example we heard the re-interpretation of the body/machine sound-image through a change in contextualising cues. In a similar way, the garden structure can be broken down through the gestural interaction of its constituents. In Example 8.5 animal-like sound-images emerge from the background (8.5a), take on a phonemic articulation (8.5b) and gesturally interact with the bird sounds (8.5c). The garden structure breaks down.

In fact, once we begin to explore the possible metaphorical ramifications of this network of sound-images, the possibilities become almost daunting. A methodology is required to allow us to make some kind of systematic search of the field of possibilities. This is certainly not a case where we can expect to set up some straightforward permutation procedure which will allow us to mark off all of the reasonably distinct possibilities, the field is in fact open. The procedure I shall describe (actually used during the composition of *Red Bird*) is meant therefore to be merely a heuristic tool, an enabling device to force the imagination to consider possibilities which might not otherwise have occurred to it. It in no sense defines or delimits the possibilities. Nor does it attempt to separate every conceivable parameter involved. In fact, definite parameters have been involved in setting up a search procedure. So long as the procedure is not meant to define our final use of the material, however, this is of little importance.

The scheme used in *Red Bird* is illustrated in Figure 8.5. Sound-images in the piece were broken down into twelve broad categories (no connection with serialism!). This included sub-divisions of the four basic categories (e.g. BIRD = birdsong consisting of the repetition of a simple element; BLACKBIRD = bird-song of more elaborate structure) and a number of subsidiary sound-images (BUZZ = the fly; BOOK, DOOR, SHARP = each a category of loud staccato sounds, in most cases made from phonemes or the slams of books or doors). Every combination of one, two,

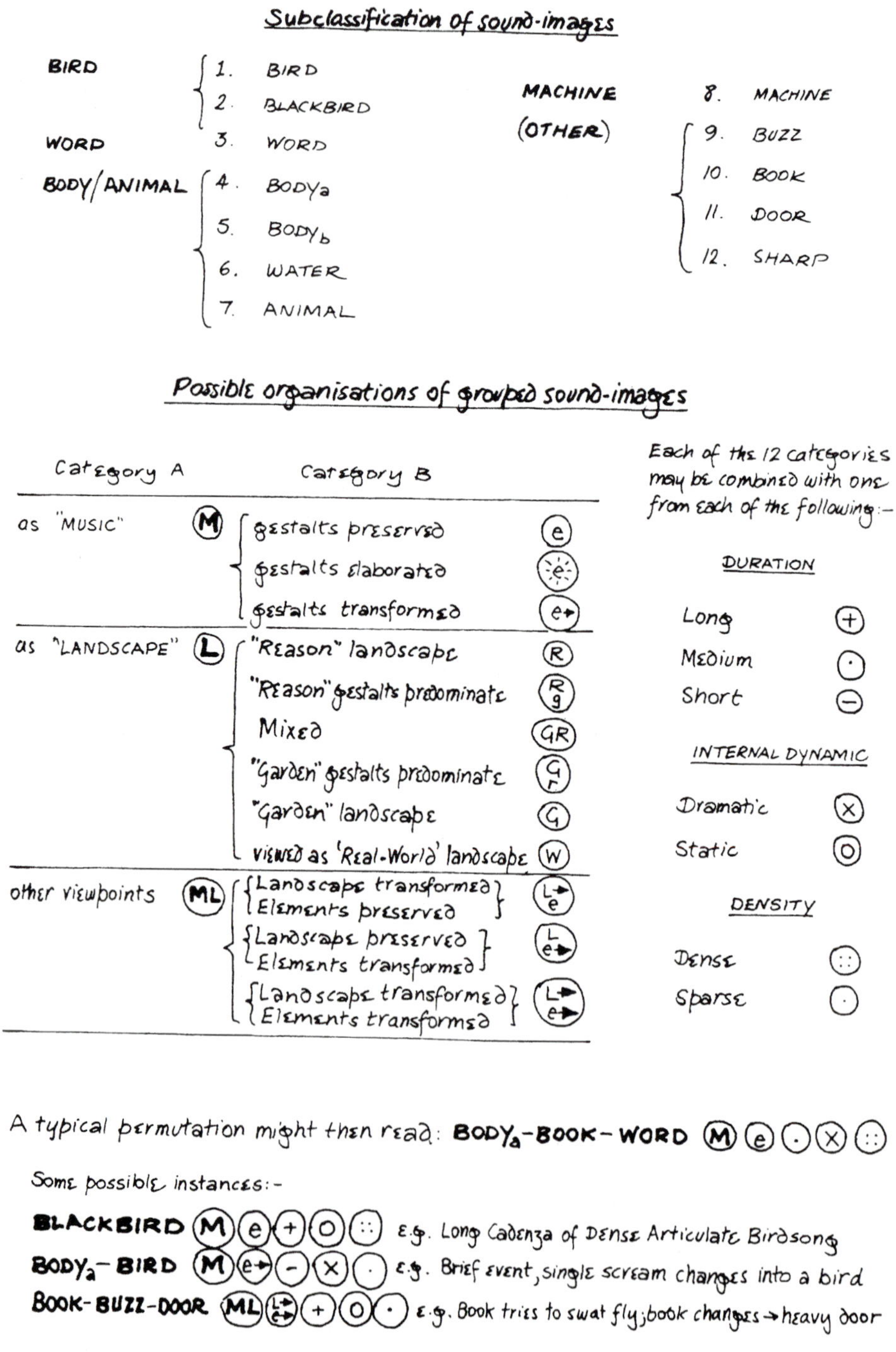

Subclassification of sound-images

BIRD		1.	BIRD
		2.	BLACKBIRD
WORD		3.	WORD
BODY/ANIMAL		4.	BODYa
		5.	BODYb
		6.	WATER
		7.	ANIMAL

MACHINE (OTHER)		8.	MACHINE
		9.	BUZZ
		10.	BOOK
		11.	DOOR
		12.	SHARP

Possible organisations of grouped sound-images

Category A	Category B	
as "MUSIC" (M)	gestalts preserved	(e)
	gestalts elaborated	(ė)
	gestalts transformed	(e→)
as "LANDSCAPE" (L)	"Reason" landscape	(R)
	"Reason" gestalts predominate	(R/g)
	Mixed	(GR)
	"Garden" gestalts predominate	(G/r)
	"Garden" landscape	(G)
	viewed as 'Real-World' landscape	(W)
other viewpoints (ML)	{Landscape transformed / Elements preserved}	(L/e)
	{Landscape preserved / Elements transformed}	(L/e→)
	{Landscape transformed / Elements transformed}	(L→/e→)

Each of the 12 categories may be combined with one from each of the following:—

DURATION

Long (+)
Medium (·)
Short (−)

INTERNAL DYNAMIC

Dramatic (X)
Static (O)

DENSITY

Dense (:·)
Sparse (O)

A typical permutation might then read: **BODYa–BOOK–WORD** (M)(e)(·)(X)(:·)

Some possible instances:—

BLACKBIRD (M)(e)(+)(O)(:·) e.g. Long Cadenza of Dense Articulate Birdsong
BODYa–BIRD (M)(e→)(−)(X)(·) e.g. Brief event, single scream changes into a bird
BOOK–BUZZ–DOOR (ML)(L/e→)(+)(O)(·) e.g. Book tries to swat fly; book changes → heavy door

Figure 8.5 Heuristic scheme for searching the field of possible sound-images for *Red Bird*.

three, etc. elements was then considered in terms of the organisational categories illustrated in the diagram. Then the imagination needed to be used! Some possible interpretations of these permutations are also illustrated in the diagram. A brief glance at these interpretations will reveal that the permutations were not regarded as definitive of the sound organisations generated. One interesting feature of this approach was that when I began the piece there was a clear distinction in my mind between organising something as music and organising something as landscape. In the actual studio construction of the piece, however, this distinction ceased to have any significance.

Aspects of landscape composition

The sound-images used in a landscape may be organised to suggest different interpretations of the landscape, or even different interpretations of the sound-images themselves. The garden landscape discussed previously, organises the sound-images in a 'naturalistic' way. Although the juxtaposition of species is ecologically impossible, our perception is of a 'natural', if somewhat dreamlike, environment. Conversely, in the *bird-cadenza* (listen to Example 8.6), the material is organised according to formal criteria derived from musical experience, but because of the sound-imagery used (various kinds of birdsong), the percept of a natural environment has not been destroyed.

In the case of the *word-machine* (Example 8.7) which we have discussed previously, our attention is not focused upon the phonemic constituents of the sound-landscape and our interpretation is of a mechanical, not a verbal, sound-image. We hear phonemes *as* a machine. In the next example phonemes are also subjected to a special kind of organisation. Here, however, the dense and diverging texture is more nearly suggestive of the flocking of birds. We hear phonemes as *if* they were flocking birds (Example 8.8).

In the next example, the phoneme 'rea' of 'reason' gradually becomes the sound of an aggressively barking dog, adding a further dimension to the three already mentioned for our presentation and interpretation of verbal elements (Example 8.9). In yet another example, the word 'reasonable' immediately becomes the sound of bubbling water. In this case the final phoneme '-ble' apparently bursts to reveal the bubbling water (Example 8.10). In another situation (Example 8.11) constituents of the landscape may be revealed to be other than we had imagined. In this particular case context has suggested that the sounds we hear are the squeals and whines of machinery. When the foreground constituents of machinery are halted, however, we can momentarily glimpse a landscape of animals, insects and frogs — or is it? Such transformations may be developed in extended sequences. In the next illustration, the screamed syllable 'rea' is first developed as a texture (Example 8.12a, see Figure 8.6 (I)), then, by a gradual shaping of the envelope and the addition of reverberation the character of the gestalt is completely altered (Example 8.12b, see Figure 8.6 (II)). Finally, it passes over imperceptibly into the ticking of a clock (Example 8.12c, see Figure 8.6 (III)).

In the penultimate section of *Red Bird* we have the most complex interaction of the many features of landscape composition. The overriding landscape image is that of the 'factory' or 'torture-chamber'. The two machines, as we have mentioned, are composed respectively of phonemes and body-sounds. The image of interminable machinery is articulated through:

(1)   changes in speed of either one or both machines, i.e. changes in the rate at which the machines cycle (not changes in their pitch) which may be achieved by shortening individual elements or omitting certain elements in the machine cycle;

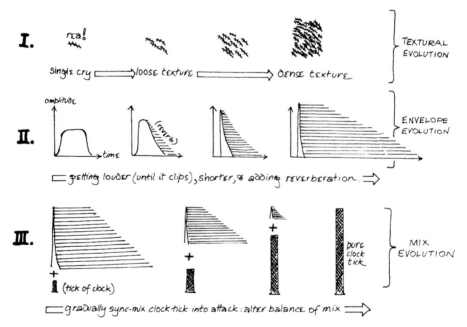

Figure 8.6   The three stages of evolution of screamed "rea-" (from reason) into a clock tick.

(2) interruption of either one machine or other or both by interpolated material. Much of this is condensed recapitulation of sound-images and events which have occurred earlier in the piece, for example, bird sounds which previously transformed into a wind-like texture now descend even further in a rushing downward glissando, voices which previously emerged into birdsong now emerge into screams, the book which attempted to swat the fly and changed into the sound of doors now pursues the human being.

At the same time animal, bird and human vocal sounds are integrated into the mechanical as the squeaks and squeals of the machinery. These may then:

(1) be revealed, as in the case of the animal sounds discussed previously; or
(2) emerge, as in the case of the human cries which become stronger, less reverberant and finally detach themselves from the machinery to complete a full vocal articulation, before being reabsorbed in the mechanical cycle.

Here we have a classic case of condensed recapitulations of materials for which we would find the model in conventional musical thought. The landscape reorganisations and transformations, however, are clearly metaphorically potent. Musical and metaphorical thinking converge in the articulation of sound-images in time. The concepts of transformation and gesture remain fundamental.

One final question remains; can any sound metaphor be said to be 'universal' in its interpretation? In his book 'The Tuning of the World' Murray Schafer has traced the almost universal symbolism of certain natural sounds:

> *The sea has always been one of man's primary symbols in literature, myth and art. It is symbolic of eternity: its ceaseless presence. It is symbolic of change: the tides; the ebb and flow of the waves. [...] It is symbolic of reincarnation: water never dies. [...] When angry it symbolises, in the words of W. H. Auden, 'that state of barbaric vagueness and disorder out of which civilisation has emerged and into which, unless saved by the effort of gods and men, it is always liable to relapse' [...] When the sea is worked into anger it possesses equal energy across the entire audible spectrum; it is full-frequencied, white noise. Yet the spectrum always seems to be changing; for a moment deep vibrations predominate, then high whistling effects, though neither is ever really absent, and all that changes is their relative intensity. The impression is one of immense and oppressive power expressed as a continuous flow of acoustic energy.*
> *(Schafer 1977: 170)*

By comparison with the barbaric challenge of the sea, the wind is devious and equivocal. Without its tactile pressure on the face or body we cannot even tell from what direction it blows. The wind is therefore not to be trusted. [...] Jung speaks of the wind as the breath of the spirit. 'Man's descent to the water is needed in order to evoke the miracle of its coming to life. But the breath of the spirit rushing over the dark water is uncanny, like everything whose cause we do not know — since it is not ourselves. It hints at an unseen presence, a numen, to which neither human expectations nor the machinations of the will have given life. It lives of itself, and a shudder runs through the man who thought that "spirit" was merely what he believes, what he makes himself, what is said in books, or what people talk about'.
(Schafer 1977: 171)

Schafer goes on, however, to point out that modern man, living in cities, sheltered from the elements in air-conditioned buildings and travelling between continents in aeroplanes, tends not to perpetuate this primeval symbolism. The sea, for example, becomes a romantic image associated with holidays. How, then, can we use any metaphor with the certainty that it will be understood? The answer, I think, lies in the embedding of the metaphor in a structure of interrelationships and transformations, as in *Red Bird*, such that various oppositions and distinctions are established. This is very much the way that musical objects (e.g. motifs) operate. The significance of the symbolisation is clarified through its relation to other symbols. Through suitable structures we could establish either the primeval or the romantic symbolism of the sea or in fact both, and generate subtle resonances and transformations between the two interpretations.

Chapter 9

IS THERE A NATURAL MORPHOLOGY OF SOUNDS?

Modes of continuation: a physical interpretation

While investigating sound-objects from a landscape point of view, it is interesting to reconsider certain categories from the acousmatic description of sound-objects given by the *Groupe de Recherches Musicales*. In particular the category of *continuation* refers, as its name suggests, to the way in which a sound-object may be continued in time. Three basic categories emerge: the *discrete*, the *iterative* and the *continuous*. Discrete continuation describes such sounds as a single (unresonant) drum-stroke or a dry pizzicato on a stringed instrument. Iterative continuation applies to a single-note 'trill' on a xylophone (i.e. the sustainment of a sound which will be otherwise discrete by rapidly re-attacking it), a drum-roll or the impulse-stream of 'vocal fry' or a bowed note on a double bass string which has been considerably slackened off. Continuous continuation applies to a sustained note on a flute, a synthesiser or a bell.

As we are here talking in terms of landscape, we shall relate our observations largely to sound-events occurring in the natural physical world (or, of course, to recordings of these heard in the virtual acoustic space of loudspeakers). We will then apply these observations to our apprehension of new sound-types generated in the studio through manipulations or synthesis. In the physical world, therefore, these three types of continuation imply something about the energy input to the sounding material and also about the nature of the sounding system itself. We may, in fact, say about any sound-event that it has an *intrinsic* and an *imposed* morphology (see Figure 9.1). Most sound-objects which we encounter in conventional music have a stable intrinsic morphology. Once the sound is initiated it settles extremely rapidly on a fixed pitch, a fixed noise-band or more generally on a fixed mass in the case of, for example, bell-like or drum-like sounds with inharmonic partials. Furthermore most physical systems will require a continual (either continuous or iterative) energy input to continue to produce the sound. Others, however, (such as bells or metal rods) have internal resonating properties which cause the sound energy to be emitted slowly

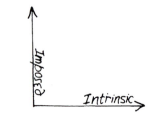

The 2 dimensions of sound morphology

Continuous	Iterative	Unsteady
Continuous→Iterative	Iterative→Continuous	Unsteady→Continuous
Continuous→Unsteady	Iterative→Unsteady	Unsteady→Iterative

9 types of imposed morphology

Figure 9.1   Nine types of imposed morphology.

with ever-decreasing amplitude after an initial brief energy input. Hence, from a landscape point of view we will split apart the category of continuous continuation to give on the one hand, sounds where there is a continuous input of energy, the continuation is due to the imposed morphology (e.g. flute sounds, violin sounds etc.), and, on the other hand, sounds where the continuation is due to the physical properties of the sounding medium (continuation through intrinsic morphology).

The reason for making this distinction is simply that the imposed morphology tells us something about the energy input to the system and ultimately relates to what we have called the gestural structure of sounds. Clearly we can gain more information about this energy input where it is continuous and least where it is in the form of an initiating impulse. Where energy (mechanical, hydraulic, aerodynamic or electrical) is continuously applied to the system, we can follow its ongoing subtle fluctuations. The sounding system is gesturally responsive. Where a sound-event is initiated by an impulse (e.g. a drum or bell-stroke), however, very little gestural information can be conveyed — effectively, only a difference in loudness relating to the force of the impulse. Iterative continuation is ambiguous in this respect. Iteration may be entirely an aspect of the applied force (as in the case of the xylophone 'trill'), purely an aspect of the physical nature of the medium (vocal fry or slack double bass strings), or an interacting mixture of the two (a drum-roll).

Clearly, on a synthesiser we can generate events of any kind without actually supplying any immediate energy input from our own bodies. Two things need to be said about this. First of all, the mode of continuation (and attack-structure, articulation etc.) of a sound will tend to be read in terms of the physical categories I have described. The distinction between, for example, continuous and impulse-based excitation is not a mere technical distinction but relates to our entire acoustic experience and 'tells us something' about the sound-object even though it may have been generated by an electrical procedure set up in an entirely cerebral manner. We can, of course, transcend these categories of the physical experience of sound-events, but I would suggest that we do so in the knowledge that this background exists. In a similar way, for example, we may generate glossolalia through the statistical analysis of letter frequencies in texts. Hayes (1983) generated the following examples from analyses of Latin (Virgil), Italian (Dante) and French (Flaubert) respectively:

AD CON LUM VIN INUS EDIRA INUNUBICIRCUM OMPRO VERIAE TE IUNTINTEMENEIS MENSAE ALTORUM PRONS FATQUE ANUM ROPET PARED LA TUSAQUE CEA ERDITEREM [...]

QUALTA'L VOL POETA FU' OFFERA MAL ME ALE E'L QUELE ME' E PESTI FOCONT E'L M'AN STI LA L'ILI PIOI PAURA MOSE ANGO SPER FINCIO D'EL CHI SE CHE CHE DE' PARDI MAGION [...]

PONT JOURE DIGNIENC DESTION MIS TROID PUYAIT LAILLE DOUS FEMPRIS ETIN COMBRUIT MAIT LE SERRES AVAI AULE VOIR ILLA PARD OUR SOUSES LES NIRAPPENT [...]
(Hayes 1983: 19)

But the reader will always hear or read the results against the background of his knowledge of one or several languages. The forms of sound-objects are not arbitrary and cannot be arbitrarily interrelated.

Composers who have weighted their activities towards live electronics rather than studio-based synthesis seem to me to have been strongly affected by the fact that a morphology imposed upon electronic sound-objects through the monitoring of performance gesture can be much more refined and subtle than that resulting from intellectual decisions made in the studio. The directness of physiological-intellectual gestural behaviour carries with it 'unspoken' knowledge of morphological subtlety which a more distanced intellectual approach may not be aware of. This is not to say that theorising cannot lead to interesting results, but that it can lead to a loss of contact with the realities of the acoustic landscape.

Even where the imposed morphology is a mere impulse, the loudness of the sound carries information about the force of that impulse. The association of loudness with power is not a mere cultural convention although loud sounds have often been used to project political potency (massed orchestras and choruses, the musicians of the Turkish army etc.). As far as we know, continuous changing in overall dynamic level (crescendos, diminuendos) were an invention of the Mannheim school of symphonic composition in the eighteenth century (though of course it was possible to differentiate different dynamic levels on instruments such as the organ in previous ages). The formalistic assignment of a series of different dynamic levels to musical objects, which was experimented with in the total serial aesthetic leaves a sense of arbitrariness or agitation (neither of which is usually intended) because it ignores the landscape basis of our perception of loudness.

Sounds undergoing continuous excitation can carry a great deal of information about the exciting source. This is why sounds generated by continuous physiological human action (such as bowing or blowing) are more 'lively' than sounds emanating, unmediated, from electrical circuits in synthesisers. The two natural environmental sounds, not of human origin, which indicate continuous excitation — the sound of the sea and that of the wind — tend to have an interesting ongoing morphology which may relate to the symbolic associations of these sounds (see the previous chapter). In the case of the sea, the excitation (the pull of the moon's gravity) may be regular but the form of the object (the varying depth of the sea) results in a somewhat unstably evolving (intrinsic) morphology. The sound 'of the wind' is usually in fact the sound of something else animated by the motion of the wind. In this case it is the exciting force (the wind itself) which varies unpredictably in energy giving the sound its interestingly evolving (imposed) morphology. Murray Schafer has pointed out in his book *The Tuning of the World* that it is only in our present technological society that continuous sounds which are completely stable (the hum of electrical generators etc.) have come to be commonplace (Schafer 1977, Chapters 5 and 6). The ability of the synthesiser to generate a continual stream of sounds says something about our society's ability to control energy sources; but if we take this continuous streaming for granted, like the humming of machinery, it tends to lose any impact it might have had on the listener. The machine has no intentions and therefore it inputs no gestures to its sound. The synthesiser can sound the same way!

Intrinsic morphology of complex sound-objects

If we accept that continuous, iterative and discrete modes of continuation can be used to describe the imposed morphology of the sound-object we can suggest a number of other possibilities. In particular, let us propose the category *unsteady* continuation. All of these categories, apart from the discrete, imply some kind of ongoing energy input and we can imagine transformations between these types of excitation. The various extensions of the modes of continuation are illustrated in Figure 9.1.

One important critique of the acousmatic analysis of sound-objects is that it reduces the two dimensions of imposed (gestural) morphology and intrinsic morphology to a single dimension. Even though the distinction between these two is not totally clear-cut and in the virtual acoustic space of loudspeaker the problem of sound-origins can be problematic; I would argue that the two dimensions continue to enter into our *perception* of sound-objects. Different kinds of intrinsic morphology affect us differently and this is something to do with the assumed physicality of the source (which is not the same thing as source-recognition). Imposed morphology we react to more directly, having an immediate relation to the workings of our own physiological-intellectual processes.

Most musical instruments have a stable intrinsic morphology. When energy is input in a steady stream or as an impulse, they produce a sound-object of the attack/resonance type. There is an initial excitation which generates a distinct spectrum (either pitched, inharmonic, or noise-based) which then dies away in amplitude either rapidly or with varying degrees of sustainment. Not all physical objects, however, behave in a similar fashion. If a steady stream of air is input to a siren it will take time to glissando up to a steady pitch and even more time to fall from that pitch once the air stream is stopped, to its lowest possible pitch. Similarly, let us compare the application of a stream of air whose pressure gradually increases to two systems. In the case of the flute we find that we set up a given fixed pitch which becomes louder until we reach a ('catastrophe') point at which the note changes rapidly to the next highest harmonic and so on. With the siren, however, we find that the pitch slides gradually upwards as the pressure is increased. Incidentally, as we will discuss in Chapter 12, the human voice is an interesting case in this respect because, although in music it is usually used to model the 'musical instruments' we have, in moments of extreme stress it tends to react more like the siren (the scream).

Thus, the flute and the siren have a different intrinsic morphology revealed by their response to a similar energy input. In this particular case the sound morphology of the siren is related in a direct (though delayed) way to the energy input. For this reason the siren is a fairly straightforward example. If, however, we take sound-objects whose intrinsic morphology is very complex or unstable how can we relate to these? Are they merely formless or random? I would like to propose that there are a number of archetypes which allow us to perceptually classify these complex sounds.

Sibelius' orchestral writing where a low bass line moves against a high melody with little or nothing in the intervening 'space' generates a sense of a vast and empty 'landscape' (Example 10.1).

Stereo reproduction on loudspeakers offers us, as we have discussed previously, a virtual acoustic space with both width and depth. There are, however, certain limitations to our perception of this (or any other) space. We can locate the direction of origin of high-frequency sounds fairly easily (our brain detects phase differences between the signals arriving at the two ears and other factors) but low frequency sounds with little energy in higher partials are very difficult to localise. In some multi-loudspeaker reproduction systems such as the *Gmebaphone*, developed by the *Groupe de Musique Expérimentale de Bourges*, the lower bass frequencies are therefore reproduced on a single large bass speaker placed directly in front of the listener, whilst higher frequency signals are distributed on loudspeakers placed in the conventional way, symmetrically to the right and left of the listener. The sense of spatial depth which, as discussed previously, may be generated in the stereo field by correlations between falling off in amplitude and high-frequency roll-off (and in certain cases reverberation) can be further extended in a multi-loudspeaker system by using planes of loudspeakers at different distances from the audience. The sound-image may thus be moved literally backwards and forwards by cross-fading from one set of loudspeakers to another (see Figure 10.1).

In certain circumstances the spatial metaphor associated with frequency may interact with real spatial motion in stereo space. I remember particularly a performance of Denis Smalley's *Orouboros* in which noise-based sounds which rose and fell in frequency band height in an undulating manner moved forward and outwards through the stereo space, creating the impression that the sound was tumbling towards the listener (see Figure 10.2). In our discussion of spatial motion in the current chapter we shall assume that the apparent location of a sound-object is unequivocal and that its motion can be adequately described. The ideas developed however cannot be applied uncritically (i.e. without listening) to arbitrary sound-material as the internal evolution of the spectrum of the sound-material may well affect the perceived motion.

A virtual acoustic space may be created all around the listener using four loudspeakers, a quadraphonic format.[1] The generation of an illusion of depth as in the stereo case allows us to expand the perceived virtual space out beyond the rectangle defined by the loudspeakers. Another perceptual problem arises in quadraphonic space. As in the real world it is not always

---

[1] Or even just three loudspeakers, in principle.

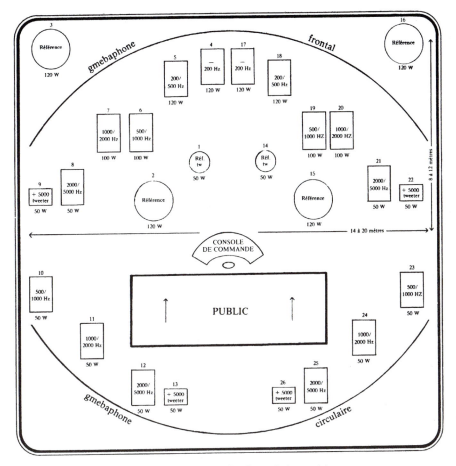

Figure 10.1 The Gmebaphone (schematic).

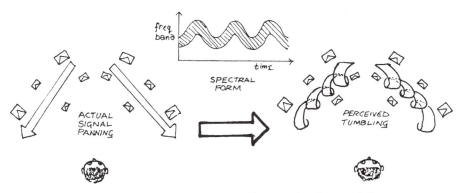

Figure 10.2 Tumbling effect produced by spatial and spectral changes.

easy to distinguish whether a sound emanates from a direction forward of the head or to the rear of the head. The doubt can usually only be resolved by moving the head itself.

Although a satisfactory quadraphonic illusion can be created through an expansion of the techniques we have described for stereo, some more refined approaches have been suggested. Through a precise analysis of the exact relationship between the fall-off in amplitude of a sound, its loss of high-frequency content and changes in its reverberance properties, John Chowning at Stanford developed a computer program to control more precisely the illusion of motion in the virtual acoustic space defined by four loudspeakers (see Chowning 1971).[2] The program also models the Doppler effect: when a sound-source moves towards us its apparent wavelength is shortened; conversely, when it moves away from us its apparent wavelength is lengthened. Thus any sound passing the hearer appears to fall in pitch (from higher as it approaches to lower as it retreats). Ambisonics on the other hand relies on phase differences generated at the different loudspeakers to convey information about the spatial location of a sound object. In some ways it may be regarded as a technical refinement of quadraphony. Ambisonic technology, however, allows the spatial image to be rotated, expanded, contracted or (if used in three dimensions) tumbled, in a technologically quite straightforward way. Recently more refined computer models of spatial encoding in loudspeaker projection have been developed.

Finally, virtual acoustic space may be expanded into three dimensions with as few as four loudspeakers (in a tetrahedral arrangement) or, more typically, eight forming a quadraphonic rectangle at ground level and a second above the audience. More ambitious three-dimensional systems have been presented. The spherical concert hall of the German pavilion at the Osaka World's Fair in 1970 had a whole network of loudspeakers distributed around the spherical surface of the auditorium walls, including beneath the platform on which the performers were suspended. The auditorium was used for performances of Stockhausen's *Spiral*[3] in which the sounds produced

---

[2] Chowning (1971) deals, strictly speaking, with an illusory space *outside of* the square defined by the loudspeakers. Other theories (ambisonics, for example) have tried to overcome some of the ambiguities which occur within the square (three distinct ways of localising a sound at the centre point of the square, for example). This does not invalidate the principles of the author's spatial morphologies, although many of the examples could not strictly be synthesised using Chowning's algorithms (*Ed.*).

[3] In fact Stockhausen's group performed many programmes of his works throughout their residency at the Osaka World's Fair. For a description of Stockhausen's spatial 'mill' see Cott, 1974: 45–6 (*Ed.*).

by the performers were picked up by microphones and made to move across the surface of the sphere. Such a multi-loudspeaker system (see Figure 10.3) conveys much more accurate information about the direction of a sound-object than any technology developed on fewer loudspeakers can. In recent years the cinema has moved from mono to stereo to surround reproduction of sound and we can expect the technology of sound location in space to develop rapidly in the coming years, particularly with the possibilities offered by computer modelling and control.

Aesthetic functions of spatial motion

In the previous chapters we have outlined one primary use of spatial localisation and spatial motion of sound-objects in the definition and transformation of musical landscape. Certain sounds (e.g. the fly) even need a spatial motion component in order to be recognisable. Spatial motion may also be used to underline contrapuntal developments and interactions between different streams of sound. At the opening of the piece *Vox I* a single stream of multiplexed vocal sounds (generated by four voices) emerges from the tape background and begins to transform and differentiate. Gradually there is a separation into a higher register stream (carried by two female voices) and a low register stream (carried by two male voices) with somewhat different timbral materials. The sense that the sound-stream has differentiated into two distinct entities (the model of growth and division of cells was consciously used) is underlined by the spatial division of the sound-stream as it moves from front centre stage through the listener and back to two separate locations on the two front loudspeakers (see Figure 10.4). One sound-object generates two sound-objects. In a similar way spatial convergence might be used to underline timbral convergence of two musical streams.

More generally, we may look on spatial movements as (musical) gestures, consider the typology and implications of different types of spatial gesture and how the spatial motion of one sound-object might relate to the spatial motion of others, and thus build up a concept of counterpoint of spatial gestures. In fact the concepts of transformation and gesture developed in earlier chapters might be extended so that gestural articulation in space might be added to our repertoire of possibilities for developing an articulate contrapuntal music. We could consider using spatial gesture independently of other musical parameters or in a way which reinforced, contradicted or complemented other gestural features of the sound-objects. The gestures of spatial motion (as opposed to the articulation of different spatial locations) occurs in Stockhausen's works

On Sonic Art

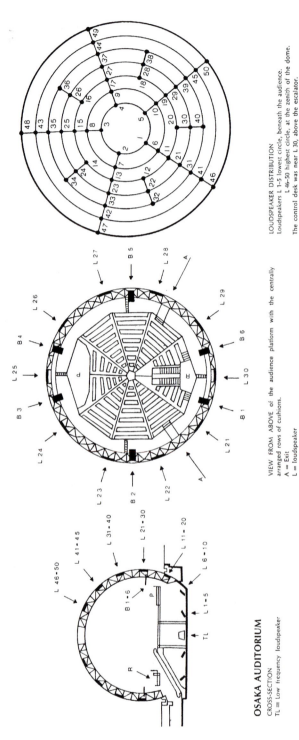

OSAKA AUDITORIUM

CROSS-SECTION

TL = Low frequency loudspeaker

VIEW FROM ABOVE of the audience platform with the centrally arranged rows of cushions.

A = Exit
L = loudspeaker
B = soloists' balcony
P = musicians' podium (c. 25 cm high)
R = control desk; in front of the control desk the double escalator by which the public entered. (Entry every 15 to 35 minutes, after a work or a section of a work; each performance was announced in English and Japanese; during a performance the auditorium lights were dimmed and only individual spotlights were focused on the soloists.)

LOUDSPEAKER DISTRIBUTION

Loudspeakers L 1–5 lowest circle, beneath the audience.
L 46–50 highest circle, at the zenith of the dome.
The control desk was near L 30, above the escalator.

Figure 10.3 The spherical auditorium at the Osaka World's Fair.

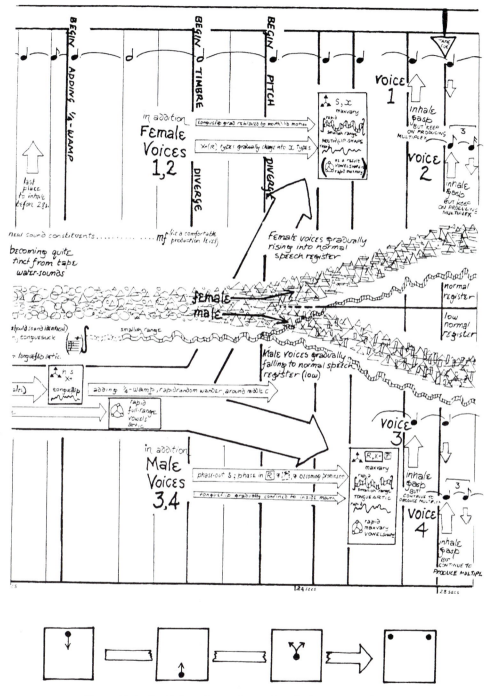

Figure 10.4   Spatial motion and sound evolution at start of *Vox-I*.

Gruppen and *Carré* where sounds are passed from one instrumental or vocal group to another, sometimes circling around the audience. In the piece *Spiral*, projected in the spherical auditorium at Osaka, spatial gestures played an essential part in the projection of the music. In this case the gestures were entirely improvised. Here we are going to attempt to analyse spatial gestures in more detail with a view to understanding the 'vocabulary' of motion but not as yet attempting to define any language.

To simplify our discussion we will confine ourselves to an analysis of the two-dimensional horizontal plane. Motions in the up-down (vertical) dimension will be referred to in passing. Furthermore we will confine ourselves to looking at connected paths, i.e. if a sound is to move from point A to point B it must pass through all locations on some line connecting these points in sequential order. That line may be as complicated or convoluted as we wish (Figure 10.5). A sound, however, which appears at A and reappears at B has not followed any connected path (this is more like a switching operation than a spatial motion). Clearly we might consider the latter kind of discontinuous motion as a special category and even consider an intermediate type of motion which traces out a path from one point to another but by a series of discrete leaps. There is of course nothing inherently impossible or unmusical about any of these kinds of motion but for the moment we shall leave them out of our discussion (Figure 10.6).

Characteristics of horizontal space

We are going to analyse the situation in which the listener is situated at the centre of a virtual acoustic space so that sound-objects may appear in front, to the left, to the right and behind the listener (see Figure 10.7). The listener, in fact, forms a frame of reference for this space which allows us to talk about

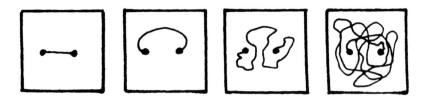

A connected path between 2 points is any line joining those points.

Figure 10.5   A variety of connected paths.

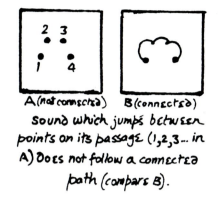

A (not connected)   B (connected)
Sound which jumps between
points on its passage (1,2,3... in
A) does not follow a connected
path (compare B).

Figure 10.6 Non-connected and connected paths.

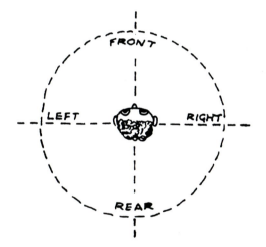

Figure 10.7 Oriented acoustic space around the listener.

'in front', 'behind', 'left', 'right'. From a purely geometric point of view the space is entirely symmetrical and there are no preferred directions. For the listener, however, certain directions have different psychological implications to others so that the frame of reference we are imposing on the space is not just a convention related to the ear-geometry of the head but a psychological/aesthetic aspect of our perception.

The principal distinction to be made is between 'in front' and 'behind'. In purely perceptual terms it can often be difficult to decide whether a stationary sound is located in front or behind the head. Motion of the sound (or the head), however, usually allows this distinction to be made. There is a slight difference in quality between the same sound heard from in front of the head and from behind the head. The orientation of the pinna and masking effects of the head itself tends to mean that most sounds are heard most clearly (in greater detail) when we turn our face towards them. More important, however, in its natural environment, on hearing a sound — particularly an unusual or frightening sound — an animal or bird will orient its face towards the direction from which the sound comes in order to be able to see the source of the sound. In the case of a sound coming from in front the creature will have probably seen the source of the sound before the sound is heard, but this is not the case with sounds coming from behind. Such sounds, therefore, tend to be more stressful, mysterious or frightening.

This separation of 'in front' and 'behind' also has a social dimension for most higher animals. We almost always turn to face the person with whom we are conversing. Sounds heard from behind may be 'overheard' or 'commands' but not usually part of a mutual discourse. At a concert or poetry reading we sit facing the performers. Metaphorically we 'face up to things' or 'face the music' and suspect things that happen 'behind our back'. The distinction, therefore, between sounds heard from in front and sounds heard from behind is not merely a function of the geometrical asymmetry of the human body in the front-back direction (as opposed to the left-right direction) but the psychological/aesthetic dimension of perception. The distinction between left and right on the other hand is not so critical. Not only is the body symmetrical in the left-right direction but (apart from sounds with no high-frequency components) it is normally very straightforward for us to differentiate between left and right in locating the source of a sound and there is no essential qualitative difference between the same sound heard from a similar angle in front, to the left or to the right.

In certain artificial test situations using specially synchronised tones played on headphones it can be shown that right-handed individuals have a tendency to orient their perception such that, for example, high-frequency sounds are assigned to the right side of the head and low frequency sounds to the left side of the head, even when such an assignment is contradicted by the physical placement of the sources. In our normal acoustic experience, however, we may assume that such effects are marginal, particularly if, like myself, you are left-handed! From an aesthetic viewpoint, therefore, a sound heard on the left, or moving from left to right does not have different implications to a sound heard from the right or moving from right to left. The distinction will only be of significance where we have different sounds placed or moving in the same space. Then, for example, a movement from left to right may be counterpointed with a movement from right to left.

Except in very special circumstances, however, playing an entire composition with the two loudspeakers switched around will not alter our aesthetic perception of the piece.

The distinction between 'above' and 'level' (or 'below'), on the other hand, has quite different psychological implications, at least for earthbound human beings (it might well become different for astronauts). Because we live on the surface of the planet to which we are bound by gravity, energy is required for any object to move upwards, whereas objects above us, unless constrained, will naturally fall down. Sounds moving upwards therefore will be linked metaphorically to flight or at least with the requirement of energy input. A sound which moves upwards, slows down and then descends has in some sense a 'natural' motion. A sound which appears from above and descends may suggest 'supernatural' or at least 'extraterrestrial' origins as it enters the horizontal plane of our normal acoustic perceptions from a plane (above) which is normally outside those perceptions. Although I have overstressed these distinctions in an exaggerated poetic way, these gravity-related orientation distinctions between 'above', 'level' and 'below' will enter into our aesthetic experience of sounds using the up-down dimension, even where the symbolic elaboration of these distinctions plays no part.

In order to analyse the qualitatively different types of motion in the two dimensional plane, I am going to assume a grid of nine distinguishable positions (see Figure 10.8). It is assumed that the listener is at the position marked 'centre', looking towards the position marked 'front'. Assuming a quadraphonic array of loudspeakers placed in the front and rear corners of the room, it should not necessarily be assumed that the positions 'front right' and 'front left' (for example) in our diagram correspond to the positions of two such loudspeakers. We are discussing positions in the

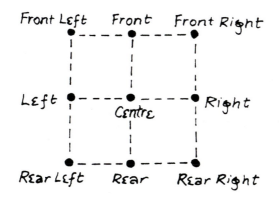

Figure 10.8 Grid of nine distinguishable spatial positions.

virtual space created by the loudspeakers and this virtual space may be much larger than the actual rectangle formed by the loudspeakers themselves (for example, by using amplitude, high-frequency roll-off and reverberation to create the illusion of depth beyond the frame of the loudspeakers). In many cases, we will be able to distinguish many more directions and distances from the centre position than these nine. This grid has been chosen for two reasons. First of all in order to make qualitative distinctions between types of motion we must be able to define the start and end points of a motion. Two motions will only be distinct (in purely spatial terms) if they start or end at positions which are qualitatively different to the listener. This grid gives us the simplest qualitative division of the acoustic space into perceptually distinguishable and qualitatively different positions. At the same time our aural discrimination of spatial position is not so refined as, for example, our discrimination of pitch. Particularly where the virtual acoustic space is projected on a limited number of loudspeakers (e.g. stereo or quadraphonic projection). Advances in computer simulation of spatial position or the general development of multi-loudspeaker concert halls may soon improve this position. However, even with just nine positions, we will find that the analysis is quite complicated enough! For the moment motion between points intermediate to the grid points may be regarded as segments of larger motions from one grid point to another (see Figure 10.9).

Considering both the perceptual limitations of the ear and the mathematics of curves it will be possible to describe all distinguishable types of motion in terms of straight line or circular motion, or some combination of these. We will also introduce the idea of random fluctuations in a motion. Finally, we may distinguish between the motion of an object and the motion of the frame (of reference). Clearly from a purely mathematical point of view, the motion of the object and the motion of the frame are but two representations of the same motion (see Figure 10.10(a)). Perceptually,

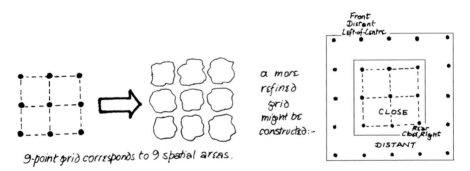

Figure 10.9   Nine-point spatial grid corresponds to nine spatial areas.

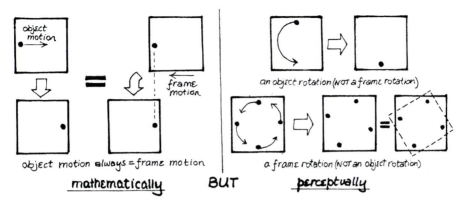

Figure 10.10 Object and frame rotations: distinction of the mathematical and the perceptual.

however, we can make a distinction between, for example, the rotation of a single object and the co-ordinated rotation of all the sound-objects in an acoustic space. The former we will refer to merely as a rotation and the latter as a frame rotation (see Figure 10.10(b)). Clearly there will be borderline cases where it is difficult to say whether we perceive the motion of objects or the motion of the frame, and certain kinds of complex motions among a group of objects may have the characteristics of both modes of perception. We will adopt what seems to be the most perceptually relevant description, indicating areas of ambiguity where these might arise.

Finally, two points should be stressed. Our analysis is a qualitative, not a mathematical, analysis. Mathematically speaking any motion in the two-dimensional plane can be expressed in terms of two separate motions along straight lines (and in many other ways). Furthermore the analysis aims at a qualitative understanding of our perception of motion in acoustic space and not as a formalisation of compositional procedures.

Direct motions

Given the left-right symmetric, front-back asymmetric nature of the acoustic space (see above) we can define just three straight-line (non-diagonal) spatial paths which pass through the listener (see Figure 10.11(a)). In the diagrams dotted line arrows indicate paths which are aesthetically equivalent to accompanying solid line arrows. However, there are four such paths along the edge of the space as motion across the front can be distinguished from motion across the back (by front-back asymmetry) and forward motion can be distinguished from backward motion (again by front-back asymmetry) (Figure 10.11(b) and 10.11(c)).

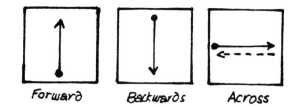

Forward   Backwards   Across

Figure 10.11a   Straight line motion: centre-crossing.

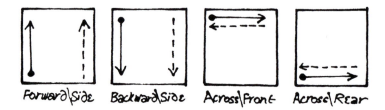

Forward\Side   Backward\Side   Across\Front   Across\Rear

Figure 10.11b   Straight line motion: edge-hugging.

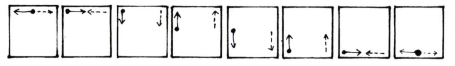

Figure 10.11c   Straight line motion: edge-hugging partial motions.

In the case of paths which pass through the listener's head, it is perceptually quite clear whether the path is a straight line or not as we can use front-back and left-right cues. Paths which pass along the edge of the space, however, are more difficult to judge in this respect as we must rely purely on distance criteria (which are not so clear-cut). We shall, therefore, for the moment assume that straight lines and arcs which do not pass through the listener's head are at least similar in their aesthetic impact. However, arcs which do pass through the listener's head will be clearly distinguishable from straight paths and we may distinguish four paths of this type (see Figure 10.12).

A second set of paths moves simultaneously along the left-right and front-back axes. We will call these diagonal paths. Backward moving and forward moving diagonals are clearly distinguishable (front-back asymmetry) and we may in fact distinguish seven types of diagonal motion (see Figure 10.13). For these paths which do not pass through the listener's head the same comments about lines and arcs apply. This means, however, that we

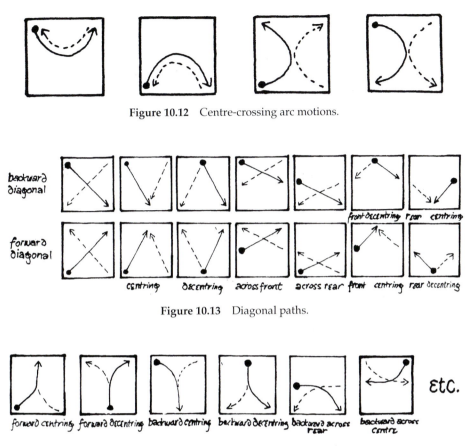

Figure 10.12 Centre-crossing arc motions.

Figure 10.13 Diagonal paths.

Figure 10.14 Centre-hugging diagonal paths.

must distinguish a further set of diagonal paths which arc through the listener's head (see Figure 10.14). In a sense, these 'centre-hugging' diagonals may be regarded as spatial articulations of the direct diagonals, a spatial gestural-articulation imposed on a spatial motion type.

A further class of movements is concerned with motion to and from the centre of the space (centring and decentring respectively). These are illustrated in Figure 10.15. Again, as these motions move to and from the listener's head, arc-like motions can be distinguished from straight lines and so we must also consider the set of spatial gestural-articulations of these ten types where the straight lines are replaced by arcs of various depths. Note that when the motion is to or from the front centre or rear centre positions (see Figure 10.16) we need make no aesthetic distinction between arcs which move out to the left or to the right; but in all other cases the initial

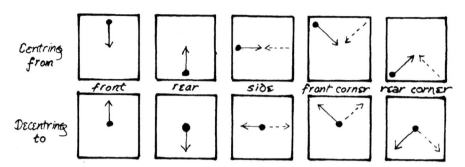

Figure 10.15   Centring and decentring motions.

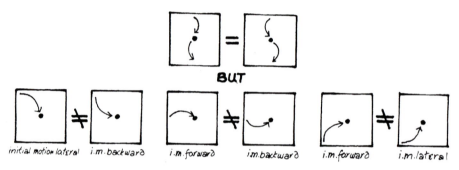

Figure 10.16   Equivalence and non-equivalence of centring arcs.

(or final) direction of the arc is of great importance because forward and backward motion are both quite different from lateral motion (Figure 10.16).

Cyclical and oscillatory motions

Next we must consider circular motion. This is the first example of a motion type which is (potentially) *cyclic*. The motions we have discussed up to this point we shall call *direct* as they trace out a path from one distinct point to a different point and therefore must take a finite time to execute. Cyclic motions, however, continually retrace the same path and therefore may continue ad infinitum. Cyclic motions have different possibilities to direct motions. In particular, they may be combined with each other or with direct motions to produce qualitatively different classes of motion (see below). In this respect they are similar to randomly wandering motions which, however, differ in that they are not cyclic. In a superficial sense diagonal motion may be regarded as qualitatively distinct from, yet derivable from, front-back and lateral motion. Although this is true, I would not regard diagonal motion as belonging to an altogether different class of motion from front-back and lateral motions. I cannot in the end give any hard and fast criteria for these distinctions; they are matters of aesthetic judgement. We might also argue that diagonal motion is nothing more than centring followed by decentring (see Figure 10.17). This is a slightly different matter, however. Whether we observe a motion as diagonal or a centring followed by a decentring in the same direction depends upon how we perceptually divide up the spatial motion into distinct spatial-gestural events; this has partly to do with the sound-material involved but also with the temporal evolution of the motions involved. This will be discussed further below.

Because left-right/front-back cues are much more reliable than distance cues, circular motion is most easily recognised when it passes right around the head of the listener (central circular motion). Circular motion which does not do this (peripheral circular motion) is much more difficult to establish in the listener's perception. The motion may however go right around the listener's head without being centred upon it (eccentric circular motion) so that in any event we can define a number of perceptually distinct circular motions (Figure 10.18). For the moment we will also not make a distinction between motions along particular closed polygons (see Figure 10.19) and related circular motions. The straight-line paths will either be distinct because of their time (and sonic) articulation, in which case we can regard the motion as a set of distinct direct motions, or these

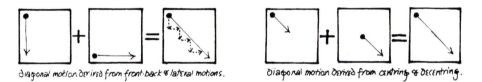

diagonal motion derived from front-back & lateral motions.   Diagonal motion derived from centring & decentring.

Figure 10.17   Possible derivations of diagonal motion.

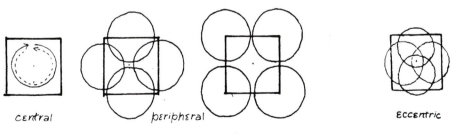

central   peripheral   eccentric

Figure 10.18   Circular motion types.

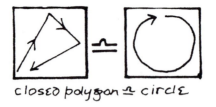

Figure 10.19   Equivalence of closed polygon and circle.

clear articulations will not be made, in which case distinguishing the polygon from motion along an arc will be quite difficult.

It is of course possible to take any direct motion and retrace the path in the opposite direction, thereafter repeating this cycle. I would, however, prefer to call this motion an *oscillation*. The motion is partly defined by its two end points and essentially oscillates between these two positions. There is no such sense of oscillation in circular motion. As all points along the circle are equivalent, there is no 'turning point'. Again, this is not a mathematical or a semantic distinction but a question of the aesthetic import of such motions. We might liken circular motion to the motion of a Shepard tone which, though apparently continually rising, never in fact moves out of its initial tessitura. An oscillation, on the other hand, is much more like a trill or vibrato. If we imagine a circular motion in which the diameter of the circle successively decreases and increases in a cyclic fashion, then the circular motion would take on the character of an oscillation. These distinctions begin to blur when we consider eccentric circular motion or narrow eccentric ellipses (see Figure 10.20).

A related movement type is spiral motion (see Figure 10.21). An inward spiral which approaches the centre slowly may be perceived as a circular motion in which the frame is contracting towards the centre (see Figure 10.22). More commonly, however, spiral motion will be perceived as direct, as it has a definite start and end point: it is not cyclic. This is

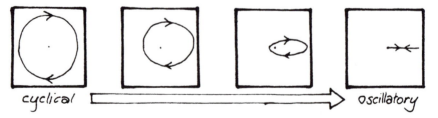

Figure 10.20   The relation of cyclic to oscillatory motions.

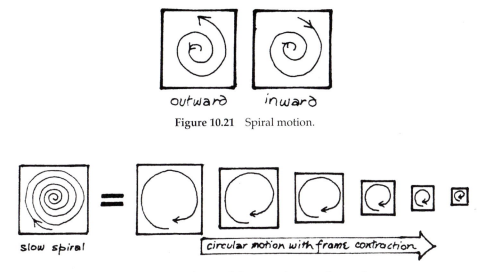

outward   inward

Figure 10.21 Spiral motion.

slow spiral   circular motion with frame contraction

Figure 10.22   Relation of slow spiral to circular motion.

particularly evident in the case of a very shallow spiral (Figure 10.23) which is more like a mellifluous spatial ornamentation of linear motion. In between the two extremes, the spiral displays some characteristics of both circular and direct motion. Like circular motion it tends to negate the orientation of the space, making all directions equivalent. In its place, however, and unlike circular motion, it establishes inwards and outwards motion as significant. Motions which spiral inward and then outward or vice versa (see Figure 10.24) should also be distinguished. Where this motion is extended into an oscillation (inwards to outwards to inwards to outwards etc.) we have the oscillating circular motion discussed previously. It seems to me unlikely that in two-dimensional acoustic space, spiral motion which is not centred on the listener's head can effectively convey the vortex feeling of spiralling.

Finally, let us consider motion along a figure-of-eight. There are two symmetric figure-of-eight pathways (see Figure 10.25). Motion along these

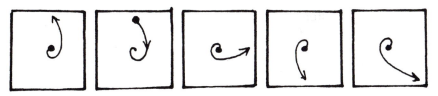

Figure 10.23   Shallow spirals.

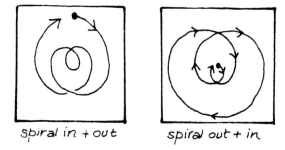

spiral in + out   spiral out + in

Figure 10.24   Inward and outwards spirals.

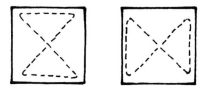

Figure 10.25   Two types of figure-of-eight motion.

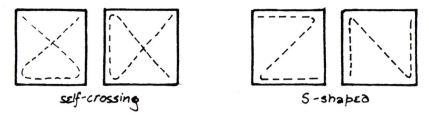

self-crossing   S-shaped

Figure 10.26   Types of pathway around figure-of-eight.

paths illustrates very well the oriented asymmetry of acoustic space. Non-cyclic paths may be divided into self-crossing and S-shaped (Figure 10.26). The important difference between these is that self-crossing paths pass through the centre of the space twice and S-shaped paths only once. Motion along an S-shaped path will be differently perceived in one direction than the other because the sound will pass either front-to-back or back-to-front through the listener, depending upon the direction of motion (see Figure 10.27). With self-crossing paths, however, there is a difference between motions which move along the edge (lateral) and motions which move along the front or back. Lateral paths pass through the centre twice in the same direction, which will be either twice forwards or twice backwards, depending upon the direction of motion along the path (Figure 10.27). With

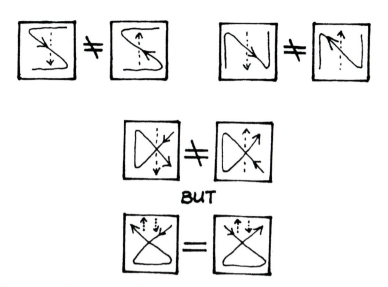

Figure 10.27   Symmetric and asymmetric motions around figure-of-eight paths.

backward self-crossing motion, however, the path crosses the listener's head in both directions — first front-to-back and then back-to-front — and, thus reversing the direction of motion, does not alter the aesthetic impact of the path (only the left-right symmetry). It does, however, make a difference whether we begin at the back of the space or the front of the space.

We can therefore classify the non-cyclic figure-of-eight motions as shown in Figures 10.28 and 10.29. Cyclic figure-of-eight motions are affected by the same asymmetry considerations so that motions which move across the front and rear of the space pass through the centre in both directions, whereas motions which pass along the sides of the space pass through the

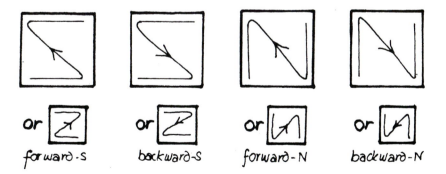

Figure 10.28   Typology of S-shape figure-of-eight motions.

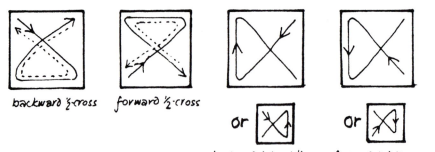

Figure 10.29   Typology of self-crossing figure-of-eight motions.

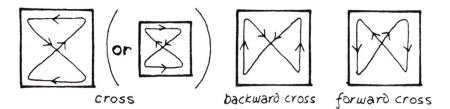

Figure 10.30   Symmetries of cyclic figure-of-eight motions.

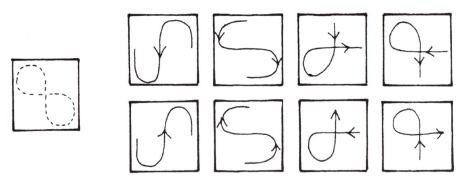

Figure 10.31   Motions along the diagonal figure-of-eight.

centre either always forwards or always backwards (Figure 10.30). Motions along the diagonal figure-of-eight are more simply asymmetric (Figure 10.31). Note also that S-shaped paths can be shaded over into arc-articulated linear paths while self-crossing paths remain quite distinct (Figure 10.32).

More extended self-crossing pathways need not be symmetrical. Figure-of-eight self-crossing motions are characterised by the reversal of

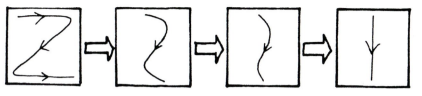

Figure 10.32 Transition of S-shape to arc-articulated linear path.

curvature of the path after each crossing of the centre. This results in a particular patterning of the directions in which the path crosses the central position. In the case of the backward (or forward) cross, this crossing is always in the same direction. In the case of the lateral cross, backward and forward crossings alternate regularly (see Figure 10.33). A quite different self-crossing motion is illustrated by the clover-leaf, in which the half-loops of the motion themselves cycle regularly around the space (Figure 10.33). This motion then carries two senses of 'circling' but lacks the 'twist' of figure-of-eight motion. This type of double motion will be discussed more fully below. Note, however, that there is a regular pattern of centre-crossings (forward, forward, backward, forward, forward etc.). We may now introduce irregular reversals and curvature into the motion to produce the irregular self-crossing motion illustrated in Figure 10.33. Here the pattern of centre-crossings is irregular (backward, forward, forward, backward etc.) and although the acoustic space is clearly articulated into centre-crossing diagonal motions and edge-hugging motions, the overall effect remains irregular or unpredictable.

Double motion

We may derive further classes of motion by combining the aesthetic qualities of motions we have already discussed. The word 'addition' used in this section does not necessarily imply that the motions can be derived by

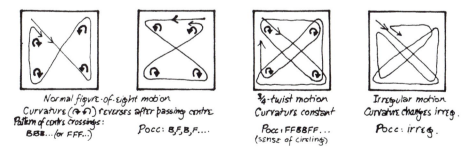

Figure 10.33 Regular and irregular paths around figure-of-eight.

mathematical addition of the two or more motions from which they aesthetically derive. As a first example, we may combine a linear oscillation with the motion perpendicular to the plane of oscillation. This gives us various types of zig-zag motion illustrated in Figure 10.34. Note that in the case of the lateral zig-zag, provided there is enough zig-zagging motion, we need not differentiate between a motion which begins at the rear and one which begins at the front as the path will spend as much time in front of us as behind us. Doubled motions, however, depend very much on the relative time-bases of the two contributory motions (more about this later) and we will find that there are limiting cases where the quality of the motion is quite different. Thus in the case of a motion which traverses a single zig-zag we must differentiate between a motion which begins at the rear and one which begins at the front (see Figure 10.35). We can also differentiate other classes of zig-zagging motion (for example Figure 10.36). These are more easily discussed in terms of the transformation of a one-dimensional frame (see below).

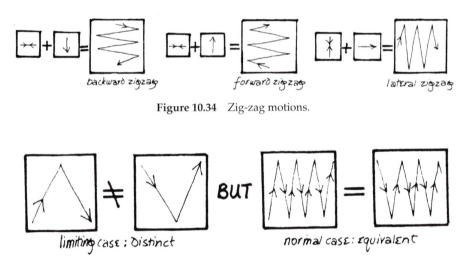

Figure 10.34   Zig-zag motions.

Figure 10.35   Zig-zag front/back symmetry/asymmetry.

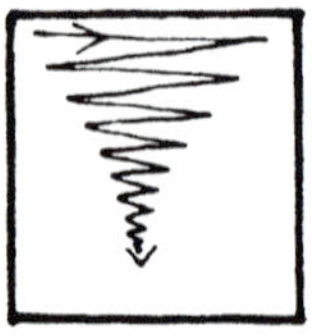

Figure 10.36   Other possible zig-zag type.

If we now combine a back-front and a lateral zig-zag motion, where the time-bases of each contributory zig-zag are quite different, we will produce merely an oscillation between backward and forward zig-zagging (or leftward and rightward zig-zagging). Where the time-bases are almost but not exactly equal we will set up an oscillating pattern in the space (see Figure 10.37). Different patterns of fluctuation between the two senses of 'diagonality' may be set up by relative fluctuations in the time-bases of the two zig-zag motions[4].

Combining circular and direct motion we produce looping motion which proceeds in a particular direction in space whilst continually looping back on itself (see Figure 10.38). If we now allow the linear motion to oscillate back and forth across the space the looping motion will do likewise. In this situation the limiting case is equivalent to the self-crossing

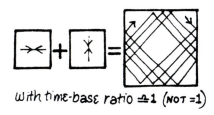

Figure 10.37   Oscillation from two zig-zag motions.

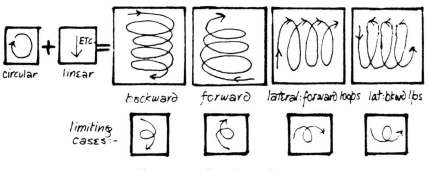

Figure 10.38   Looping motions.

---

[4] Note that the precessing ellipse motion discussed below may be mathematically described in terms of a front-back and a lateral oscillation with appropriate time bases. It is, however, discussed in a different context here because it is perceptually related to circular and elliptic motion and not to linear oscillations.

motions discussed earlier. Applying linear motion to an inward-outward spiral we obtain a pulsating looping motion (see Figure 10.39).

If we now expand the linear oscillation into a narrow ellipse we may differentiate between two distinct senses of the 'addition' of the qualities of motion. If we apply the circular motion to every point along the path of the ellipse we obtain the path illustrated in Figure 10.40(a). If, however, we apply this circular motion to a particular defining parameter of the ellipse — in this case the position of one focus of the ellipse — we obtain the precessing ellipse illustrated in Figure 10.40(b). Both of these motions have the quality of circling and of elliptic motion but they are combined in a qualitatively quite different sense. The first I will refer to as *internal* addition (of the circle to the ellipse) and the latter as *external* addition. Note that we can look on this addition the other way round and regard the first motion as imposing an elliptic motion on a defining parameter of the circle (the position of its centre point) and the latter motion as the internal addition of elliptic motion to all points on the path of the circle.

Similarly we may add zig-zag motion internally or externally to circular motion (see Figure 10.41). The process of addition of motion in this

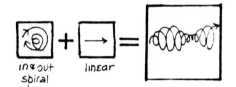

Figure 10.39   Pulsating loop motion.

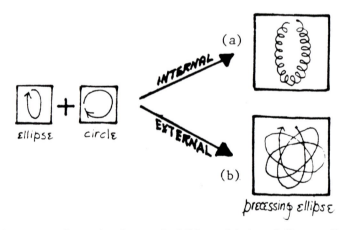

Figure 10.40   Internal and external additions of circle and ellipse motions.

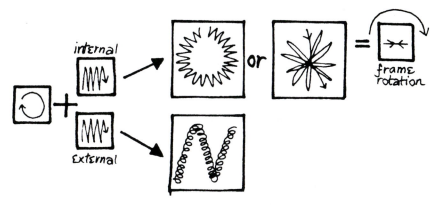

Figure 10.41   Internal and external additions of circle and zig-zag motions.

sense may be elaborated even further (see, for example, Figure 10.42) but, at least for the moment, there are distinct limitations on our ability to perceive the characteristics of such complex types of motion. We may also add cyclical motion to itself, producing the circling loop motion illustrated in Figure 10.43. This motion has several special cases, from the rotating single loop (Figure 10.44) to circular and elliptic four-cloverleaf formations (see Figure 10.45). We may also describe three-cloverleaf formations and, even within this category, we can define two distinct types, the normal and the maximally-swung (see Figure 10.46). The latter is produced by varying the time-base of the motions appropriately. By a similar process we can produce

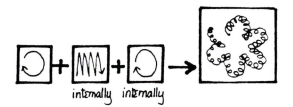

Figure 10.42   An elaboration of additions of circle and zig-zag motions.

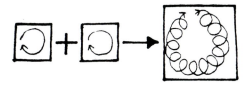

Figure 10.43   Addition of circular motions.

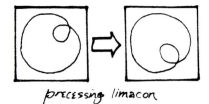

precessing limacon

Figure 10.44   A rotating single loop.

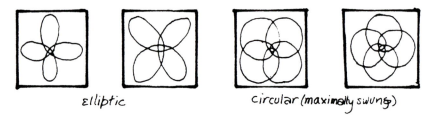

Elliptic   *Circular (maximally swung)*

Figure 10.45   Four-cloverleaf formations.

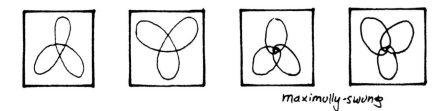

maximally-swung

Figure 10.46   Three-cloverleaf formations.

two different kinds of four-cloverleaf pathways (see Figure 10.47) and even motions which are asymmetric with respect to the acoustic space (for example, the 'butterfly' motions illustrated in Figure 10.48). Finally we may imagine motions which loop closely around the centre, throwing out larger loops of either regular or irregular sizes at irregular intervals. These may be regarded as irregularly oscillating circular motions (Figure 10.49) and lead us into a consideration of randomness in spatial motion.

Irregular motion

We may also consider motion-types which involve irregular paths through the acoustic space. Such a path may be completely unlocalised or localised in

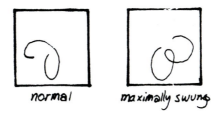

normal   maximally swung

Figure 10.47 Two types of four-cloverleaf formations.

    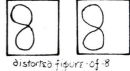

lateral forward   lateral backward   front   rear   cf.   distorted figure-of-8

Figure 10.48 'Butterfly' pathways.

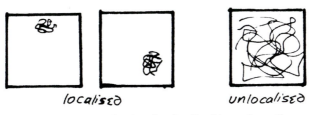

Figure 10.49 Irregular oscillating circular motion.

localised   unlocalised

Figure 10.50 Localised and unlocalised irregular paths.

a particular area of the space (see Figure 10.50). Alternatively, an entirely unlocalised (or partly localised) motion may be weighted so that the sound-object spends more of its time in particular areas of the space than in others (Figure 10.51). We will leave consideration of such time-averaged properties for a later section. Clearly irregularity is a matter of degree and we can imagine a whole array of paths between completely unlocalised irregular motion and small fluctuations around a direct motion. Movements of the

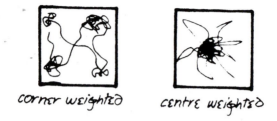

corner weighted   centre weighted

Figure 10.51   Time weighted irregular paths.

latter type are best considered as double motions, combinations of motion types we have already discussed and irregular motion. Clearly, irregular fluctuations in space can be applied to any direct motion. If, however, we apply them to double motions, we are able to do this internally or externally as before. Consider for example zig-zag motion. We may apply irregular motion internally to the zig-zag paths themselves or externally to the defining end-points or centres of the zig-zag motion (Figure 10.52). Clearly the perceived qualities of the three motions are quite different. In the first case we have an unsteadiness within the zig-zagging motion itself. In the two other cases, however, the zig-zagging motion is quite definite but its orientation is unpredictable.

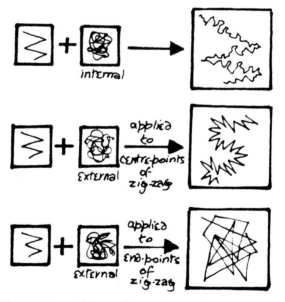

Figure 10.52   Addition of irregular and zig-zag motions.

We may similarly combine irregular motion with circular motion, or looped circular motion (see Figure 10.53) or to pulsating looped motion (Figure 10.54). In the case of these circular motions, the external addition causes the circle centre to wander about in a random manner. With the

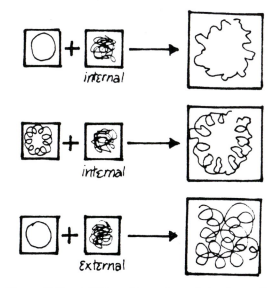

Figure 10.53   Addition of irregular and circular motions.

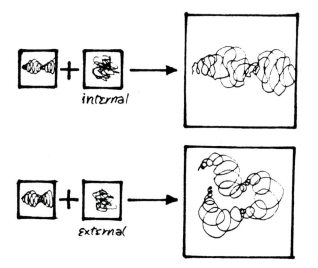

Figure 10.54   Addition of irregular and pulsating looped motions.

pulsating loop motion, however, there is another external parameter, the rate of oscillation of the pulsation. This, too, may be made to fluctuate randomly. These variables combine to produce a motion with one degree of order (looping) and two degrees of disorder (random circle centre and random pulsation rate (time-base randomness) (Figure 10.55)).

Clearly, when a motion becomes too complex we cease to perceive any pattern in it at all. Thus internal addition of irregularity will be perceived as a 'jitteriness' of the motion only where it is a small component of the motion. Beyond a certain point the motion will appear quite random. External addition of irregularity is in fact more interesting because the zig-zagginess, or loopiness of the motion is preserved. These qualities should differentiate one kind of randomly wandering motion from another.

Time

A motion is characterised not only by its path in space but also by its behaviour in time. We may distinguish the first order time properties (different speeds of motion) and second order properties (the way in which the speed changes through time, the acceleration or deceleration of the motion). We might even consider in some cases third order properties of the motion (the way in which the acceleration or deceleration changes through time) but for the moment we will assume that this degree of precision is not generally audible.

The absolute speed of the motion will determine its perceived aesthetic character. A very slow motion will be experienced as a mere relocation of position or even as 'drift' rather than a movement with some definiteness or 'intention'. As the speed of the motion increases the apparent energy associated with that motion is increased. Motion at

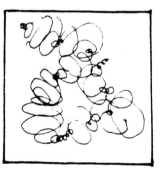

Figure 10.55 Pulsating looped motion with two degrees of randomness.

intermediate speeds has a feeling of definiteness or 'purposefulness', an intention to get from one location to another. Fast motions carry a feeling of urgency or energy. Where fast motion is introduced suddenly into a relatively static frame, there is a sense of sudden surprise. The similar introduction of a very slow motion into a static frame may induce a sense of gentle disorientation. Very fast motion in a circle may even induce a sense of head-spinning dizziness.

Considering now different categories of speed change we may broadly differentiate six classes of motion (see Figure 10.56). Accelerating motions, with their sense of rushing towards a final position, thus increase in spatial 'definiteness' or 'intention' and point to the significance of their target point. They are a kind of spatial 'anacrusis'. Decelerating motions, on the other hand, have exactly the opposite effect, a definiteness in leaving their point of origin and a sense of coming to rest at their target, a calming or spatial 'resolution'.

Accelerating-and-decelerating or decelerating-and-accelerating motions allow us to define some new types of linear motion. Figure 10.57 defines a whole class of there-and-back linear (or narrow elliptical) motions. Where these have a decelerating-accelerating time-contour they are perceived as 'thrown' elastic motions. It is as if the sound-object is thrown out from its point of origin on an elastic thread whose tension slows down its motion and then causes it to accelerate back towards the source. Simple constant speed motion along any of these paths would usually break down in our perception into two separate motions, one in the outward and the other in the inward direction. The time-contour, however, gives the whole motion a special kind of unity. Conversely, the accelerating-decelerating time-contour gives the feeling of 'bounced' elastic motion, the motion gathering energy and then being forcibly repelled by the edge of the space it defines, losing energy as it returns. Again, the overall there-and-back motion is unified by the time-contour.

Where a motion cyclically accelerates and decelerates, our aesthetic interpretation may depend on our position in relation to the motion. Consider the maximally-swung elliptic four-cloverleaf motion of Figure 10.47. We may apply a synchronised pattern of accelerating and

Constant   Accelerating   Decelerating   Accel-Decel   Decel-Accel   Irregular

Figure 10.56 Time contours (classes of motion).

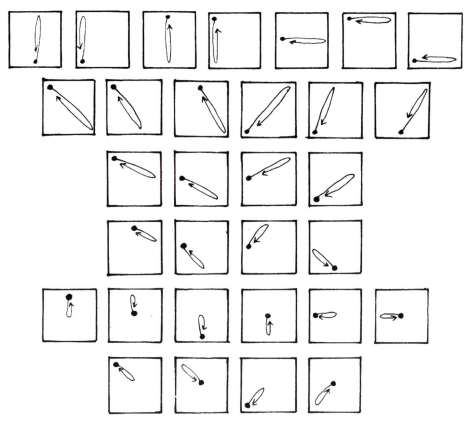

Figure 10.57   Elastic or bounced motions.

decelerating motion to this path in one of two ways. In the first case the movement on the elliptic outer loops will accelerate whilst the motion close to the observer will be slow. As the sound-object will therefore spend most of its time circling slowly around the observer's head, the motion will appear rooted in the centre but making dramatic swings out into the distant space. The motion will thence appear 'bounced' elastic. In the opposite case, however, the motion along the outer ellipses will be slow, accelerating towards the centre and moving very quickly around the observer's head. Here the sound-object will spend most of its time on the outer edges of the space, making sudden (and perhaps disturbing) close loops around the listener. The motion will then appear 'bounced' elastic but in the opposite direction (inwards) to the first case (see Figure 10.58). We can imagine a third situation in which the motion around the listener's head is at a medium pace, suddenly accelerating before it moves off along

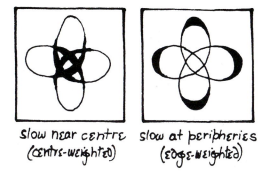

slow near centre   slow at peripheries
(centre-weighted)   (edge-weighted)

Figure 10.58   Bounced elastic four-cloverleaf motions.

the outer ellipses where it decelerates. In this particular case the motion at the centre has a stable phase (where it is moving at a medium rate) and the listener may thus feel that the sound is rooted in the centre of the space but ejected to the edges by 'thrown' elastic motion. This example illustrates the way in which subtle interactions between motion contour and spatial path may influence the aesthetic impact of a particular spatial motion. As another example, consider the inward spiral (see Figure 10.21). Where this motion accelerates towards the centre we have a sense of the sound-object rushing towards, or being sucked into, the centre of the vortex. Conversely where the motion decelerates there is a feeling of the sound-object coming to rest at the centre of motion.

In the case of cyclical and oscillatory motions, changes in the motion contour may synchronise with the rate of oscillation. In this way, a cyclical or oscillatory motion may be given an entirely new character. For example, a circular motion may start slowly at the front and accelerate as it moves towards the back of the space, decelerating as it moves back to the front. The circle thus no longer defines all directions as equivalent. It becomes oriented as with most other motions in acoustic space. In the case of double motions, the relationship between the time-cycles of the contributory motions will determine the type of spatial pattern traced out by the path of the sound-object. Aesthetically, however, it is more profitable to analyse the paths of the resulting patterns and this we have done in a number of cases in the previous section.

There is, however, another sense in which temporal considerations enter into our perception of spatial motion. Returning to Figure 10.51 we may remember that random motion may be weighted in the sense that the sound-object may spend more of its time in particular areas of the space than others. The otherwise random motion does have certain time-averaged characteristics which allow us to distinguish it from other random motions. There is an interesting parallel here with our perception and analysis of noise-based signals. Taking a time-average of a white noise signal would show it to contain all possible frequencies with equal probability. We may, however, filter the noise such that the occurrence of certain frequencies becomes more probable, and we then obtain a different sound, a noise with a distinctive 'colour'. The weighting of an unlocalised random motion corresponds exactly to this concept of filtering.

We may go even further. Even more patterned motions such as circling-looping motion may be time-weighted so that the sound-object spends more of its time in a particular part of the space (see Figure 10.59). This is equivalent to stressing a particular 'formant' (or quadrant) of the motion; as the analogy with filtering time-averaged sounds still stands but we are dealing with a regular pattern. This analogy with filtering procedures gives us a powerful tool for analysing our perception of complex types of motion. We might, for example, apply it to discontinuous motions (where a sound appears and disappears in various locations in the space without passing through the intervening positions).

Frame motions

In certain situations a group of sound-objects, or a single oscillating sound-object, may define a line (which need not be straight) in the space. This may be regarded as a one-dimensional frame and we may investigate motions of the total frame (as opposed to motions of the individual objects). In a sense, a frame motion could be seen as merely a set of simultaneous motions of independent objects. If, however, certain types of symmetry are preserved between the objects (or in the nature of the oscillation) we will perceive the group of objects to move as a whole. As well as the fairly straight-forward

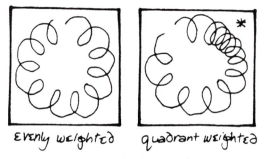

Figure 10.59 Time-weighted circling-looping motion.

motions we will consider here, a frame may be considered to 'writhe' in all sorts of strange ways if the objects defining it move in elaborate relative motion. There is no clear dividing line between a complex frame motion and a sense of independent motion of the sound-objects.

We may consider frame translation, swing, twist, flip and rotate. These are illustrated in Figure 10.60, together with their application to a one-dimensional linear oscillation. Note that a frame twist is only effective with an asymmetric one-dimensional sound-image. Otherwise it will be read merely as a frame translation which contracts towards the centre and then expands outwards again to beyond the centre (a three-dimensional twist would be different). The frame may also be contracted or expanded and these operations may be combined with the previous class of movements (see Figure 10.61).

We may also consider motions of a two-dimensional frame. The frame defined by the entire acoustic space may rotate, contract or expand

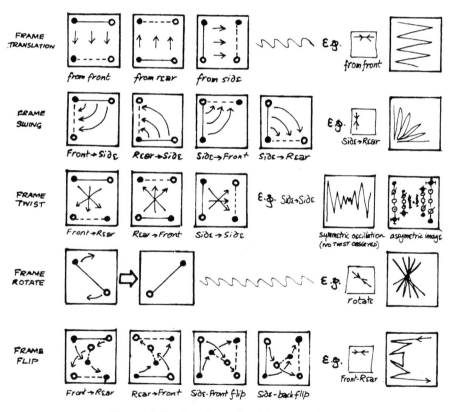

Figure 10.60 One-dimensional frame motions.

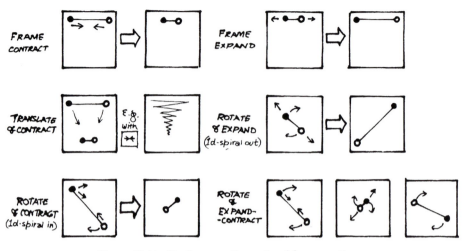

Figure 10.61   Further one-dimensional frame motions.

(see Figure 10.62). By combining these types of motion the frame itself may spiral inwards or outwards (Figure 10.63). We might also consider translations of an entire two-dimensional frame (Figure 10.64(a)). The change in the listener's perspective implied by this motion, however, would be better suggested by a corresponding expansion and contraction

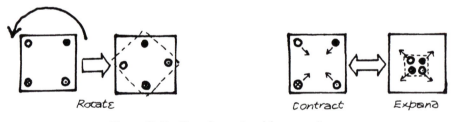

Figure 10.62   Two-dimensional frame motions.

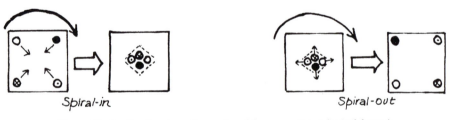

Figure 10.63   Further two-dimensional frame motions (spiral forms).

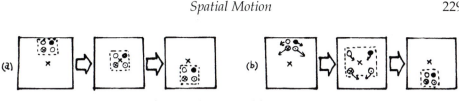

Figure 10.64 Further two-dimensional frame motions (translations).

(Figure 10.64(b)); the observer passes through the acoustic landscape (or vice versa). We might also consider various distortions of the two-dimensional frame as illustrated in Figure 10.65. We cannot go too far along this road, however, without the sense of 'frame' being lost and the sound-objects appearing to move independently of one another. There is a sense in which any mutual movement of the sound-objects in the space which preserves certain symmetries can be considered a frame motion or distortion, but how we actually perceive this will depend upon the particular circumstances.

Two types of frame motion are of particular interest: the first (see Figure 10.66) involves the expansion of sound-objects from the centre into the surrounding space. If this is accompanied by an accelerated motion it

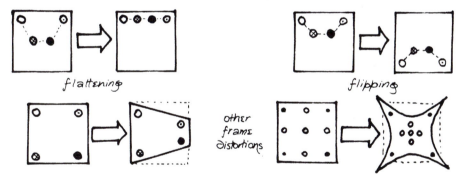

Figure 10.65 Two-dimensional frame distortions.

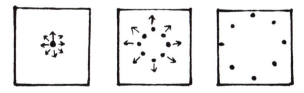

Figure 10.66 Frame motion (expansion).

should give a sense of growth, whereas if accompanied by a decelerating motion which is initially quite fast, a sense of exploding will be conveyed. Conversely (see Figure 10.67) all the elements in a space may collapse into the central position and, if this is achieved with an accelerating motion, a sense of imploding will be created. In more complex situations we may imagine most of the objects in the acoustic space undergoing a symmetrical rotation whilst a single object pursues an independent course. How we perceptually group the objects in these situations will depend partly on the various relative motions of the objects and partly on various landscape aspects of our perception (for example, recognition or sonic relatedness of the sound-objects).

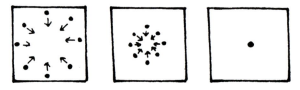

Figure 10.67   Frame motion (contraction).

Some principles

We may draw the following set of conclusions to this part of our discussion:

(1)   acoustic space is an oriented space: in particular, front and back are to be clearly distinguished from one another;
(2)   individual motions in the space may be direct or cyclical/oscillatory;
(3)   motions may have more than one characteristic;
(4)   a degree of irregularity may be imposed internally or externally on any basic pattern of movement;
(5)   the temporal characteristics of a motion will significantly affect its character: with direct motion (or cyclical motions which have directed characteristics such as the cloverleaf) the motion contour will determine the 'gestural' feel of the motion, while with cyclical double and random motions the motion contour will contribute to the spatial structure of the path;
(6)   in certain cases we may consider a one-dimensional or the entire two-dimensional frame of reference to move.

The counterpoint of spatial motions

Having now established an enormous potential vocabulary of spatial motion, we may consider how the motion of distinct sound-objects in the acoustic space may be counterpointed with one another. Direct motions (or directed aspects of motions, either spatial or temporal) may in this respect be distinguished from cyclical or oscillatory motions. This distinction, we will discover, is akin to that between sounds of dynamic morphology and sounds of stable mass or tessitura in that the former motions may be organised gesturally whilst the latter may be organised in a sense 'harmonically'. Any directed aspect of a motion may be considered as a spatial gesture, These gestures may then be made to move independently, to interact, or to trigger one another just as with sonic gestures.

For example, we may have three sound-objects in the acoustic space: sound A wanders slowly around the edges of the space, sounds B and C, however, dart about rapidly in the space always avoiding each other. In this situation we would tend to hear the movement of A as a separate and independent spatial layer, not interacting with B and C. B and C, however, would form an interactive contrapuntal system because their spatial motions clearly interact with one another. In Figure 10.68, various motions of the sound-objects B and C are plotted. These motions might be independent, interactive, or triggering. In the latter case, for example, the arrival of sound B at a particular location will suddenly cause sound C to move off (the two locations in question need not be the same). Just as with sonic gestures, gestural interaction relies on the relative temporal coordination of the gestures in time and their intrinsic qualities. We may for example make gestures which have similar temporal structures but different spatial qualities, for example, motions which are accelerating in a synchronised way but which move differently in direction and spatial contour (see Figure 10.69). Similarly, the spatial interrelatedness (or lack of it) between two gestures may be established in many ways, particularly with reference to the symmetry of the space (see Figure 10.70). In this way we may establish a subtle interplay between the relative timing and the spatial characteristics of various spatial gestures which is akin to the counterpoint of gesture and transformation. This was discussed in Chapter 6.

Gesture and transformation in space may underline or counterpoint other (possibly gestural) properties of the sound-objects themselves. Clearly

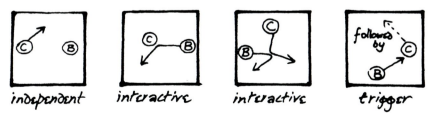

Figure 10.68 Gestural interactions of spatial motions.

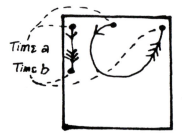

Figure 10.69   Synchronised motions with different spatial contour.

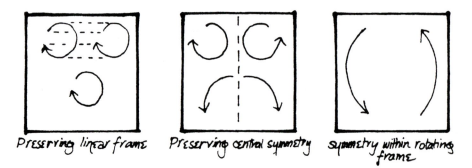

Figure 10.70   Multiple motions symmetry considerations.

a motion accelerating towards a point through a crescendo has a quite different feel from a similar motion accelerating through a diminuendo. In cases such as the merging and divergence of sonic streams, the coordination of spatial motion and timbral transformation is obviously of the utmost importance. Conversely, it is not possible to conceive of a collision between two sound-objects having identical sonic structures. We would perceive at worst a mono image as our ears located the sound-object between the two (hypothetically) moving sources or we would achieve a merge; a sense of collision could only be created between two objects of quite distinct sonic properties.

The symmetries (or lack of them) established between the relative spatial positions of the sound-objects simultaneously help to define the total space itself. Once all objects in the space are in motion — particularly if these motions are asymmetric — a sense of disorientation can be created as there is nothing left to define the limits or orientation of the space (this is where closing the eyes becomes important as we can always establish a visual reference grid). Conversely, if such motions are set against a background of distant but static sound-objects, a sense of energetic activity within the frame may be achieved. A cyclic motion on the other hand may be regarded as a kind of spatial 'resonance', mapping out as it does a particular way of dividing up, and in many cases orienting, the space (see Figure 10.71). Various motions may then be spatially or temporally coordinated in order to create various degrees of 'consonance' or 'dissonance'.

The harmonic analogy is not so far fetched as it may at first sound. Consider for example the motions in Figure 10.72(a). Here two motions follow the same circular pattern, the same direction. Clearly when the two objects start from the same point at the same time we hear the rotation of a single image. Alternatively, if the objects are placed exactly at opposite sides of the space (Figure 10.72(b)) they are symmetrically oriented with respect to the head and we hear what amounts to a one-dimensional frame rotation. These may be regarded as harmonically related states of the rotation of the system. If we now make the two objects rotate at slightly different speeds (Figure 10.72(c)) they will continually pass through the states of parallel rotation and anti-parallel rotation (Figures 10.72(a) and (b)). We are producing a kind of portamento between two harmonic states of the system.

We can discover not only spatial 'harmonics' but temporal 'harmonics' in a rotating system. Let us imagine two objects rotating along the same circular path but in opposite directions. If they rotate at the same speed, they will always cross at the same points on the circle (at $0°$ and $180°$) (Figure 10.73(a)). Similarly if one rotates twice as fast as the other they will always cross at the same four points of the circle ($0°$, $90°$, $180°$, $270°$)

Figure 10.71 Spatial division and orientation from cyclic motion.

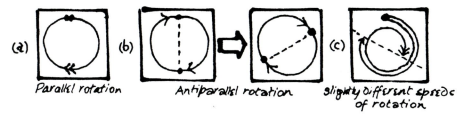

(a) Parallel rotation (b) Antiparallel rotation (c) slightly different speeds of rotation

Figure 10.72 Spatial 'harmonics'.

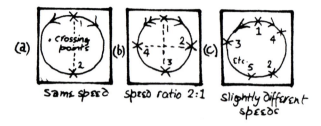

(a) · crossing points · Same speed
(b) speed ratio 2:1
(c) etc. slightly different speeds

Figure 10.73   Temporal 'harmonics'.

(Figure 10.73(b)). All of these may be regarded as temporal harmonics of the system. Again, we may make one of the sound-objects move slightly faster than the other and we may observe the motion pass through these various harmonic states (Figure 10.73(c)). A temporal portamento of motion has been created.

In Figure 10.74 the two objects move on different paths. The two paths, however circulate around the space in the same direction (always anticlockwise). They are therefore in some kind of spatial 'harmony' with one another. If at the same time the cycle times are coordinated so that, for example, they are both at the centre rear of the acoustic space at the same time a further temporal 'harmony' is achieved between the two motions. In Figure 10.75 a group of sound-objects rotates around the centre of the space. If they all preserve the same angular velocity we hear merely a rotation of a one-dimensional frame around the centre. If, however, they all have the same linear velocity the outer objects will gradually lag behind the inner objects. The motions of the various objects are however spatially 'harmonised' with each other or at least they set up a particular feeling or structuring to the space which is more vaguely akin to an inharmonic resonance. Examples of this type may be multiplied *ad libitum*. Furthermore, gestural motions may be superimposed on these situations, either through the movement of other objects through gestural articulation of the cyclic

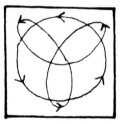

Figure 10.74   Spatial coordination of two motions.

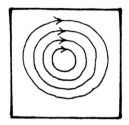

Figure 10.75 Coordination of rotations.

motions, or through the consecutive use of gestural and 'harmonic' modes of organisation. The counterpoint of spatial motions is thus in itself an extremely rich field for the sonic artist to explore.

Conclusion

There is clearly even more we can say about spatial motion. We have not yet considered the up-down dimension; we have not considered oscillating motions which are so fast as to produce amplitude modulation of the signal (the timbral effects of spatial motion); we have not considered analogies with the sphere of dance.

As the technology is further developed which permits us to analyse and control the various parameters which enable us to accurately locate sounds in space and, as reproduction facilities and acoustics are improved, we can expect this analysis to be expanded and refined; certainly at this stage it cannot claim to be complete. The organisation of spatial motion is undoubtedly a growth area in sonic art.

Part 3

Utterance

Chapter 11

UTTERANCE

Man's languages have objective status as internally organised systems that are independent of the people who speak them, whereas animal communication is precisely the social interaction of the animals. Notice that this difference is not just a matter of the cultural rather than genetical transmission of human languages, for many animal signaling actions, references, or significances may be culturally acquired either separately or together. [...] Because languages are, as such, not behaviours, their properties cannot be compared with the properties of animal communication.
(Bastian 1968: 589)

If [...] verbal language were in any sense an evolutionary replacement of communication by kinesics and paralanguage, we would expect the old, preponderantly iconic systems to have undergone conspicuous decay. Clearly they have not. Rather, the kinesics of men have become richer and more complex, and paralanguage has blossomed side by side with the evolution of verbal language. Both kinesics and paralanguage have been elaborated into complex forms of art, music, ballet, poetry and the like, and, even in everyday life, the intricacies of human kinesic communication, facial expression, vocal intonation far exceed anything that any other animal is known to produce. The logician's dream that man should communicate only by unambiguous digital signals has not come true and is not likely to.
(Bateson 1968: 614–5)

Imagine that we switch on the radio and tune into the sound of an orchestra playing a familiar piece. The music proceeds for a short while but then we begin to hear the sound of falling masonry. Performance of the music becomes disorganised and stops. We hear the sound of chairs being knocked over and running footsteps and then people screaming. How do we interpret this sequence of events? The most likely interpretation is as follows: when we begin to listen we hear the soundstream as music. For many listeners (though not for all) even the landscape of 'people playing instruments' will be 'bracketed-out', their attention will be focused on the syntax of pitch relations. Once the masonry starts to fall, however, people's attention will switch very rapidly to the landscape. It will be apparent that some event is taking place in a location. The landscape of the musical performance can no longer be bracketed-out. Finally when the screams are heard we perceive an utterance, that is we assume the sounds that the people are making have some fairly immediate intent and are not just some new development in avant-garde musical technique. It may, of course, be objected that the original musical performance is a type of utterance but it is clear even at this stage that there is a marked distinction between the two types of sound-event. In the first (orchestral) case, the utterance is highly formalised, the sound is patterned according to conventional syntactic rules and we do not even ascribe the patterning to the performers themselves. They are (up to a point) merely the agents involved in producing the structure. In the latter case (screaming) we assume, however, that the individuals involved 'mean' their utterances in some immediate sense, i.e. fear, danger. Although we can make no absolute distinction, for the moment at least we will not describe the conventionalised case as an utterance. As we proceed with our argument these distinctions and their ramifications will become clearer.

Now imagine that all of a sudden the pandemonium ceases and an announcer comes on the air to inform us that we have just been listening to a new electroacoustic work by a certain young composer. In a sense, with hindsight, we can now say that the entire experience was a formalised utterance, a piece of clever tape montage created by a composer, but clearly it is not as simple as this. Even where we know that we are dealing with a conventionalised situation, we cannot normally completely obliterate from our minds the interpretation in terms of (direct) utterance. If we compare two extreme cases, for example: I tread on my dog's foot and it yelps; someone says something which he does not mean which is then quoted in a play by an actor, a recording of which is then used as the basis for a tape composition which is overheard on the radio by someone who speaks a different language. Here we feel we can make a clear distinction between what is a direct utterance and what is a completely different kind of sonic 'communication'.

In most normal cases, however, where human beings are heard to produce sounds, then we will tend to impute intention to the sonic event. We will hear it at some level as an utterance. In particular, whenever the human voice is used as a source of sound in whatever context, the concept of utterance will enter at some level into our apprehension of the event. This becomes particularly important in the sphere of electro-acoustic music projected in the virtual space of loudspeakers where we can no longer rely on the physical and social cues of the concert hall to conventionalise and sanitise the vocal events. In general, sounds produced by individual creatures may be taken to indicate or express something about internal state, reactions to environmental events, responses to utterances by other creatures and so on, becoming more involved, convoluted and to some extent detached as we move up the cerebral hierarchy, finally reaching the etiolated heights of artistic manifestation. At whatever level, the sense of utterance, whether as indicator, signal, symbol, sign or syntactic or semantic-syntactic stream, enters into our perception of the events.

The study of utterance will have a bearing on sonic art in two related ways. First of all, wherever voices enter into sonic structures, we will have to deal with the special characteristics which pertain to the sonic architecture of utterance, for example, universal utterance-gestures, para-language, phonemic objects, language-stream articulation. At the same time, aspects of utterance may be observed in, or structured into, the morphology of other sound-objects and events. Just as we can imagine a landscape containing an utterance, so we can imagine an utterance containing a landscape (a crude example would be vocoded sea sounds). Either of these may be aspects of an essentially musical composition.

Animal communication; intrinsic and imposed morphology

In order to consider the utterances of various creatures, we are going to return to our analysis in terms of intrinsic and imposed morphology of sound-objects. This will be a useful starting point for the analysis but, in fact, in the case of utterance, we will find that these distinctions become difficult to maintain. When dealing with instruments it is intuitively clear what properties of the sound-object are determined by the intrinsic properties of the vibrating medium and what properties are determined by the way in which that is articulated by the human performer. Superficially it will also seem that we can make a clear distinction between these two on the grounds that the former is, in a sense, inevitable, while the latter is a result of conscious choice or intention. Unfortunately, however, matters are not so simple.

Let us consider first the human voice: the physical structures which make up the 'vibrating medium' are complex and constitute an integrated system from lungs to larynx to mouth and nasal cavities, tongue, lips etc.. These various components can be set in so many different ways that talk of an intrinsic morphology of the sound-source is, to say the least, extremely problematic. Furthermore within the physiology of the organism there is in no sense a dividing line between the vibrating medium and the musculature used to articulate this medium. They are one and the same and are furthermore intrinsically connected to the nervous system and thence to the brain. In this case, then, to talk of intrinsic morphology becomes meaningless.

Considering, on the other hand, a much simpler organism, such as the cricket, the idea of an intrinsic morphology makes more sense.

> *For many of the lower species, the signal's morphology is a close physical expression of the mechanical structure of the emission apparatus. These signals have thus a sort of obligatory physical form, rigidly determined by the elementary movement of the organs.*
> *(Busnel 1968: 137)*

We may thus, at this level, make an analysis in terms of intrinsic and imposed morphology. However, now the concept of intention comes into question. To what extent can we say that the cricket intends the sounds that it makes. Here we get into interesting philosophical hot water. We can deal with this problem initially in a somewhat clinical manner, as René-Guy Busnel writes:

> *Other signals, on the contrary, have a flexible physical structure due to the possibility of varied uses of the same organ (such as the bird syrinx, higher vertebrate vocal cords, and the delphinid larynx) and to a directing brain capable of making choices.*
> *(Busnel 1968: 137)*

> *The higher we go in the animal kingdom, the more diffuse and heterogeneous become the motor zones, introducing a notion of the degrees of freedom. The production of complex signals depends upon numerous centers which interfere with each other, and thus no longer permit the 'all or none' responses of invertebrates or lower vertebrates. In mammals, zones corresponding to a specific signal are not found. Instead, generalised phonation zones can be described which are diversely activated by other centers concerned with different emotional behavior patterns.*
> *(Busnel 1968: 135)*

In order therefore to understand the sound emission of the cricket in terms of intrinsic and imposed morphology we must for the moment sever the connection between imposition and intention. As we move up the 'mental hierarchy' of the animal kingdom, we will need to consider the different degrees of voluntariness or involuntariness of utterance, and this will at the same time deepen our conception of the nature of human utterance.

The biological instrumentarium

> *The range of sound emission organs found in the animal kingdom is quite varied; they are usually bilateral in invertebrates and very often unpaired in vertebrates. They may be restricted to one sex, or they may present a considerable sexual dimorphism. They are found on all different parts of the body. For example, the following may be found functioning as sound emission organs in invertebrates: chitinous toothed files which, by friction, stimulate a vibrating body — wing, elytra, antenna, thorax, leg, abdomen (Orthoptera, Crustaceans); friction or vibration of nonspecialised organs such as the wings (mosquitoes and some moths); semi-rigid plates on a resonant cavity stimulated by neuromuscular contractions (Tymbal method — cicada); reed-like organs which function by aspiration and expiration of*

air (death's-head hawk moth, Sphinx atropos). [...] two species have been found [...] which can automate legs. These species have no special stridulatory organ; however, when the legs are separated from the body, they emit sounds. When they are intact, they are silent. The hypothesis is that the noise emitted by the leg attracts predators, leaving the animal free to flee [...].

In lower vertebrates, [...] nonspecialised organs may produce friction, as do vomerine teeth in certain fish; osseous, rattle-type apparatuses may be found, made up of moving, oscillating parts which knock each other when agitated, as in rattlesnakes; whistling or vibrating apparatuses which function by air expulsion through a more or less differentiated tube (larynx) ending in an aperture (glottis) with more or less functional lips. The expelled air is supplied by the lungs themselves or by being in contact with an air pocket reserve [...] (vocal sac of some amphibians); and finally, membranes may be stretched over resonating pockets (as is the swim bladder of fish). These apparatuses are activated either by external percussion (fin beating) or by contraction of muscles disposed in different ways around the cavity.

Sounds produced by nonspecialised organs are also found in higher vertebrates. These include breast-beating in the gorilla, organ-clapping, such as wing-beating of the wood pigeon, drum-rolling in the hazel grouse and gold-collared manakins and trembling of remiges (primary) and rectrices (tail feathers) in the woodcock and snipe. Owls and storks use their beaks, and some bats [...] and some insectivores [...] use their tongues. In many higher vertebrates specialised organs are found, usually working by propelled or aspirated air in a more or less differentiated tube equipped with modulating membranes or slit systems. These organs are vocal cords, muscular glottal lips, the larynx [...] and the bird larynx and syrinx. These apparatuses often have additional organs which form air reservoirs or resonators (clavicular and cervical air sacs) as found in the bustard, ostrich, crane and morse. In some monkeys these features are found in the thyroid cavity, as is the gibbon's vocal sac or the hyoid bone resonating chamber of the New World howler monkey. Curious peripheral sound organs are also found, such as the fifteen-spined sound apparatus in tenrecs, [...] and the tail bell of the Bornean rattle porcupine.
(Busnel 1968: 131–132)

Figure 11.1 illustrates two examples of the many forms of stridulatory apparatus found in insects: on the left the pointed rostrum scratches the striations on the prosternum. On the right the apparatus is situated on the antennae; a plectrum (Pl) is rubbed against a row of small tubules, the pars stridens (PS) situated on the other antenna. Figure 11.2 shows a typical bird syrinx: on the left it is illustrated from behind (A), from in front (C) and laterally (B and D). The trachea may be greatly extended as in the Trumpet Bird (right). The syrinx is surrounded by an air-sack and this, in combination with the tympanic membranes, makes up the sound-producing system of the bird. Figure 11.3 shows the human vocal tract (above) and changes in the vocal cords during speech (below). It should be emphasised of course that sound is not the only means of communication for animals. Two important areas which may often be associated with the use of sounds are the use of gestures of physical movement of the body, face etc. (kinesis)

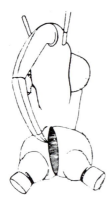

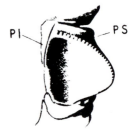

Figure 11.1 Two examples of stridulatory apparatus in insects.

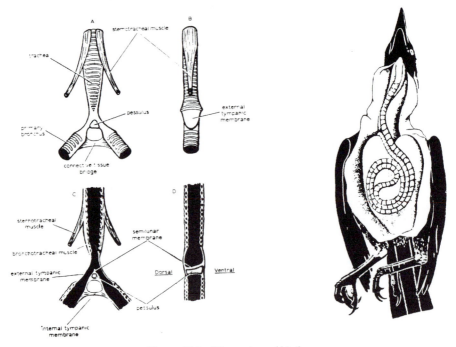

Figure 11.2 The syrinx of birds.

and, in humans, the use of written language. The temporal patterning of kinesics may be analysed in a similar fashion to sonic utterances (see Figure 11.4). For the purposes of this book, however, we will not concern ourselves with either the relationship between written text and the resulting sound or with the kinesic pathway of communications either in animals or in

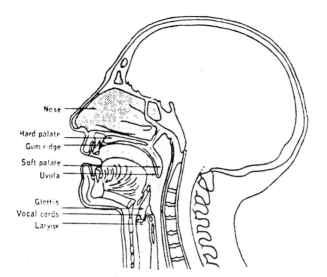

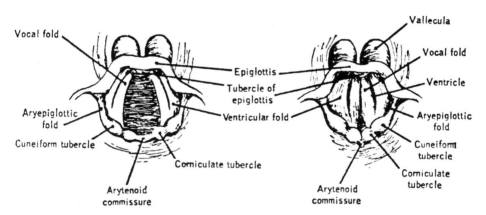

Figure 11.3   The human vocal tract and vocal cord changes during speech.

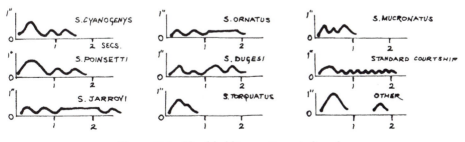

Figure 11.4   Head-bobbing patterns in lizards.

Art performance, with one exception: in particular circumstances, physiological postures and motions will directly influence the morphology of sounds, thus the characteristic turning-down of the corners of the mouth which can be observed both in humans and in many primates, visually indicating a state of 'sadness', also influences the formant structure of vowels and the articulation structure of various consonants. Similarly the 'deep ululation' of sobbing (or laughing) influences not only kinesic signals but also the nature of the sounds emitted. It is the sounds, however, with which we are concerned.

Indicators

Cicadas, crickets and grasshoppers have a very simple sound-producing mechanism. This may be a specialised stridulatory apparatus (crickets), specialised convex portions of the abdominal body wall (tymbals) which are crinkled at rapid rates, or specialised hind legs which are rubbed against the wings or abdomen. In most of these cases the individual sound-event is some kind of impulse whose sonic characteristics are determined by the nature of the biological materials which come into contact. Generally, however, these impulses appear in short or long groups at a (usually very rapid) speed. They may also vary in loudness according to their specific contour (Figure 11.5).

   The individual impulse, then, is not open to articulation by the creature itself; the intrinsic morphology is quite clearly defined. On the other hand, these impulses may be grouped differently or changed in intensity (or intensity variation) or speed. This gives a limited number of imposed morphological characteristics to the signals produced. In our original schematisation (see Figure 11.6) the sounds of these creatures may be thought of as occupying a position down to the far right where intrinsic morphology has a more strongly determining role on the sound-object than imposed morphology.

   However, we run into a new difficulty here. To what extent is the 'imposed' morphology imposed? In the case of the cicada, the tymbals are crinkled by a large pair of muscles to which they are attached. These in turn are activated by nerve impulses sent out by the cicada's brain. It can be demonstrated that the sound of a particular species of cicada will vary according to particular situations, for example, external threat, sexual arousal, etc.. In this sense the different signals can be taken to indicate the cicada's state. But does the cicada *intend* to indicate? Even in human beings certain acoustic utterances may be taken to indicate the state of the organism, but are not necessarily voluntary emissions. Consider, for example, what happens when we hear someone laughing and, against our

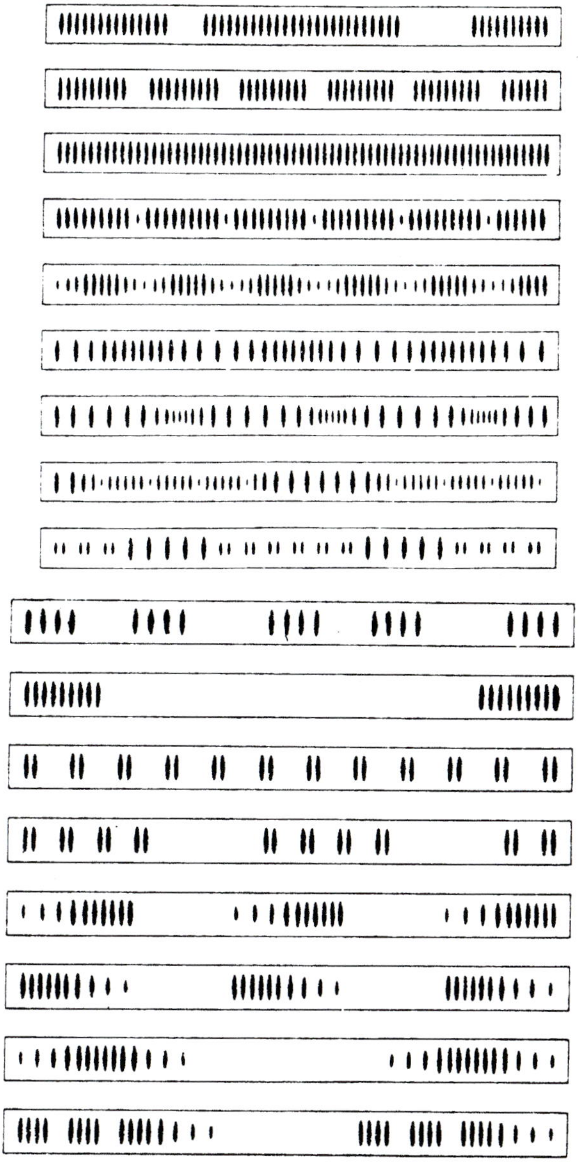

Figure 11.5 Examples of stridulatory patterns in crickets.

conscious will, we find ourselves laughing. Here a signal received has triggered a response which is outside the control of our conscious intent.

There is, however, an even deeper division between the functions of acoustic emissions.

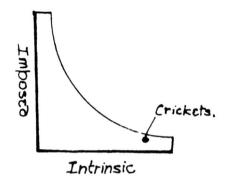

Figure 11.6   Morphological classification of cricket sounds.

No cry leopard frogs emit in the laboratory, however, is comparable in intensity to the scream heard near midnight on one occasion when a mixed chorus of over a dozen species of frogs called from a single pond. Microphones were being disconnected when a piercing scream came from a smaller pond nearby. A beam of light disclosed a raccoon scarcely twenty feet away carrying a leopard frog in its jaws. The raccoon had seized its prey in shallow water where numerous other frogs continued to call as though oblivious of its presence.
(Bogert 1960: 204)

In this particular situation the frog's utterance obviously can be taken as an indicator of its state (terror). However, the indicator does not appear to have been received by its fellow frogs as a signal.

Clearly in any system of communication at least two features are involved. We can discuss the sound emissions of one individual in terms of their being indicators, signals, symbols or signs, only in relation to how they are perceived by the listening creature. Clearly to us the scream of the leopard frog is a signal, we recognise its terror. To its fellow frogs, however, (or so it would seem) the *indicator* is not a *signal*. Assuming, however that we are producing sonic art for human beings, indicators emitted by beings will tend to be perceived as signals. Thus the sound of a metal rod falling to the ground is an indicator of the presence of a metal rod. The scream of a frog, however, not only indicates its presence, but also signals its internal state to us.

In fact, natural sounds may act as indicators, so that thunder or the relative pitch of the wind blowing through telegraph wires indicates the state of the weather. In some cultures humans have imputed intentions to such sounds and have read the indicators as signals (or even signs) — the voice of God or the spirits of nature. In the virtual acoustic space of loudspeakers, we can play with the ambiguity between indicator and signal. In the recording of a person speaking, for example, we have a nested system of signalling which may be represented by the schemata: (signal recorded and presented by recordist (signal emitted by vocalist (utterance))). In normal listening we bracket out the signalling intention of the recording engineer and we are left merely with our interpretation of the signalling behaviour of the recorded voice. In an electro-acoustic work we may play with the recognition of the sound-objects as utterances by beings or mere indicators of inanimate events. As a simple example, the anthropomorphic interpretation of thunder may be hinted at by a formant-like articulation of a recording of thunder.

Returning to the case of crickets how are we to distinguish an imposed but involuntary morphology from an intrinsic morphology of the sound-object? Here we begin to get into deep philosophical water concerning the nature and degrees of differentiation of voluntariness and consciousness. It is interesting to note, however, that, even in higher animals certain emitted sounds are involuntary indicators of an internal state (sneeze, cough, belch) and some of these may be involuntarily emitted and received signals (laughter, screaming, both of which may elicit the same response in a human being without passing through the process of conscious decision to emit a signal). In most of these cases also our analysis would be similar to that for the cricket. The 'intrinsic morphology' of the sound-event would be a function of the involuntary conformation of the organism (resonance of the oesophagus in belching, tense glottis and wide open vocal cavity in screaming) and the 'imposed morphology' would be an involuntary kind of articulation (such as the deep ululation of breath flow in laughter).

Of course, for human beings it is possible to utter all these sounds voluntarily. The contention here is, however, that such basic indicators/ signals always retain some of their primeval communicative power. Such universal indicators not only transcend our attempts to formalise them, they even transcend the barriers between species. We may divide them roughly into three classes:

(1) involuntary physiological indicators;
(2) extremal indicators;
(3) other.

Amongst the involuntary physiological indicators we may cite coughing, sneezing, vomiting, yawning, biting, chewing, belching, etc. which are produced not only by humans but by many primates. Furthermore, the general physiological tone of the creature may be determined from the nature of breathing. We may distinguish tiredness, ill-health, sexual arousal etc.. Darwin, in *The Expression of the Emotions in Man and Animals* remarks:

As fear causes all the muscles of the body to tremble, the voice naturally becomes tremulous, and at the same time husky from the dryness of the mouth, owing to the salivary glands failing to act.
(Darwin 1965: 92)

Tremulous breathing is therefore indicative of fear. Note also that such indicators may be carried over into the articulation of conventional wind instruments. Crying and laughing which, as Darwin pointed out, can also be observed in chimpanzees, orang-utans and baboons are semi-involuntary in nature.

The main extremal indicator is the scream. This may be characterised as a continuous, high-frequency, loud, broad-spectrum emission. It usually indicates a state of extreme terror or pain and may be heard in humans, chimpanzees, frogs, birds (see Figure 11.7), pigs and even a normally silent hare when it is torn to pieces by hunting dogs. In birds and mammals, at least, the similarity of the sound-object 'scream' may be related to the physical properties of a windpipe and throat and a wide open mouth aperture, an oscillator such as the larynx or syrinx and its activation by a maximally high energy sustained stream of air.

In fact this indicator is so universal that we may assume that any sustained high-frequency, loud (and usually broad-spectrum) signal will carry the connotations of terror. Even in the highly-formalised musical context of Schoenberg's *Erwartung* the sustained, high-frequency, loud but pure-toned pitches which are sung at certain points retain the 'resonance' of screaming (Example 11.1).

There do, however, appear to be trans-special universals. Comparing the signals of the Great Northern Diver (or Loon), the wolf, the whale and the red squirrel (Example 11.2) we notice a striking similarity. The signal initially rises (often a harmonic series step), is sustained and then falls away in pitch as it ends. It may also include a secondary upward pitch motion during the pitch-sustained section (see Figure 11.8). These signals should also be compared with certain human cries. In none of the cases is this particular utterance the sole utterance of the creature (quite the contrary). Is there, however, some shared, internal, gestural experience which creates this particular sustained contour?

Totemics

The analysis of indicators is yet more complex. Clearly, some utterances indicate the internal state of the being emitting them, regardless of whether fellow-creatures interpret these as signals or not. Indicators or signals may

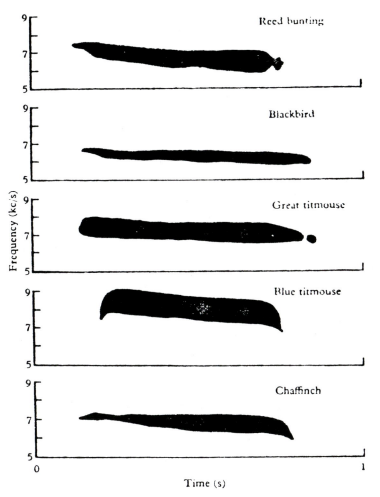

Figure 11.7 Scream spectrograms of five small birds.

have another function, however; they serve to differentiate one species from another. Thus different members of the same species of cricket produce the same set of signals but the set of signals is different from the set of signals produced by a different species of cricket. This may be the case whether or not the signal is involuntary or (at least semi-) voluntary. Thus, certain species of birds sing a genetically determined song which characterises the species and differentiates it from other species. The song is achieved by the adult bird even where it has no opportunity to hear other birds of the same species singing the song. In other cases it can be shown that such species-specific song is learned by the young birds from the adult (and there are

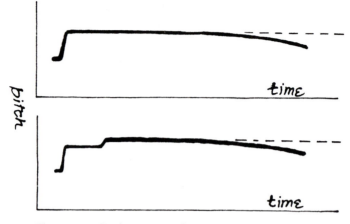

Figure 11.8 Pitch contours of one type of 'universal' call.

various stages in between the two). Whether or not the creature intends to emit the sound-signal of its species, that signal serves two important functions. First of all it can be a territorial indicator and secondly it can serve to attract a mate of the same species. It is important, however, to realise that it can fulfil both of these functions without any 'intention' to fulfil either. This I would describe as a kind of involuntary totemic communication. The sound, in a sense, stands for the species and is understood to do so, whether or not it is intentionally emitted with that purpose.

This *sound-totemism* can be observed in situations where the involuntariness of the structure of the signal can no longer be assumed. Thus, in birds such as the British blackbird which has a repertoire of song-phrases which it can articulate and sequentially combine in multifarious ways, the song 'style' as a whole still serves as a territorial and mate-attracting totem (it is wrong to assume that this is a sufficient explanation of the intent and format of song-production in this case). Even with human beings, certain musical styles (for example styles of rock-music also associated with particular types of clothing, hair fashion and even speech; even the Western classical repertoire in middle-class white society in South Africa[1]) can fulfil a basic totemic function, indicating membership in a particular and exclusive social group and binding one to others of the same 'species'. At the level of nations, particular 'song-formulae' known as national anthems may serve as sound totemic symbols. In Stockhausen's work *Hymnen* an important

---

[1] At least at the time of writing (1983) during the apartheid era [*Ed.*].

aspect of our perception is the distancing from, and commenting upon, this national totemism through techniques of electronic transformation of the 'song-formulae'. The use of widely-known melodies in mediaeval practice (*L'Homme Armé*) and more recently in concert music ('BACH') and jazz may be viewed from the perspective of sound totemism whereby religious, intellectual, or merely 'in', groups serve to identify themselves.

Repertoire: gesture and sequencing

As we ascend the cerebral hierarchy of the animal kingdom, our simple 'cricket' model rapidly becomes inapplicable. The sound-producing organs of higher creatures are more complex and are capable of producing a greater range of sound-objects. There is in fact a *repertoire* of sounds. At the same time, and intrinsically tied up with this development, the means and ability to articulate this repertoire develops — but, as noted before, one can make no hard and fast distinction between the vibrating media and the muscles involved in controlling these in the vocal tract of most higher organisms.

> It begins to appear that a repertoire of from about 10 to about 15 basic sound-signal types is rather characteristic of nonhuman primates as a whole. In some it may prove to be smaller or larger, but it is doubtful if the limits will be exceeded by very much.
> (Marler 1965: 558)

This assertion is, however, misleading (as will be discussed further) as it depends essentially on where human beings choose to draw lines of differentiation between different types of signal. Given this qualification, certain creatures such as birds, dolphins, killer-whales and human beings display a wonderfully replete repertoire.

The existence of such a repertoire brings other considerations into play. Apart from the gestural articulation of the individual sound-objects, we must also now consider the concepts of *ambiguity* and *sequencing*. Whereas with a single sound-source we may talk about a simple iconic relationship between the state of excitation of the organism and the sound-emission (i.e. more excited, afraid etc. equals louder or faster), we now have a multi-dimensional situation. Most sounds of higher animals are of complex spectrum and dynamic morphology (see previous chapters). There are therefore a large number of dimensions in which expression of these may be varied and, in fact, by such variations we may transform one type of sound-object into another.

For example, in the case of the rhesus monkey (see Figure 11.9), nine signal types have been described but —

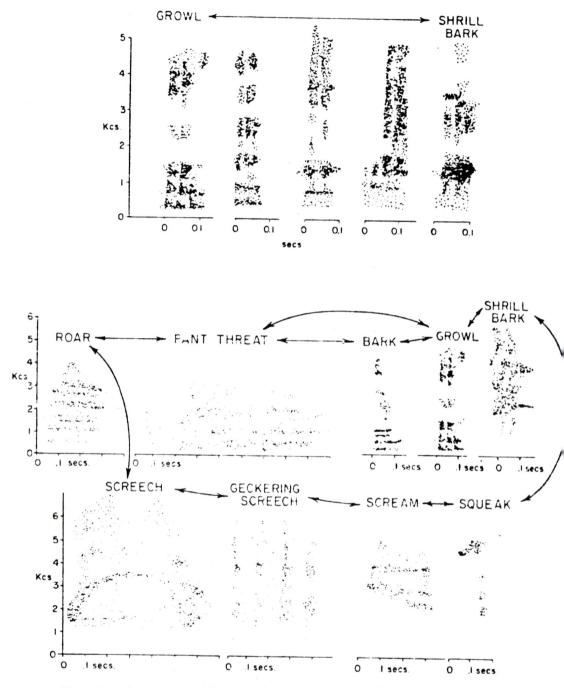

Figure 11.9   Spectrograms of rhesus monkey sounds (after Rowell (1962) and Rowell & Hinde (1962)).

> *Rowell (1962) has been able to show that these nine sounds actually constitute one*
> *system, linked by a continuous series of intermediates. Moreover there is one example of*
> *multi-dimensional variation, the pant-threat grading independently into three other calls*
> *[...] Rowell's descriptions also demonstrate correlations with a continuously varying set of*
> *social and environmental situations [...]*
> (Marler 1965: 561)

Hence, just as with a sound-object of dynamic morphology we are able to make gestural articulations in different dimensions simultaneously, the rhesus monkey is able to 'present' its internal state in a multi-dimensional field of utterance. We might imagine a single articulated signal carrying information simultaneously about, for example, dependency, sexual arousal, aggression and territoriality, a rich communication medium without the benefit of the arbitrary sign of a language system. This state of affairs also reflects the fact that the 'internal states' of such organisms have themselves become multi-dimensional, complex worlds and further underlines a point made in an earlier chapter about the inadequacy of a discrete verbal vocabulary of 'emotional states' as a means of describing what is going on within a being.

In addition, however, the repertoire of sound signals may be sequenced in particular orders and gestural information conveyed through this sequencing. Most animal studies are heavily concerned with the development of denotative and arbitrary signs; they are searching for the roots of human language and there is a tendency to assume that syntax (rules of sequencing) implies semantics (in the sense of language). As every musician knows, however, this does not follow. Just as previously we were able to make a distinction between an indicator and a signal, we must now note that there is some confusion between a signal and a symbol. Therefore a certain combination of fear, aggression and sexuality may produce a particular level of arousal and a particular articulation of the internal state causing the vocal apparatus to emit sounds of a particular form. As another organism of the same species will recognise these sound-objects as if it itself had emitted them, they may be taken to symbolise the particular state of the first organism. However, we cannot therefore assume that the emitter *intended* this symbolisation. Apart from the bringing into action of the vocal apparatus as a whole, the resulting evolution of the sound-objects may have been substantially involuntary, a direct utterance.

For the emission to be a symbol to the producer, an act of self-mimesis is necessary. Mimesis (the imitation of sounds external to the organism) can be observed in a number of animal and bird species. For example Indian Hill Mynahs can mimic almost any noise presented to them, mocking birds incorporate an enormous variety of other bird-sounds into their repertoire and parrots may be taught to imitate human speech (mimetic factors in fact enter into natural human languages; see the next chapter). We may imagine now that a creature may mimic the fear cries of its fellow creatures and finally that it may mimic its own fear cries, in other words that it may pretend fear. At this point the signal "fear" becomes a symbol for fear. This, however, is a difficult point to define. On seeing a predator a monkey might emit a particular sound which we might take to be a signal of fear or a symbol of the predator. If the predator is nearer the emission may be louder. Does this mean, therefore, more-fear or predator-nearer? Where does the signal end and the symbol begin? We may assume in fact that at least until the emergence of the arbitrary linguistic sign, there is no absolute separation. All symbols carry with them an element of physiological-intellectual signalling to which other creatures respond in a very direct manner. Once, however, we are able to sequence different signals, we may convey gestural information in the overall sequence and contour of the expression. The more this is the case, the less need the individual sonic gesture units carry immediate signalling information. We generate a separation (not unknown in music) between the microstructure and the macrostructure of an utterance. Here, however, nothing is referential in the sense of the arbitrary sign of language and although the microstructure gestural units no longer carry such intense and immediate internal gestural information, there is still a remnant of that original physiological-intellectual response which allows us to differentiate and respond to them. We have thus created an articulate gestural syntax which exists on (at least) two levels.

In such a way we can evolve a multi-level syntax without the linguistic 'arbitrary sign'. We can even imagine referring to hypothetical situations within the context of a real situation, once this operation of syntactic levels is generated. I am not suggesting here that I know of any non-human animals which have evolved such a system! Only that such a system, without language, is conceivable.

Invention; convention

As noted previously, birdsong which serves the function of defining territory or attracting a mate may arise out of a genetic programme or through learning from parents or some combination of these two. Certain birds have a repertoire of possible song phrases which they may articulate and sequence more or less freely. Given that the song has the totemic function of representing the species of the bird in question, what more can we say about it? We have here the first example of a conventionalised utterance structure which is, however, not language. This is possible because of the redundancy involved in the system. Thus each phrase of the blackbird's song might be taken to mean 'blackbird' or 'blackbird territory' etc. but this gives us no linguistic reason for ordering these utterances. We might perhaps read from an overall string of phrases 'self-confident, ebullient blackbird' (!) but we do not associate with the sequencing of phrases the sequencing of immediate gestures ('happy blackbird', 'wakeful blackbird', 'unsure blackbird', 'frightened blackbird' etc.). The individual units have become distanced from any immediate gestural implication. The syntax has become conventional.

We may make a similar argument about (at least certain types of) music. Thus whereas an overall sequence of events may convey a sense of exaltation, defeat, distancing or whatever we do not therefore associate every microstructural musical gesture with a particular nameable internal state. Nevertheless, the microstructural, gestural articulation remains more closely tied to our visceral/physiological response system than the detachment of the linguistic sign. Without this remnant of 'direct utterance'/'immediate response', our response to music at the microstructural level would be arbitrary and the details of our musical experience would cease to have any significance.

The fact, therefore, that structured musical utterances are conventional and, even on a large scale, refer to (at the most) hypothetical internal states does not mean that they are detached, formalistic exercises in the arrangement of sound-objects. In particular, a conventionalised utterance structure (such as music or birdsong) (a) contains the traces of direct utterance at several levels, (b) can integrate aspects of direct utterance and (c) can be confused (intentionally, unintentionally or inevitably) with direct utterance.

Virtuosity, sincerity, acting

The Western classical art music tradition is often noteworthy for its rejection of the concept of utterance. This may in some respects be traced to the totemic function of music within society to emphasise group solidarity in various ways. In situations where the activities of a large group of musicians are co-ordinated to fulfil a certain predetermined musical end (for example, fixed ritual observances associated with religious practice), individual utterance is intentionally negated for the furtherance of a group utterance manifested through the organisation of the musical materials re-presented. Here also a second level of conventionalisation arises. Not merely is a conventionalised structure of musical gesture used, but our attention is directed away from the personal intent of the performers. In music of the standard Western repertoire, the conventionalisation of utterance is many-layered. The composer, conductor and the individual performers each contribute a level of conventionalised utterance to the overall sonic experience.

Utterance in the special sense in which we have used it in this chapter can occasionally come to the forefront of our perception of the musical experience. The display of virtuosity draws our attention to the technical expertise or ebullience of the individual performer. The veil of convention is broken. In the gospel singing of Mahalia Jackson or Aretha Franklin, conventional musical syntax is gesturally articulated in an extremely elaborate way which suggests a sense of immediacy (rather than hypothesis) in the utterance. In contrast a typical *Lieder* recital normally presents a sense of distancing; the utterance is clearly of a hypothetical nature. The singer is not directly involved in the actions or internal states suggested by texts or musical architecture. In the case of opera singing, however, a further state is reached. Here (just as an actor adopts a persona in a play), the singer attempts to present musical material as if it were the direct utterance of the character represented. In fact the situation is even more complex, because we of course know that the character represented would probably not sing about his or her grief, joy, etc. but would more likely speak about it. We might then schematically represent the situation as follows: (conventional utterance — opera singer (direct utterance — character represented (conventional utterance — singing))).

Even without the further level of characterisation we have in opera, music may be presented in such a way that the utterance aspect is played down, for example, Xenakis' *Pithoprakta*, where the large-scale structure is dominated by slowly-evolving events, many of which seem gesturally neutral while the activities of individual players are amassed in dense or semi-random textures which negate the possibility of individual articulations emerging through the total structure, or pushed forward, as in Schoenberg's *Erwartung*, a monodrama about a frightened woman lost in a wood sung by a single female singer. The use of the voice in modern Western popular music presents an interesting case. Whereas in the classical tradition the singer strives towards the perfection of a particular kind of voice which is a social convention and is felt to be transferable from one work or one expressive context to another (liturgical, concert etc.), popular music projects the idiosyncratic features of the individual singer's voice.[2] The audience is assumed to be more interested in music as a personal utterance rather than as a socially conventionalised utterance. We are clearly not dealing here with direct utterance in our original sense of the term. The popular

---

[2] See Roland Barthes' essay 'The Grain of the Voice' (Barthes 1977) for a parallel view (*Ed.*).

singer adopts many levels of conventional utterance-structures in order to communicate with an audience. It is usually assumed, however, (whether or not it is justified) that at some level the singer is not 'acting', that the conventionalisation stops and that the singer is presenting his or her personal utterance. This is pretty obvious in the case of protest singers, but may be much more indirect. For example, the idiosyncratic features of the particular voice may be felt to carry the mark of personal tragedy, grief or difficulty (if in a somewhat distilled format), for example, Edith Piaf, Judy Garland or Janis Joplin.

Often such personalised utterances will be expressed through widely-known popular and often totemic song-structures. This is taken to an extreme in the case of blues, where an almost claustrophobically rigid structure of music and text is used as a vehicle for sophisticated gestural expression. This is akin to the highly articulate gestural articulation of 'stock phrases' in vernacular speech where the linguistic content can be the least significant communicative element. The concept of 'sincerity' in the world of popular music can only be understood in relation to these ideas about utterance.

A more interesting interrelation between conventional and direct utterance can be observed in ecstatic behaviour. The state of ecstasy achieved in various religious rites and sometimes in music or dance improvisation is experienced as a loss of conscious control. In glossolalic speech, possessed dance, ecstatic gospel music, etc. the performer is able to articulate the voice or the body to a degree or extent and with a fluency which is not possible where the conscious mind retains control over the intellectual-physiological sphere. However, this articulation usually takes place over a field of conventionally-established possibilities (phonemic strings, dance movements, musical scales) an intense and immediate utterance swirls upwards through the conventional structures. How can we explain this?

When a child begins to walk, it must learn how to do so. It begins with difficulty to co-ordinate the necessary muscular movements and the signals about balance and posture received from the ears by the brain. Eventually, however, all these activities become 'second nature' and we are able to do all sorts of intricate tricks (avoiding objects, hopping over things, changing our pace to match another person) without consciously thinking about any of these. Although there is probably a lot of genetic input into our development of the walking skill, the development of second-nature skills does not stop when our ontogenetic development ceases. Thus the motions of the fingers and the fingering patterns required by an experienced concert pianist are not normally thought about as such in detail during a performance. They are second-nature. Furthermore, it can be argued that speech itself (except perhaps among heavily contemplative intellectuals) is a second-nature activity. High level conscious control is only required at the most general semantic level. Once this is released, ecstatic glossolalic speech becomes possible.

Confidence tricksters and psychopaths

One recurring trend of Western art is the movement away from any kind of direct and ecstatic utterance towards the conventionalisation of all parameters of the event. The conventionalisation may be an aspect of social distancing where the conventions are generally understood and accepted as a medium through which social messages may be transmitted. They may also, however, be personal conventionalisations of the artist, ways of distancing himself or herself from the social conventionalisations and even the implications of direct utterance. Thus the sound poet may plan and execute a sequence of rhythmic screams or sobs during the performance. Similarly, a composer like Berio may sit in the studio and coolly edit together segments of tape carrying verbal gestures which are erotic, funny, terrifying and so on. Although we know of the artist's detachment from such utterances, we do not normally distance ourselves entirely from the utterance-implications of the sounds involved. There is, however, a fine balance to be preserved between distancing from and involvement in the utterance whether by the artist or the listener. To quote Gregory Bateson:

> *I suggest that this separate burgeoning evolution of kinesics and paralanguage alongside the evolution of verbal language indicates that our iconic communication serves functions totally different from those of language and, indeed, performs functions which verbal language is unsuited to perform. [...] There are people — professional actors, confidence tricksters, and others — who are able to use kinesics and paralinguistic communication with a degree of voluntary control comparable to that voluntary control which we all think we have over the use of words. For these people, who can lie with kinesics, the special usefulness of non-verbal communication is reduced. It is a little more difficult for them to be sincere and still more difficult for them to be believed to be sincere. They are caught in a process of diminishing returns such that, when distrusted, they try to improve their skill in simulating paralinguistic and kinesic sincerity. But this is the very skill which led others to distrust them.*
>
> *It seems that the discourse of non-verbal communication is precisely concerned with matters of relationship — love, hate, respect, fear, dependency, etc. — between self and vis-à-vis or between self and environment and that the nature of human society is such that falsification of this discourse rapidly becomes pathogenic. From an adaptive point of view, it is therefore important that this discourse be carried on by techniques which are relatively unconscious and only imperfectly subject to voluntary control. [...]*
>
> *If this general view of the matter be correct, it must follow that to translate kinesics or paralinguistic messages into words is likely to introduce gross falsification due [...] especially to the fact that all such translation must give to the more or less unconscious and involuntary iconic message the appearance of conscious intent.*
> *(Bateson 1968: 615)*

The point at which the artistic manipulation of materials collapses over into formalism (in the listener's perception) is very difficult to judge. The type of artist we are discussing needs to be sufficiently removed from the immediate utterance implications of his or her materials to explore new areas of statement or expression. If these implications are ignored, however, the artistic result is likely to be perceived in some way not intended by the artist or, worse still, it will be rejected as the artistic equivalent of a 'confidence trick'.

The problem of detachment has particular significance in Western society. As an aspect of a professional pursuit, particularly the pursuit of science, it has proved highly socially fruitful. A detachment from the social sphere, however, is normally (except in the case of politicians and military personnel) regarded as a form of mental illness. Mental detachment in science is useful because it enables us to develop instruments which may then be useful to the social body. Social detachment in the research which precedes an artistic work may also be useful in that it enables us to look at our materials in new ways. Social detachment in the artistic work itself, however, makes it intrinsically meaningless except as a solipsistic activity for the artist or an interesting intellectual game for analysts. There is a certain psychopathology in the scientific method where it is applied to other beings such as in the pseudo-science of behaviourism and in the pseudo-art of the notational formalists.

Towards language

Retracing our steps somewhat we have established that a hierarchic structure of groupings — a syntax — can be established for a stream of utterance. Birdsong, human music and human language are three examples of utterance systems using syntax. As explained previously, certain kinds of birdsong and music can be described exclusively in terms of a hierarchical structure of gestures from the level of the single event to, for example, the motif, the phrase, the line, the section, the movement or the work. With human language, however, another quite separate element enters into our description: the *arbitrary sign*. Linguistic signs differ from the symbols we have discussed previously in that they need not be related in any way (either causal or mimetic) to the objects, activities, or just syntactic operations, which they represent.

From the standpoint of this book we are only interested in the sonic implications of this fact about human language. First of all we should note that although the linguistic sign *need* not mimic or otherwise relate to what it represents, it may do so. Secondly, linguistic signs are only defined up to a certain point. There are always dimensions of the sound-object which do not enter into its definition as a sign. These other dimensions may be articulated, either using independent conventions (the organisation of pitch in song), interrelated conventions (conventional aspects of paralanguage) or in other non-linguistic imposed or involuntary ways.

Finally, and most importantly, we now find that the repertoire of the human voice is divided in a new way. We now have a special class of sound-objects called phonemes which are used to make meaningful linguistic utterances. All other sounds, whether voluntary or involuntary, form a separate category. Strings of phonemes will also have a particular kind of imposed morphology, including the conventional paralanguage associated with the particular language (for example the rising tone at the end of a sentence in English to indicate questioning). Some aspects of this morphology will be more or less involuntary, such as the vocal transitions involved in phonemic connectedness. Excluded from this class, however, is a whole set of alternative imposed morphologies some of which may be involuntary (such as the contour of a yawn or the physiological idiosyncrasies of the individual speaker) while others may be intended. Finally there will be patterns of sequencing of phonemes which will be syntactically and semantically valid, standing in opposition to all other types of sequencing. From the sonic artist's point of view, these divisions may be transgressed in multifarious, multi-dimensional and subtle ways. In the following chapters I shall try to discuss many of these, but the number of possibilities and their aesthetic implications are (fortunately) limitless. Furthermore, all these aspects may enter into our construction and interpretation of a landscape or any musical structure — in whatever way we wish to define this term — in which a vocal source is present.

In the following analysis of human utterance we may divide the subject on the basis of these initial investigations into a consideration of repertoire (in the sense discussed in this chapter), phonemic objects, language stream and paralanguage phenomena, and utterance interaction (duet, antiphony, discourse, chorus, etc.).

Finally, a special word about electro-acoustic music. In the real physical world we are able to say quite clearly that the sound of a metal bar falling to the ground is not an utterance whereas a sound produced by a being is. In the virtual space of loudspeakers this sort of distinction may become difficult to make. An artificially created sound-object may be articulated in such a way that we pick up cues of an utterance or not. We may, in fact, play with the 'utteranceness' of a sound-object, just as we may play with its landscape interpretation. This aspect of the electro-acoustic medium is another feature contributing to its potentially dreamlike quality, the creation of an artificial universe in which our conventional presuppositions are called into question and where we may be brought to see the world from an entirely different perspective.

Chapter 12

THE HUMAN REPERTOIRE

Voice is the original instrument.
(Joan La Barbara 1976)

We are now at the point where we can describe the human repertoire, the fund of possible sonic objects and their articulations which is available to the human utterer. The following taxonomy is based on an earlier analysis of mine published in *Book of Lost Voices* (Wishart 1979). Recent discussions with the *lettriste* poet Jean-Paul Curtay have clarified a number of physiological and other distinctions enabling me to present a more systematic classification of the sound-materials discussed in that publication. Curtay has presented a physiological analysis of vocal technique (Curtay 1981) whereas my own approach is oriented to a description in terms of sound-objects. This leads to two different notational approaches to the sounds (both of which will be discussed below). Furthermore, the analysis here will be confined to sounds related to the vocal tract. Body slaps, hand rubbing and other sounds may of course be produced by human beings (and these are discussed in Curtay (1981)) and no aesthetic preference is implied by their omission here. Furthermore, I will not claim that this is a complete analysis as I have been discovering new sounds almost every week since the completion of *Book of Lost Voices*. This listing does include several sounds not mentioned in the earlier publication.

The analysis does treat sounds of intrinsically short-duration separately from sounds which can be sustained. Of course any of the sustained sounds can be made into a short sound merely by curtailing its duration. Furthermore I have not made the distinction between 'iterations' and 'vibrations' simply because any iterated sound becomes a vibration if it is sufficiently speeded up. Some sounds (e.g. rolled-r, lip-flabber) appear at first sight to be intrinsically iterative as we normally produce them in a range where we can hear the individual pulsations; however, as will be demonstrated, these sounds can be made to rise into the normal audio vibration range (the first by increasing tongue pressure on the roof of the mouth, the second by hand tensioning the lips) and even at their normal rate of iteration a pitch can be perceived (particularly if it is stabilised). Slow iteration may be looked on as sub-audio vibration, for example, the glottis (vocal chords) can be made to vibrate in a sub-audio mode and even to emit individual impulses (particularly when activated on inhaling).

Oscillators and other sources

For the moment we will assume that the flow of air is outwards from the lungs (exhaled). The principal sound-sources in the vocal tract are physical oscillators in the sense that they produce sound by physically moving to and fro (just like the reed in a reed instrument). Certain other parts of the vocal tract can be made to resonate and hence produce pitched sounds.

(1) The *glottis* is the source of the normal human singing voice. Sounds are produced by oscillations of the vocal cords, and we will refer to these sounds either as glottal vibrations, or vibrations of the larynx. Vibrating the larynx produces an impulse which is normally iterated (Example 12.1). At normal rates of vibration this is heard as a pitched sound (Example 12.2). At least two separate registers can be perceived within the range of pitch produced by the larynx. For the male voice these are usually referred to as normal voice and falsetto voice. A completely seamless transition can be made between the two registers. It is also suggested that there is a further break in the voice permitting an even higher range of pitches to be obtained. My own (male) voice will at the moment reach to the G two octaves and a fourth below middle C (the lowest part of the range is very relaxed and quiet) and as far as the G one octave and a fifth above middle C (in falsetto).

(2) The *windpipe*. If air is expelled very forcibly from the lungs a low pitch is produced which does not originate in the larynx but somewhere below it (Example 12.3). The sub-glottal vibration may be stabilised on a definite pitch. This pitch, as far as I can tell, cannot be altered and may be combined with glottal pitches. Note that this sound is quite different from sub-harmonics (see below) and is the basis of the famous 'Satchmo' gravel-voice. A similar effect may be observed in the windpipe above the larynx (Example 12.4). Although I have no direct medical evidence that these sounds are produced where I suggest, they are quite distinct from glottal vibrations because it is possible to combine them with glottal vibrations. Examples 12.5–12.8 illustrate the sound below the larynx, the same combined with the sound of the larynx, the sound

above the larynx and the same sound combined with the sound of the larynx.

(3) *Subharmonics.* If glottal production is made very relaxed, it is possible to instigate a note one octave below the original glottal note and sounding simultaneously (Example 12.9). This note varies in pitch along with the original glottal note, always remaining at the interval of one octave and is produced either by the larynx or by the false vocal folds resonating (half) in step with the larynx. With practice, a note one octave and a fifth, or even two octaves, below the glottal note can be produced.

(4) The *oesophagus* is resonated during belching. The sound is used as a basis for speech by people who have had their larynx removed for medical reasons.

(5) The *tongue* may be vibrated against the roof of the mouth. This may be done using the tip of the tongue towards the front of the mouth (Example 12.10), upwards onto the soft palate (Example 12.11) or strongly retroflexed (Example 12.12). Alternatively the tongue may be arched so that the middle of the tongue is in contact with the roof of the mouth, producing the characteristic French 'r', either in the middle of the mouth (Example 12.13) or towards the back of the mouth (Example 12.14) and finally against the uvula, the sound associated with snoring (Example 12.15). By suitable use of tongue pressure and placement these sounds can be brought into the range of normal sung tones, particularly the arched tongue type (Example 12.16).

(6) The *lips* may be made to vibrate either in normal position (Example 12.17) or strongly folded inwards towards the teeth (Example 12.18) or strongly pouted outwards (Example 12.19). Pitch formation with the lips may be assisted by using the hands to stretch or relax the lips. This also helps to stabilise the vibrations so that lip notes can be sustained for long periods (Example 12.20). The available aperture and tension of the lips can also be manually controlled to produce a variety of different kinds of oscillations (Example 12.21) and in particular two independent sets of vibrations can be set in motion at different corners of the mouth simultaneously (Example 12.22).

(7) The *cheeks* may be vibrated independently of the lips and the pitch controlled by varying tension by use of the hands (Example 12.23). These vibrations may be sub-audio (Example 12.24). The two cheeks may also be set in vibration independently (Example 12.25) with possibilities such as producing patterns of beats between two sub-audio frequencies.

Filters

Sounds produced within the vocal tract have not only a fundamental frequency but also formants, frequency areas within the spectrum where energy is concentrated. Formants are generated by various resonances within the oral and nasal cavities and it is quite possible to vary these in a continuous fashion. This may be done in four ways: by varying the size of the oral cavity, by varying the position of the tongue's arch, by greater or lesser rounding of the lips and by greater or lesser nasalisation (i.e. varying the amount of sound which is passed by the nasal passages). The latter will be discussed separately as it is of less importance and applies only to glottal and windpipe sounds. (Vowels, Example 12.26.)

Sounds produced prior to the oral cavity (glottal, oesophageal and windpipe sounds) may have their formant structure altered by any of these four methods. The oral (nasal) cavity may thus be regarded as a complex filtering device. As an initial approximation we will omit lip-rounding from our analysis. Fortunately there is a notation immediately to hand for specific formant types as the vowels of human languages are determined by their formant colour. As a first approximation we may draw a two-dimensional map (see Figure 12.1) of the 'formant space' available. Note that we may move from the open *a* sound of English 'father' to the small aperture vowel with the tongue arched against the front of the mouth (German *ü*) by either

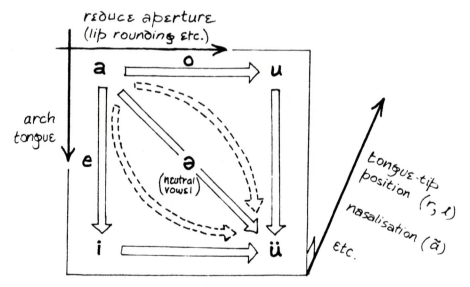

Figure 12.1 Map of the 'formant-space' of vowels.

first closing down the mouth aperture to reach the vowel *u* as in North of England 'mud' and then moving the tongue arch position forward, or we may begin by moving the tongue arch forward, passing through the vowel *e* of English 'red' and arriving at the vowel *e* of 'she' and then closing down the mouth aperture. Between these two extremes there are any number of roots from the *a* to the *ü* through the vowel space (Example 12.27).

In this analysis in fact we have compounded lip-rounding with aperture effects. The effect of lip rounding on various formant types can be heard in Example 12.28. A further dimension is also added by moving the tip of the tongue into the *r* or *l* position, producing a clear changing colouration of the formant spectrum. Finally by using the tongue arch to stop off the flow of air through the oral cavity (the *ng* position) the sound is projected entirely through the nasal cavity; varying the degree of contact of the arch with the roof of the mouth will vary the proportion of the sound which is projected through the oral cavity.

The international phonetic alphabet provides a concise and fairly detailed means of notating particular formant structures (Figure 12.2). It also has the advantage over a physiological notation (see later) that we may establish links with language utterances quite easily. However, the notation does need to be modified for use in sonic art. For example, if we wish to produce a formant which has a mouth formation for *e* but in which the tongue-tip is half moved towards the *l* position, or a sound with the mouth-shape of *i* but the tongue-tip halfway towards the *r* position, an extension of the notation is required (as illustrated in Figure 12.3). The same thing is also true of the notation of consonants. When we produce the phoneme *le* we normally assume that the mouth is already in the *e* formant position during the production of the *l* apart from the tongue position for the *l*. This need not be the case. We may for example put the mouth in the *u* position for the *l*, changing with the articulation of the *l* to an *e* formation (Example 12.29). A notation for this is illustrated in Figure 12.4.

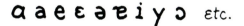

Figure 12.2 Some vowel signs from the International Phonetic Alphabet.

Figure 12.3 Examples of extensions of phonetic notation.

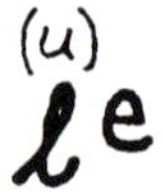

(u)

l e

Figure 12.4   Indication of specific formant-structure for consonant.

The filtering techniques we have been discussing can be applied not only to exhaled pitched sounds but also to inhaled and/or pulsed sounds, e.g. inhaled glottal clicks (Example 12.30).

These filtering techniques can also be applied in modified form to both tongue and lip vibrations. Vocal aperture and lip-rounding variations may be applied to tongue vibrations. In fact, with practice an analogue of the Shepard tone effect can be generated vocally where the fundamental pitch of the rolled-r vibration falls while the pitch area stressed by the filtering rises (Example 12.31). In fact the position of the tongue's arch can also be moved smoothly from one position to another, but this is more easily classified as a sound transformation (see below).

Because lip vibrations take place in front of the oral cavity filtering effects are less effective with these sounds but they are in fact possible (Example 12.32). Cheek vibrations may be filtered in an altogether different fashion by hand manipulation of the cheeks. What appears to happen is that the cavity between the cheek and the gums is varied in size, changing the pitch of the resonance (Example 12.33).

In addition, a second level of filtering may be added by the hands which may either form a cup external to the mouth or a funnel-shaped aperture (made with one hand) partially closed off (with the other hand). Any sounds whatever produced in the oral cavity may be filtered using these techniques. A particularly interesting effect can be produced with the funnel technique if the other hand is waved very rapidly backwards and forwards away from and towards the mouth of the funnel. With noise-based sounds (see below) this produces an effect akin to electronic phasing (Example 12.34).

The technique of formant filtering may also be used to emphasise particular harmonics of a tone. In this way it is possible to play the harmonic series components of (for example) a glottal tone (Example 12.35). The production of very high harmonics allows the continuous sliding of the upper partials as they are close enough together to meld into a continuum. Harmonics may also be 'played' above sub-harmonic production and even (though the effect does not seem to be particularly strong) over high-pitched tongue vibrations (Examples 12.36, 12.37).

Noise

Noise-type sounds may be generated by setting up turbulence in the air-stream travelling through the oral (or nasal) cavity. Such sounds are most usually indicated by the various noise-based consonants (see Figure 12.5). Most of these are distinguished from one another by the particular placement of the tongue except for the *f* which is produced by a contact between the teeth and lips. Given the particular conformation of the tongue each consonant corresponds to a particular formant structure but these may themselves be varied in average pitch by changes in the size of the mouth cavity (Example 12.38). In addition, by changing the formation of the tongue we may pass from one formant formation to another and these two types of filtering motion may be combined (as was the case with vowel sounds) (Example 12.39). We may also extend the phonetic notation to indicate noise-states which lie halfway between states to which the phonetic signs refer or are in fact combinations of these states (as in the case of *x* and *f*; listen to Example 12.40) (see Figure 12.6).

With noise sounds, however, the filter may be made sufficiently narrow that it 'rings' and we produce the characteristic sound of whistling. Because whistling is essentially a filtering effect it is difficult to alter the formant spectrum of a whistle sound (though not totally impossible).

Normal whistling is produced by a filtering at the lips. Pitch is varied by altering the size of the oral cavity and two registers may be distinguished according to whether the tongue arch is to the back or to the front of the mouth cavity. A third and higher register can be produced by filling the cheeks with air and pushing the tongue forward (Example 12.41). Whistling may also, however, be produced over the tongue. This may be with the tongue arch in its rear position (Example 12.42) which does however not

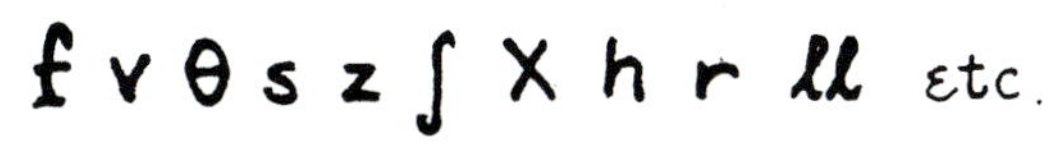

$$\mathbf{f \; v \; \theta \; s \; z \; \int \; X \; h \; r \; ll} \quad \text{etc.}$$

Figure 12.5 Phonetic notations for various noise-band consonants.

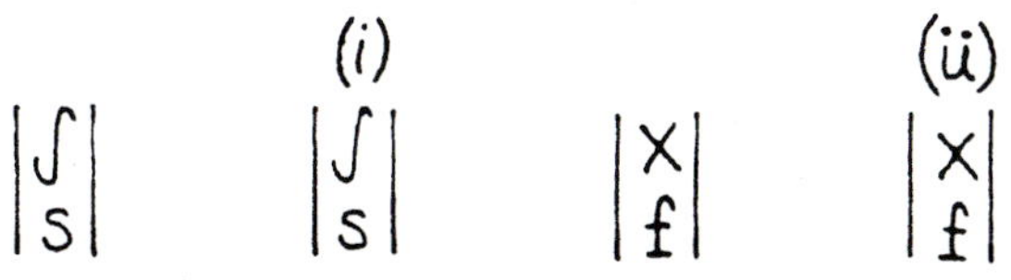

(i)   (ii)

$$\left|\begin{matrix}\int\\s\end{matrix}\right| \qquad \left|\begin{matrix}\int\\s\end{matrix}\right| \qquad \left|\begin{matrix}X\\f\end{matrix}\right| \qquad \left|\begin{matrix}X\\f\end{matrix}\right|$$

Figure 12.6 Examples of extensions of phonetic notation for noise-consonants.

produce a very strongly focused pitch like normal whistling. Alternatively the tip of the tongue may be used either in the *sh* position (Example 12.43) or in the *s* position (Example 12.44). Finally, whistling may be generated with both the tongue and the lips, producing a double whistle (Example 12.45). In this case, as pitch is produced almost entirely by varying the oral cavity aperture, the two pitches almost inevitably move in parallel motion.

Double and treble production

Within the vocal tract, it is clearly possible to set in motion two oscillators or other sources simultaneously. This may of course produce merely a mix of two kinds of sound, but in many cases the two vibrations interact with each other and intermodulation effects are produced. Figure 12.7 charts all the

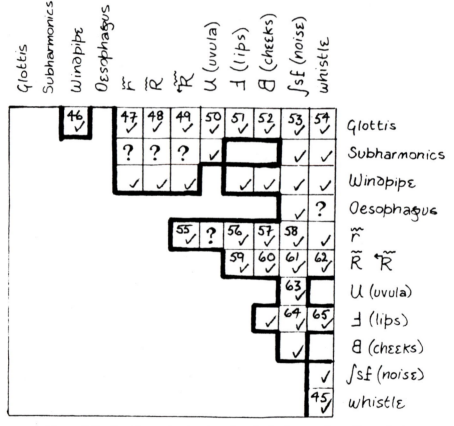

Figure 12.7   Double production (numbers in the boxes refer to Examples).

double production sounds. In certain cases I am not sure whether a certain sound can be produced or not and I have therefore entered a question-mark in the chart. The numbers in the chart refer to sound examples on the tape (Examples 45–66).

The types of sound available are not as simple as this chart might suggest; the particular nature of the individual oscillations, their relative amplitude and pitch and the extent to which they interact may vary or be varied, thus producing quite distinct classes of sound-objects. Thus, when we combine glottal vibrations with windpipe vibrations, the latter may be of the stable low-frequency type which gives us the 'gravel voice' or the less clear and more forced 'air' type which interact with the larynx sound to produce a sound-complex like a roar or bark (Example 12.46).

Where glottal sounds are combined with tongue oscillations in speech discourse, the amplitude of the glottal vibration is usually much higher than that of the tongue oscillation which thus appears as a mere colouring of the glottal pitch. However, if the strength of the tongue vibration is increased we become more strongly aware of the amplitude modulation which is taking place (the tongue is an audio rate amplitude modulator of the glottal pitch stream). If the tongue vibration is made even louder and the glottal vibration reduced in level the glottal pitch becomes a mere decoration of the strong tongue vibration. In addition the two oscillators may be tuned to one another. Where they are of equal strength and in similar register this tends to take place 'naturally'. As the physical system of the oral cavity seeks positions of lowest energy, we discover ourselves producing octaves and fifths almost automatically and it is much more difficult physically to produce other intervals. By slightly detuning one of the oscillators, beating effects can be produced which may be physically felt within the mouth (or on the lips) (Examples 12.47–12.50). In glottal/cheek and glottal/lip vibrations there may be a remarkable difference between 'rounded' slow-stream impulses with glottal pitch colouration and chordal effects produced by the inter-modulation of mid-frequency glottal and lip or cheek vibrations (Examples 12.51–12.53).

If a highish glottal note and a whistle are tuned to an octave and then the whistle tone moves slightly away from the octave intermodulation will produce chord-like colouration of the resulting sound. This process is exactly analogous to what takes place (electrically) in a synthesiser. If on the other hand a very high s-whistled note is produced fairly quietly against a deep (male) glottal note, an almost grain-like amplitude modulation is imparted to the note (Example 12.54).

Windpipe sounds can be combined with other articulations but currently I would not recommend anyone to try these too much! It is also possible to vibrate the tongue in two modes (rear arch and tip) simultaneously (Example 12.55). The forward vibration tends to be a subharmonic of the rear vibration. In a similar fashion the lips and tongue can be simultaneously vibrated. Tongue-tip vibrations can be easily combined with loose-lip and manually-stretched-lip vibrations, often producing intermodulations which can be felt in the lips (Example 12.56) and either low register or high register pitches may be tuned. Noise bands are easily and effectively amplitude modulated by low-frequency tongue, uvula and lip vibrations and noise may also be made to colour the more high frequency vibrations of these types (Examples 12.57–12.64 give some examples of these combinations). Even whistling can be amplitude modulated by tongue-vibrations (easier with rear-arched tongue than with tip of tongue). The lip modulation of whistling is the basis of the 'trimphone' imitation which became a craze in Great Britain in the early 1980s (Example 12.65).

We can go beyond this and generate three or even four sounds at once, for example noise turbulence, tongue vibration, lip vibration and glottis vibration may all be activated simultaneously and controlled independently of one another (Example 12.66). Some special cases can be observed, for example, if a glottal/tongue-tip vibration in the male low falsetto register is passed through pouted lips, they may be caused to vibrate in a very subtle way, producing a trumpet-like colouration of the sound (Example 12.67).

Air-stream and other effects

Many of the sounds discussed so far can be altered or articulated by modifications of the air-stream which initiates them. The manual and physical control of the air-stream (discussed below) in particular may be applied to lip and tongue vibrations as well as glottal vibrations. The other techniques apply to glottal vibrations except where otherwise stated. If the glottis is activated by a sudden rush of air, we produce the roaring sound discussed previously. If, however, the glottis is activated very quietly by a strong and fairly constant stream of breath we first produce a mix of pitch and air sounds ('half-wamp'). If the glottal sound is made even quieter it begins to destabilise and the pitch content breaks up ('quarter-wamp') (Example 12.68).

If the glottis is fairly relaxed and the air-stream is restricted at (I believe) the epiglottis a sub-harmonic is produced which differs from the usual sub-harmonics in being produced in this state of tension (normal sub-harmonics need great relaxation of the vocal apparatus). If only a very small amount of air is allowed to pass the epiglottis and much pressure is applied to make this pass we produce a multi-phonic. Such production may be called half-lunged (Example 12.69) (these sounds are called 'constipation multiphonics' in the *Book of Lost Voices*). Half-lunged sounds must be differentiated from unlunged sounds which are produced when no air passes through the oral cavity. In the case of short pulses (discussed below) these may be difficult to distinguish. The surest indicator is that during the production of an unlunged sound it is possible to breath normally through the nasal passages as if no sound were being produced. Half-lunged sounds, however, need sufficient air and 'back pressure' that independent breathing during their production is impossible. An example of an unlunged sound is the unlunged whistle (Example 12.70) which can be produced by sucking air into or pushing air out of the mouth cavity by a movement of the tongue. Notations for these are given in Figure 12.8. These are not entirely consistent with my previous use (in *Anticredos* and *Vox-I*) but are more systematic.

Various (tremolo-type) amplitude modulations of the breath-stream can be achieved manually or physically (flutters). Manual pressure on the diaphragm can be used (Example 12.71). If the glottal signal is quiet and the formants are high whilst the diaphragm is drummed rapidly with the fingers, the stream of glottal pitch can be broken up into a series of short staccato sounds (Example 12.72). Shake-head flutter (Example 12.73), drum-glottis flutter(Example 12.74), shake-body flutter (Example 12.75), drum-cheeks flutter (Example 12.76), strum-lips flutter (Example 12.77), strum-nose flutter (Example 12.78) and hand-cup flutter are all that they seem. Some of these may be applied to tongue vibrations (Example 12.79) and lip vibrations (Example 12.80).

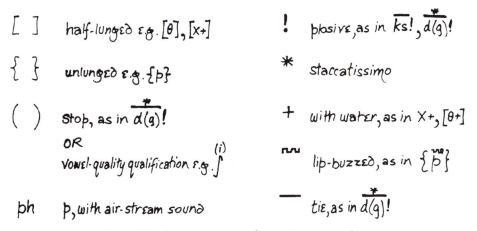

Figure 12.8 Some suggestions for notation conventions.

A natural oscillation is that known as *ululation* (Example 12.81). This may be used across a break in the voice to produce an alternation in pitch (Example 12.82). The 'depth' of the ululation may be increased, producing a sound more like laughter (Example 12.83).

Water effects

Saliva (or externally introduced water) may interact with the articulation of vibrations. Gargling is the most obvious example of this. Saliva often affects the sound quality of arched-tongue vibrations (Example 12.84). In particular, the noise sound x has a great number of possible modes when it is combined with saliva-water sounds (Example 12.85). The sound may be filtered in various ways (Example 12.86). It may be half-lunged and then filtered again (Example 12.87). It may be plosively attacked with a k and a short rush of air to produce the children's 'gun' sound (Example 12.88). It may be half-lunged, filtered to produce very high partials and produced staccato and plosive (Example 12.89). A rational notation for the distribution of harmonics in this sound is very difficult to achieve because although the high partials are strongly emphasised, it is clearly still possible to vary the resonance of the mouth cavity that is produced. The notation shown in Figure 12.9 uses the 'stave of harmonics' to indicate that this is a high partial sound but a simpler mnemonic is proposed. This sound incidentally can be combined with tongue-tip vibration (Example 12.90). Saliva-water effects also account for the pitch content of the sounds indicated in Figure 12.10 (Example 12.91).

Most of these half-lunged water sounds can also be produced inhaled. Inhaling, however, also generates a number of other sounds such

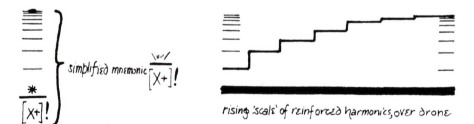

Figure 12.9   Stave notation for harmonics.

Figure 12.10   Notation for unvoiced sounds with water content.

as the modifying of inhaled lip vibrations by water held behind the lips (Example 12.92) and various sounds around the sides of the tongue (Example 12.93).

Transformations

Within this huge class of exhaled sustainable sounds it is possible to make transformations from one type to another. The simplest transformations are those of formant change demonstrated earlier. We may also make transformations between the different kinds of oscillations produced by the tongue (Example 12.94). We may add or subtract water (Example 12.95). We may move from the lunged to the half-lunged or vice-versa (Example 12.96) or from the normal to under- or over-breathed (Example 12.97). We may make transformations from normal to fluttered production (Example 12.98) and we may also make a transformation between two sounds by passing through an intermediate mix, as for example moving from a tongue vibration to a lip vibration (Example 12.99).

Inhaled sounds

Sounds may also be produced when air is inhaled. In many cases these are the same or quite similar to those produced on exhaling, but in a number of cases quite different sounds are produced. Many of the sounds produced in this way exhibit instabilities, either in pitch, spectral content or sub-audio attack rates.

Vibrating the lips by inhaling can produce pure tones, trains of pulses or multiphonics (Example 12.100). The vibrations may be controlled and articulated by using the heels of the hands (Example 12.101). All these sounds are unlunged. The tongue may be made to vibrate, both in retroflex position unlunged (Example 12.102) or at the uvula as in snoring (Example 12.103).

Finally, the glottis (and possibly the windpipe) may be made to vibrate while inhaling. If a lot of air is drawn inwards the effects produced by (I believe) the larynx and windpipe are heard. A better method of production, however, is to draw air in regularly and slowly (as air would be expelled during normal singing). By varying the tension of (I believe) the larynx and the filtering in the oral cavity a great number of different kinds of sounds can be produced: from pure tones (Example 12.104) which may be outside the normal range, click trains (Example 12.105), sub-harmonics (Example 12.106), more complex multiphonics (Example 12.107) to complex and unstable oscillations (usually produced at the end of a long in-breath when the pressure inwards is difficult to maintain) (Example 12.108). The instabilities in these latter sounds can be felt as a kind of irregular beating in the larynx. In the various complex sounds different aspects of the complex spectrum can be emphasised by the filtering process (Example 12.109).

As some of these inhaled sounds are unlunged it is possible to simultaneously produce inhaled and exhaled sounds. For example, one can produce inhaled lip vibrations while projecting glottal vibrations through the nose. Furthermore, various of the flutter techniques can be applied to the air stream.

Pulses

Short sounds or pulses may be produced in a variety of ways in the vocal tract. The pulse may be released or initiated by the epiglottis (Example 12.110), the arched tongue which may touch the roof of the mouth at the rear, in the centre or at the front (Example 12.111), the tip of tongue (against the roof of the mouth) which may be retroflexed or further forwards (Example 12.112), the tongue and the teeth, the tongue and the top lip (Example 12.113), the teeth and the lips (Example 12.114) or the lips (Example 12.115). Pulses may be lunged, half-lunged or unlunged (Example 12.116).

Pulses may be either normal or plosive. If they are lunged, plosive production tends merely to make them louder but if they are half-lunged or unlunged plosive production may produce a quite different sonority by slight modification of the process of production. Thus the half-lunged sound *d* can be made plosive by retroflexing the tongue and releasing it plosively forwards (Example 12.117). Similarly the half-lunged *p* may be made plosive by folding the top teeth and lip over the bottom lip and releasing air plosively (Example 12.118). The same technique can be applied to the unlunged *p* (Example 12.119).

If pulses are lunged they may be voiced or unvoiced. The voicing may be dominant as in the normal production of voiced consonants in the language stream or secondary, and various amounts of breath may be added (Example 12.120). The 'voicing' need not be a glottal sound but may come from the windpipe, tongue vibrations or even whistling (Example 12.121).

If lunged they may have more or less air-stream content (Example 12.122) and of various kinds (Example 12.123). The air-stream may also be glissandoed (Example 12.124). In fact the pulse itself may be suppressed to produce a plosive air-stream effect (Example 12.125). If lunged or half-lunged they may be stopped. In this procedure the air-stream is cut off abruptly, almost as soon as it has been initiated. This may be achieved with the epiglottis, by moving the tongue into the *g*, *k* or *t* position but not releasing it from the roof of the mouth or by plosively closing the lips. The stops may be used to make the pulses exceedingly short and this alters their character. A *g* may be used to alter the character of a plosive *d* (*d(g)!*) (Example 12.126). When a *p* is used as a stop its slight buzzing may alter the character of the pulse (Example 12.127). Such very short stopped sounds may also be used as envelope shapers for glottis vibrations, producing for example (with *d(g)!*) extremely loud impulses or, with a quiet, low frequency and slightly glissandoed glottal vibration, an excellent drum imitation (Example 12.128).

Stops may also be used to produce end-pulses, such as those produced by a *ch*- or a *k*-stop on an *h*-air-stream (Example 12.129) or a *p*-stop on the end of a *s*-stream (Example 12.130). The slapping of the tongue into the 't' position on the roof of the mouth (unlunged) and the slapping together of the teeth provide two other pulses (Example 12.131).

If pulses are produced by the lips, the lips themselves may be buzzed whether the pulse be lunged (Example 12.132), half-lunged (Example 12.133) or unlunged (Example 12.134). During an unlunged lip-buzz of this type air may be pushed out of the mouth with the tongue, producing a glissando as the mouth opens (Example 12.135). Lip pulses may also be manually initiated. In this way quite loud unlunged and unbuzzed sounds may be produced (Example 12.136).

In all cases the pulses produced can be filtered by altering the shape of the oral cavity (Example 12.137). This applies even to unlunged *p* sounds where the position of the arched tongue and the degree of pouting of the lips can alter the resonance of the mouth cavity (Example 12.138). Even with such very short sounds the filter may be made to glissando, for example, with the plosive click (discussed below) (Example 12.139).

Certain pulses may be produced simultaneously, for example *g* and *k* (Example 12.140) or *t* and *k* (Example 12.141). Pulses may also be paired and iterated as in *tktktktk* which may be lunged (Example 12.142), half-lunged (Example 12.143) or, if produced by a lateral movement of the tongue, unlunged (Example 12.144). The physiological limits of this iteration may be extended to produce *g* and *th* (Example 12.145). Lip and tongue pulses may be thus iterated as in *ptptptptp* which may be lunged (Example 12.146), half-lunged (Example 12.147) or unlunged (Example 12.148). Lip pulses may also be iterated manually and may be lunged (Example 12.149) or unlunged (Example 12.150).

Pulses may also be produced during inhaling at the epiglottis (Example 12.151) and variously with the tongue and lips. The most interesting of these are perhaps the unlunged clicks such as the lateral tongue movement (Example 12.152), the vertical downwards tongue movement (*kl*) (Example 12.153), the plosive, pure-resonance, vertical downwards tongue-click (Example 12.154), the *t* (or *tut*) click (Example 12.155) but also the *th*-click (Example 12.156) and the 'kiss' with various degrees of lip pouting (Example 12.157). As with exhaled pulses some of these may be combined. For example, the plosive and the kiss (Example 12.158) or the lateral and the kiss (Example 12.159).

Transitionals and percussives

A number of sounds used as consonants in language are essentially transitions from one formant state to another, produced by movements of the tongue or lips. The consonants *l, m, n, ng* and 'deep' *ng* (i.e. with the arch of the tongue towards the rear of the mouth) are of this type. By controlling the oral aperture it is possible to use these consonants to make transitions between harmonics of a given glottal pitch (Example 12.160). Transitionals may also be iterated as in *mnmnmn* and *n-ng-n-ng* (Example 12.161).

A number of short sounds may also be generated by the use of the hands. For example, hand-clapping in front of the mouth used as a variable resonator (Example 12.162), tapping the teeth with the mouth used as a variable resonator (Example 12.163), popping the finger out of the closed lips (Example 12.164), filling the cheeks with air with the lips tightly closed and then striking them with the fingers to expel the air (Example 12.165) and the now-famous 'water-drop' discovered by the *San Diego Extended Vocal Techniques Group* (see 1974): an unlunged sound where the finger strikes the cheek with the teeth parted and the mouth open and as it does so the tongue pushes air out of the mouth in an unlunged whistle (Example 12.166).

Multiplexes and complex articulations

Using the multiplex notation described in Chapter 5 (an example is shown in Figure 12.11) we may combine various short sounds into a more complicated stream. In Figure 12.11 the iterated string *pkʃlgr* is combined rapidly and randomly with lunged and half-lunged *X+* sounds and lip-flabber while the box containing vowels is a mnemonic for 'maxvary' mouth vowel shape (Example 12.167). The horseshoe shaped symbol indicates that the vowel formants are to be varied as rapidly as possible. We may now further articulate this multiplex by putting the tongue in and out of the mouth as rapidly as possible (Example 12.168).This sound may now be super-imposed, for example on a glottal pitch which glissandos rapidly and at random over its maximum range (Example 12.169). Using these symbols, together with the continuum and transformation signs (see Figure 12.12) and our general

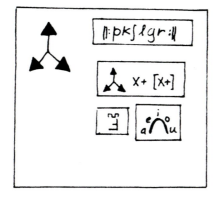

Figure 12.11   An example of multiplex notation.

Production	Phonetics	Graphics
Glottis (voiced)	(bold type-face)	▬▬▬▬
Subharmonics		▰▰▰▰▰
Windpipe (trachea)	⊥	/////////////////
Tip-tongue: forward	ȓ̃	∿∿∿∿∿
normal	r̃	ditto
backward	ȓ̃	ditto
Mid-tongue: normal	R	ditto
rear	ˤR	ditto
uvular	ʮ	ditto
Lips	ʒ ɟ ʃˤ	⊓⊔⊓⊔ OR, subaudio ⊓ ⊓ ⊓ ⊓
Cheeks	ᴇ	ditto
Noise-consonants	ʃ,s,f,h,x etc.	▨▨▨▨▨▨ (etc.)
Whistle		●●●●●●●●●●
Complex sounds	e.g. [x+], inhaled complexes etc.	▰▰▰▰▰ (etc.)

Figure 12.12   Further examples of extended vocal technique notation.

knowledge of the sound repertoire of the vocal tract and the individual physiological parameters, we can develop rapidly articulated and evolving sound-streams of great complexity.

Notation

In Figure 12.12 various other aspects of the notational system for voice-sounds are indicated. The vowel and consonant symbols are derived from the international phonetic alphabet (Figure 12.13). In assembling a score a three-level representation is used (see Figure 12.14). At the upper level durations and loudness are indicated in the traditional musical fashion, at the bottom level detailed phonetic and extended-phonetic notation is used to indicate the details of the sounds. In the central level these sounds are notated using graphic symbols which allow us to indicate pitch, pitch motion, transformation, intermodulation and so on.

The international phonetic alphabet has been developed for linguistic analysis of phonemes. In a performance situation, however, such diversity of symbols may become confusing and it seems more practicable to use a smaller set of symbols and methods of combining or modifying them (see previous diagrams). In addition the phonetic alphabet has been derived from natural languages and does not cover the whole human repertoire, therefore modifications and extensions are required.

The system of notation developed here has a degree of redundancy. In particular information is given both in a 'phonetic' format and in a graphic format. This redundancy is useful when it comes to reading notation during a rehearsal or performance. The notation is also somewhat eclectic, using devices drawn from standard repertoire music, contemporary music and phonetic research. This, however, has the advantage that we are able to pass over into conventional musical or conventional linguistic use of the voice without any abrupt change in the way we represent the sounds.

It is also possible to present a systematic physiological notation for the sounds of the human vocal tract (and the body in general). This has been developed by Jean-Paul Curtay (Figure 12.15 which is from Curtay (1981)). This notation is in fact more systematic and is used by Curtay in his performances. However, I would still tend to prefer the eclectic method which retains the links with language and conventional music and allows us to notate complex sounds such as multiplexes while using physiological descriptions as a very useful aid to performance practice. Furthermore, just as traditional music notation tends to channel the aesthetic possibilities (Chapter 2), even these extended notations have some bias towards a physiological and a sound-object-oriented perspective respectively.

Natural morphology

In the next chapter we will return to some of our ideas about a natural morphology of sound-objects in relation to phonemes. However, even at this

The International Phonetic Alphabet

	Bi-labial	Labio-dental	Dental and Alveolar	Retroflex	Palato-alveolar	Alveolo-palatal	Palatal	Velar	Uvular	Pharyngal	Glottal
Plosive	p b		t d	ʈ ɖ			c ɟ	k g	q ɢ		ʔ
Nasal	m	ɱ	n	ɳ			ɲ	ŋ	ɴ		
Lateral Fricative			ɬ ɮ								
Lateral Non-fricative			l	ɭ			ʎ				
Rolled			r						ʀ		
Flapped			ɾ	ɽ					ʀ		
Fricative	ɸ β	f v	θ ð s z	ʂ ʐ	ʃ ʒ	ɕ ʑ	ç j	x ɣ	χ ʁ	ħ ʕ	h ɦ
Frictionless Continuants and Semi-vowels	w ɥ	ʋ	ɹ	ɻ			j (ɥ)	(w)	ʁ		

CONSONANTS

VOWELS

		Front	Central	Back
Close	(y ʉ u)	i y	ɨ ʉ	ɯ u
Half-close	(ø o)	e ø		ɤ o
Half-open	(ɛ œ)	ɛ œ	ɜ ʌ ɔ	ʌ ɔ
Open	(ɒ)		a ɐ	ɑ ɒ

(Secondary articulations are shown by symbols in parentheses.)

Figure 12.13   The International Phonetic Alphabet.

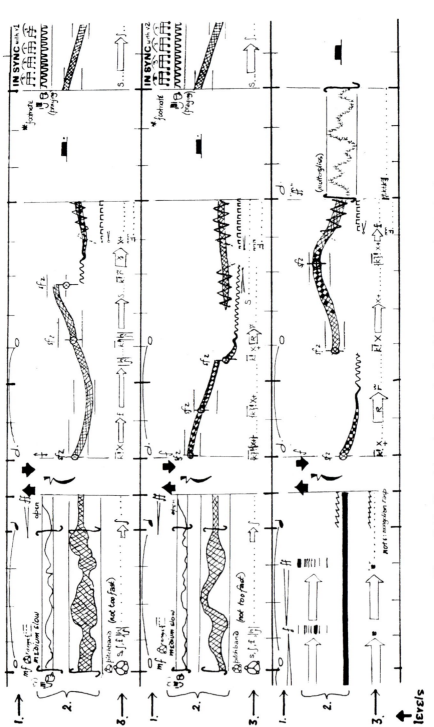

Figure 12.14   Use of three-level notation (used in three voice parts) in *Anticredos*.

Figure 12.15   Examples of Jean-Paul Curtay's iconic notation (after Curtay (1981)).

level we can note certain distinctions which may relate to our natural morphology classification. Curtay has suggested a gross classification of the human repertoire into *gaseous*, *liquid* and *solid*.[1] This might be given a more general interpretation as an aspect of natural morphology. Sounds of solid objects are generally of stable mass (or pitch) — this includes the air resonances within fixed-shape objects, e.g. a flute. Liquid sounds on the other hand will often have changing mass, tessitura, spectrum and other features but this change will exhibit a specific class of form (like a bubble archetype). Gaseous sounds however, will be varying continuously in various parameters (particularly mass) without a definite class of morphological forms emerging. Clearly there is very much more to be said about this. Air columns or liquids vibrating within solid objects (the water-in-saucepan effect) or air passing through liquids would need to be considered but there is certainly an interesting natural morphological aspect here. For example, the sounds of a classical synthesiser can be very stable in their spectral properties, implying a 'solidity' of the source. The sounds of the human voice, on the other hand (and of course of musical instruments articulated by human beings), even when they attempt to be stable, in fact contain micro-fluctuations of pitch, dynamics etc. partly because the musculature acting as a physical source or articulator is not a rigid object. We tend to prefer even in normal musical practice a certain small degree of 'liquidity' in our musical objects.

Moving outward

From this repertoire of human sounds we may lay out areas of sonic discourse. Focusing on the repertoire as physiological acts and perhaps complementing them with visceral sounds recorded from within the body (flow of the blood, etc.) we may evolve sound-structures which become a kind of physiological diagnosis of the state of the organism. Something of this feel is achieved in Curtay's *Abridgement* (Curtay 1981) where the physiological landscape becomes the basis for sonic exploration. We may treat the repertoire as a class of (intertransformable) sound-objects and organise music accordingly (for example in my *Anticredos*) though we

---

[1] Although mentioned in the spoken introduction to 'body music' on the cassette (where *solid* is strictly referred to as *tissue*), Curtay (1981) concentrates on a discussion of *method of production* which he divides into three levels: *excitation*, *emitter* and *modulation* (or *resonance*) indications. Wishart interviewed Curtay at the time of his visit to London in 1981 and his material has been elaborated through this personal communication and through Curtay (1983) (*Ed.*).

cannot entirely avoid physiological (and para-linguistic) aspects of the landscape adhering to the events at least on a first hearing. The sound-objects may be extended into the electronic (as in McNabb's *Dreamsong*) or into the world of recognisable sound-objects such as the transformation from *ss* to birdsong in *Red Bird*. Given a good computer model of the human voice as in the language *Chant* we may manipulate the form and structure of the voice beyond that which is physiologically possible so that, for example, individual glottal pulses may become bells (the formants are narrowed and ring) or the energy in the formants may be refocussed and the pitch articulated in such a way that we produce birdsong.

We may focus upon the mimetic abilities of the human voice made possible by its enormous repertoire. The imitation of instruments such as drums or trumpets has been touched upon earlier. Natural morphology in relation to phonemes will be discussed in the next chapter as will the idea of phonemic analogy (phonemic objects which are akin to but not exactly mimetic of other sounds). We may extend the human repertoire by the use of external resonances; thus brass instruments amplify and stabilise lip vibrations extending their range of loudness and controllable pitch. We may model the voice on musical instrument technology, separating out pitch as a parameter and developing the field of song.

We may focus upon the paralinguistic articulation of the sound-objects. Such paralanguage may be based on (originally) involuntary physiological states, gestural expression or linguistic conventions. In this way we produce a kind of phoneme-free poetry. Such paralinguistic articulations may enter into instrumental practice, particularly in relation to pitch and timbre control on the trombone or pitch, timbre, breathiness control on the saxophone. Finally we may select specific sound-objects from the repertoire and combine them in particular ways to produce phonemic objects. We then enter the sphere of language, of linguistic syntax and semantics. In the following chapters we will look more closely at this world from a sonic art viewpoint.

Figure 12.16 indicates some of these many possibilities. (Fine arrows indicate areas between which there is a continuum of intermediate possibilities or an interaction of perceived categories.) Note, however, that these cannot truly be represented on a two-dimensional surface. The implications of human vocal utterance are multi-dimensional. The biological, paralinguistic, linguistic, mimetic and musical may all be present in an utterance. In sonic art we will structure this material in order to focus in upon one or several aspects of this amazing universe of sounds. Although the archetype of the keyed musical instruments, fashioned in the image of

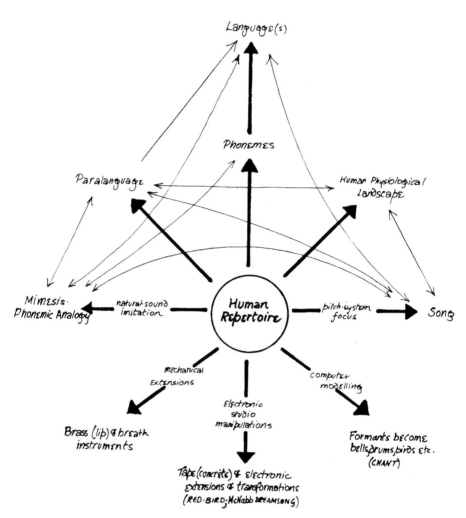

Figure 12.16   The relation of the elements of the human repertoire.

a theory of pitch, has been the dominant focus for musical thinking in the West for at least 300 years, at this moment of enormous technological and musical change there can be no doubt that we shall return to the human voice for our inspiration as "voice is the original instrument".

Chapter 13

PHONEMIC OBJECTS

gadji beri bimba
glandridi lauli lonni cadori
gadjama bim beri glassala
glandridi glassala tuffm i zimbrabim
blassa galassasa tuffm i zimbrabim [...]
(*Hugo Ball 1974: 70*)

We must return to the innermost alchemy of the word, we must even give up the word too, to keep for poetry its last and holiest refuge.
(*Ball 1974: 71*)

Sequence and Morphology

From the vast array of possible sound-objects available from the human repertoire any natural language selects only a small proportion and combines these phonemes into phonemic objects. These are the basic sound units of any language and correspond roughly to the notion of the syllable. Phonemes themselves are then combined sequentially to form morphemes (words), the smallest independently meaningful units of language. We will not go into this in greater detail, however, as this is not a linguistic analysis but an attempt to explore the world of phonemic objects as a special class of sound-objects for the purposes of sonic art.

Any particular language will exclude a large number of possible human utterances from the sphere of the phonemic. If, however, we scan all existing (and extinct) languages, we will discover that quite a large proportion of the sounds in the human repertoire are being (and have been) used in human language discourse. For example, inhaled clicks are used as consonants in a number of Southern African languages but not in any European languages.

Phonemic objects are almost paradigmatic examples of sound-objects of complex morphology. For example, if we consider the word 'when', its written form suggests that it contains four consecutive objects. A superficial listening might suggest that it contains three separate sound entities (a 'w', an 'e' and an 'n'). If, however, we speak this word very slowly we will discover that it is one coordinated sound articulated by the opening of the lips (and associated widening of the oral aperture) and the coordinated motion of the tongue concluding where the tongue tip reaches the roof of the mouth and cuts off the air stream. As a sound-object, therefore, this event consists of a complex but continuous motion through the formant space, most likely simultaneous to a slight movement of the fundamental pitch. This kind of continuum exists in most verbal objects, except where it is explicitly chopped up by stops and pauses. Thus, in the word 'say' it may seem superficially that we have two distinct objects 's' and 'ay'. If, however, we speak these two objects (even very carefully) and record them onto tape and edit the two together we will not reproduce (except approximately) the word 'say'. In the speech stream there are subtle transformations both of formants and into and out of noise turbulence. The speech stream is thus an archetypal example of complexly evolving timbral morphology. This will be discussed again in the next chapter.

For the purposes of linguistic analysis it is necessary to separate off the distinct units which form the basis of the 'digital' coding of language. From a sound morphological point of view, however, this can be quite misleading. For example, the computer model of the singing voice encapsulated in the programme *Chant* had by 1981 very successfully modelled vowels in terms of definable and fixed formant structures which could be reproduced by simulating the effect of a related system of filters on an impulse stream. Modelling many of the consonants, however, proved to be more difficult as their absolute characteristics varied very greatly with context, both in absolute formant structure and, for example, onset time of noise turbulence. They were thus characterised more by second order characteristics (characteristics of the process of change itself) than by any absolute properties. It is therefore important not to confuse the economy of print with the reality of this speech stream.

A similar complexity of timbral morphology may be found in the utterances of other creatures. For example, various kinds of birdsong which appear superficially as trills or bubblings of fixed pitch have in fact a complex internal structure which can be heard when they are slowed down (Example 13.1). I would not agree, as some observers have suggested, that these internal complexities do not exist for the human listener. On the contrary, it is possible to predict with some accuracy what the internal structure of a sound will be when slowed down if one develops one's ear for dynamic morphological properties. Even without this degree of discrimination, however, the listener can usually observe a qualitative distinction between various songs which derive from these rapid internal articulations, even if he or she is unable to describe how they arise.

Phonemic objects, then, are interesting sound-objects from the point of view of the musician interested in sound-objects of dynamic morphology. Interest has also arisen, however, from an entirely different direction. In 1947, the Rumanian Isidore Isou published *Introduction à une Nouvelle Poesie et à une Nouvelle Musique* (Isou 1947) In this book Isou proposed a new type of poetry based on the letter, to be known as *lettrism*. Isou's view of the development of poetry is illustrated in Figure 13.1. The lettrist movement led to many interesting developments, including *aphonic poetry* (see Figure 13.2) and also to a deeper interest in the expressive possibilities of phonemic sound-objects beneath the level of the word. Curtay's work (discussed in the previous chapter) develops out of this tradition. This is an interesting juncture of fields of thought about the world of sound, that springing from music and that springing from poetry and language. As we begin to consider larger units of language (such as words, phrases, sentences etc.), considerations of semantic meaning (or the lack of it) will enter increasingly into our field of view until we finally arrive in an entirely different area of human discourse (didactic or scientific prose). At the level of the phoneme, however, we are still deeply embedded in sonic art.

We may also note that from the human repertoire described in the previous chapter we can create imaginary phonemic objects and in fact construct imaginary languages and linguistic streams from these. (We can also construct imaginary linguistic streams from 'valid' phonemic objects, as we shall see.) This kind of imaginary language retains our material for the field of sonic art as questions of semantics cannot enter into the listener's perception (though paralinguistic and other signs and signals may remain part of the experience). The four-voice piece *Vox-I* concludes with the peroration of such an imaginary text.

Mimesis and phonemic analogy

Language divides the human repertoire into two distinct fields. Those sounds (or sound combinations) which may enter into the construction of language sounds and those sounds (or sequences) which may not. If we do not make any restriction on the sounds we can use, the immense pliability of the voice makes it able to mimic an enormous variety of sounds. In the previous chapter we discussed how it was possible to use plosive consonants and stops to imitate drums very accurately. Similarly, various entertainers and serious investigators are able to imitate birdsong sufficiently accurately to fool other birds, to imitate the idiosyncratic features of another person's voice, or to imitate the sounds of natural objects or machines. Even approximate mimesis makes the construction of the kind of transformations into other recognisable sounds used in *Red Bird* a possibility. Once, however,

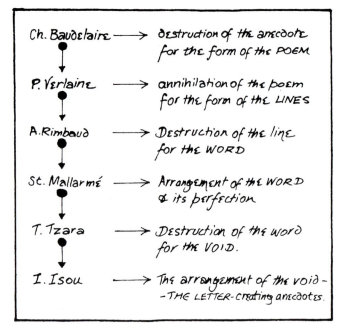

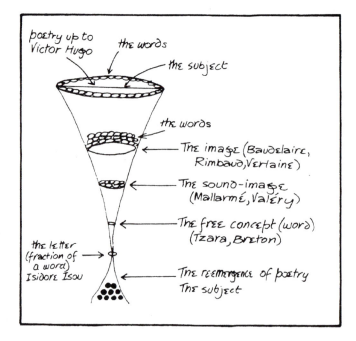

Figure 13.1 Isadore Isou's view of the development of poetry (adapted from Isou (1947)).

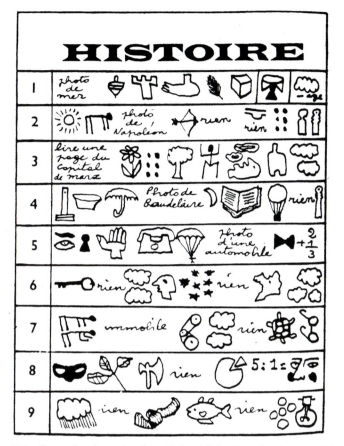

Figure 13.2 Example of notation from Roland Sabatier aphonic poem *Histoire*.

we restrict ourselves to those sound-events deemed suitable for use in a particular language this type of mimesis becomes more problematic.

Instead, we must substitute the technique of phonemic analogy. Here, sounds may be imitated by a closest possible approximation constructed out of sounds available as phonemes for language. Thus we might indicate a drum sound by the syllable *du* or *bom*. This imitation retains certain characteristics of the sound it imitates. It has the initial attack, though now somewhat soft-edged and the resonance of the drum skin is suggested by the fixed resonance of the vowel formant. In the case of *bom* the slight natural reverberation of a deep drum with a loose skin is suggested by the *m* continuation of the vowel. As the mouth moves into the *m* formation the formants of the *o* are rapidly filtered out from the top downwards, a process similar to the rapid damping of the drum skin. There is no way, however, in which any listener would mistake these syllables for the sound of a drum. Phonemic analogy need not, in fact, use the phonemes of the language. For example the children's gun imitation *kX+* uses the sound *X+* which does not occur in the English language. Nor, in fact, does the sound-object sound at all like a gun but more like a small explosion. The object is also interesting because it is clearly not based on the restricted phoneme set but the use of such sound analogues may be seen to relate to the kind of vocal set induced by speaking a particular language, i.e. particular settings and articulations of the vocal tract muscles become 'second-nature' to the speakers of a particular language and they will therefore seek to make such analogies using these second-nature articulations. *kX+*, though not within the phonemic set of the language, is not outside the second-nature vocal set.

A second aspect of phonemic analogy is illustrated by ornithologists' attempts to write down birdsong using specially created syllables. Figure 13.3 (adapted from Schafer 1977: 30 citing Nicholson and Koch (1946)) shows a number of examples. Their most interesting feature is the way in which formant movement is used to 'track' pitch movement; thus in the great titmouse, the syllable 'tsoo-ee' clearly indicates a figure which moves upwards in pitch. In fact, if this is a good imitation the birdsong should slide up in pitch as the speech stream transition from *oo* to *ee* involves a spectral glide from low formants to high formants. The formant tracking of

Hawfinch	*Dɛak … warsɛ-rɛɛ-rɛɛ Tchɛɛ … tchɛɛ … tur-wɛɛ-wɛɛ*
Greenfinch	*wah·wah·wah·wah·-chow·-chow-chow-chow-tu-wɛ-wɛ*
Crossbill	*jibb… chip·chip·chip·-gɛɛ-gɛɛ·gɛɛ·gɛɛ*
Great Titmouse	*zɛ-too, zɛ-too, p'tsɛɛ-ɛ́ɛ, tsoo-ɛ́ɛ, tsoo-ɛ́ɛ ching·-sɛɛ, ching·sɛɛ, ðɛɛðɛr·ðɛɛðɛr·ðɛɛðɛr, biplɛ-bɛ·wit-sɛ̆-diddlɛ*
Pied Flycatcher	*Tchɛ́ɛtlɛ, tchɛ́ɛtlɛ, tchɛ́ɛtlɛ diddlɛ·diddlɛ-dɛ́ɛ; tzit-tzit-tzit, trui, truí, trui*
Mistlethrush	*trɛ-wir-ri-0-ɛɛ; trɛ-wir-ri-0-ɛɛ-0; trɛ-uɛ-0-wɛɛ-0-wɛɛ-0-wit*
Corncrakɛ	*crɛx-crɛx, krɛk-krɛk, rɛrp·rɛrp*
Common Snipɛ	*tik·tik·tik-tuk·tik·tuk-tik·tuk·chip·it; chick-chuck; yuk-yuk*

Figure 13.3   Phonemic analogues of birdsong used by ornithologists.

pitch is not confined, however, to the vowel. In the greenfinch, for example, *wah-wah* is perceived as spectral glides up through the formants and presumably represents a rising pitch figure. At the same time other consonants, as in *tchee* or *tic*, may indicate spreading of the spectrum during the attack (or decay) portions of the bird tones producing 'impure' tones which cannot thus be represented simply by a formant-tracking procedure. Similarly, iterated sounds such as the rolled *r*, may be used to indicate rapid streams of impulses in the song.

These formant-tracking and spectral-analogue procedures were also used in an art context by Raoul Hausmann in his poem *Birdlike* (1946), for example in this extract:

> *Pitsu puit puittituttsu uttititi ittitaan*
> *piêt piêt pieteit tenteit tuu uit*
> *ti ti tinax troi troi toi to*
> *Iti iti loi loi loiouttouto!*
> *(Motherwell 1989: 316)*

There may of course also be direct analogies with birdsong as certain birds (such as parrots) are able to articulate clear formant structures (such as in their imitations of human speech).

Phonemic analogy and formant tracking of pitch can also be found in human names for animal sounds. These vary in the 'goodness of fit'. For example, a cow, which produces a low-pitched sound, 'moos'. A mouse, producing a high-pitched sound, 'squeaks'; a wolf, which sings a sustained pitch which then gradually falls, is represented by a formant structure which falls as in 'howl' (say it slowly). On the other hand, the low frequency glottal/windpipe multiphonic (which humans can produce) of the pig or the lion is only loosely represented by 'grunt' (where the 'gr' hints at the subaudio oscillation of the windpipe) and 'roar'. Such phonemic analogy may breach the distinctness of natural languages, such as the various words for the sound of the cockerel (*cock-a-doodle-doo* in English, *kikeriki* in German, *kokke kokko* in Japanese, *kio kio* in the language of the Lokele tribe of the Congo) or of sneezing (*kerchoo* in American, *atishoo* in English, *atchum* in Arabic, *cheenk* in Urdu, *kakchun* in Japanese and *ach-shi* in Vietnamese).

Natural morphology; mouth symbols

We may go one stage beyond the concept of mimesis and ask whether we can apply the criteria of natural morphology to the sound-objects produced in the vocal tract. Clearly these sound-events are generated by processes which may be physically described (turbulent air-streams, plosions, opening and closing of apertures, etc.). Is there a natural morphological description of certain kinds of phonemic (and other) vocal objects?

Jean-Paul Curtay has approached the same problem from a slightly different point of view. Hence he considers both the motions and shaping of the vocal tract organs in his conception of *mouth symbols*. These two conceptions are very close indeed and it is worth considering the slight difference that does arise. In considering, for example, the word *stop*, Curtay talks of "*st*- evoking a sudden interruption of movement in a rigid vertical posture" (Curtay 1983).[1] The rigid vertical posture is suggested by the tight downward movement of the tongue and this particular *st*- formation can be associated with a number of words (*stake, stalk, stand, stare, statue, staunch, stick, stiff, stop*). Another way of describing this would be that we hear a continuously sustained sound which is suddenly interrupted by an impulse. The feeling of interruption of flow is equally apparent from such a description and in fact, of course, the sound morphology arises from the physical morphology of the sound production process. If, however, we now consider the phonemic object *sp*-, Curtay states that this is "evoking a circular movement" (*spin, spiral, spool*). The circular movement is presumably suggested by the circularity of the lips, a kind of spatial metaphor. Looking at it temporally (and in terms of what is heard) we would suggest that the (air) flow of the *s*- is momentarily interrupted by the constriction *p*- and then released into the rest of the word. This is more evocative of the whipping of a top where a sweeping motion of the whip is applied suddenly (the strike) to the stable spinning motion of the top. Similarly, when a dancer spins it is necessary to tense the musculature in a particular way and then suddenly release this energy, allowing the body to spin as a result. The sense of stored energy and sudden release into a stable motion is evoked by the time morphology of the word *spin*.

It is interesting to consider some other examples. The phonemic object *sl*- consists of a stream (or store) of energy (*s*) which is gently released (*l*) into the stable motion of the vowel. The sense of gentle release into movement is of course caused by the sliding of the tongue. We may bring this motion to an abrupt end by the insertion of a stop consonant such as *p*, to produce the word *slip*. This motion is so analogous to someone slipping on ice, where the move into the continuous sliding motion is abruptly interrupted by a fall that it seems unlikely to be coincidental. Curtay quotes the related words *sledge, sleigh , slide , slime, slip, slough, slug, slant, slope, slash, slat, slit, slice, slither, slot, slender, slim*. Some of these associations are

---

[1] See Chapter 12 footnote 1. Curtay (1983) is unpublished.

undoubtedly metaphoric or tangential (for example, *slope* from *slip* and possible also *slap* from the act of killing by sliding a sword into someone). Furthermore, the reader can now think of many words which do not conform to this archetype. The point being made, however, is not that all language is somehow made up of symbolic or metaphorical sound-objects, but that some parts of language may originate in such symbolism.

Spr-: a flow (or store) of energy (s), passing through a constriction (*p-*) and continuing but being broken up into an iteration, (*r-*), as in *spray, sprinkle* and, more metaphorically, *sprout, spring*.

Spl-: in which a continuous air stream (*s-*) meets a constriction (the initiating mouth formation for *p-*), leading to a double release (*pl-*), as in *split, splice, splinter, splay, splash* and, by metaphor or association, *splendour*.

Gr- and *scr-*: in which an impulse or contact (*g-*) is followed by a non-continuous (iterative), or we might say abrasive, motion as in *grate, grind* (and possibly *grip*) and *scratch, scrape, scrawl* (even perhaps *scream*).

Cl-: a double, rather than a clean, attack as in *clang* (as opposed to *dong*), *clatter, clink, clash*. Certain word endings are also interesting from this point of view, such as *-ng*, a resonant extension of vowels in which the higher formants are gradually filtered off — sound is gradually directed through the nasal cavity — as in many naturally decaying resonances. This is found in *bang, clang, bing, ding, ping, ring, dong, song*. '-ash', a resonance which breaks up into turbulence, as in *dash, smash, clash, splash, bash, crash* and, perhaps as a metaphor for the visual after-effect, in *flash*. The word *clash* thus has an unclear (double) attack onto its resonance which rapidly dissipates into turbulence.

These sound morphologies (which are illustrated graphically in Figure 13.4) point in two directions. Curtay has suggested that the linking of these phonemes with objects and activities in the real world is to a great extent kinaesthetic, i.e. we feel the formations inside the mouth and thereby associate them with activities or the shapes of objects in the external world. This naturally leads us into the sphere of representation and language. At the same time the sound 's' which we feel as a store of tension because it is produced by constricting the passage of air with the use of the tongue, is also indicative of a similar or related physical situation in any natural world event. These forms, therefore, also point towards a natural morphology of timbral gesture.

Expletives and paralanguage

Phonemic objects may, however, carry gestural information outside their timbral morphology. This may be suggested by pitch articulation, dynamic

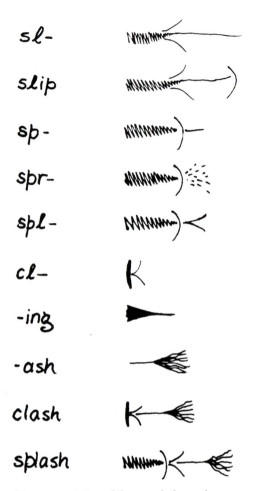

Figure 13.4 Graphic representation of the morphology of some consonant clusters.

or rhythmic articulation or physiological indicators such as breath state etc.. An interesting case to consider is that of expletives. If we consider four words of equivalent meaning which might be used as obscenities: *fuck, screw, copulate, make love*, we find that only the first is used regularly as an expletive. This can be related to its timbral structure. A restricted flow of air *f-* is released very briefly *u* into an abrupt stop *k*. This intense and brief release of energy is like a verbal punch, a violent physical action is mapped into violent verbal action and the tension caused by anger or pain is symbolically released. Compare for example the words *shit* and the (slightly less satisfying) *damn*.

RED BIRD
vocal sources

CHART ONE....

Speak the following list of Words, Phrases, Phonemes & Syllables in the ways indicated on the right hand side of the page:—

1. "L" 2. "LI" 3. "LIS"
4. "T" 5. "LISTEN"
6. "STEN" as in listen
7. "EN" as in listen 8. "T"
9. "TO" 10. "R" 11. "REA"
12. "REAS" as in reason
13. "EA" 14. "REASON"
15. "SON" as in reason
16. "LISTEN TO REASON"
17. "REASONABLE"
18. "NABLE" as in reasonable
19. "BL" as in reasonable

(each to be treated as a separate entity...do NOT string together in a sentence-type delivery)

If you cannot speak the syllable/word in the manner suggested, say it as best you can and pass on to the next...

Types in brackets apply only to full words. "Long"-variants do not apply to "L" and "Listen to Reason"

CONSIDER THE EXPRESSION OF EACH SYLLABLE ON ITS OWN MERITS

You may take 1 or 2 syllables(words) at a time, or all, together; whichever seems most appropriate to you, and easiest for you.

EXPRESSION	long	extra long	EXPRESSION	long	extra long	EXPRESSION	long	extra long
Flippant	X		Determined	X		Squeaky	X	
Poignant	X		Fervent, Fanatical	X		Question (...?)	X	
Passionately	X		Triumphant	X		Answer (Yes) (....)	X	
Lovingly	X		Wicked, Demoniacal	X		2nd Question (...??!!)	X	
Drunkenly, Stupidly	X	X	Aggressive	X		2nd Answer (...!!)	X	
Sneering imitation of person	X		Menacing	X		3rd Question (...????!!)	X	
Annunciated	X	X	with foreboding	X	X	3rd Answer (...::!!!!!)	X	
Stressing the meaning	X		Insidiously	X		(Rhythmically)	X	
Incredulous	X		Frantically	X		(Rhythmically, different)	X	
Laughingly	X	X	Histrionic	X		(Rigid, Starchily)	X	
Weepily	X	X	Screechy	X	X	(Tersely)	X	
Resignedly	X		Sincere	X		(Jabber)	X	
Indignant	X	X	Sacred	X		(very rapid)	X	
Enraged	X		Concerned	X		(woodenly, whispered)	X	
Jolly, Bouncy	X		Beseeching	X		(fitfully, awkwardly)	X	
Delighted	X		Coaxing	X		(encouraging, friendly)	X	
Feebly, (Shakily)	X	X	Seductive, Enticing	X	X	(authoritatively)	X	
Ponderous, Learned	X		Lewdly	X		THE FOLLOWING, WHISPERED...		
with Loathing	X	X	Cutely	X	X	Stupidly	X	
as if rejecting the words from the mouth like bad food	X	X	Coyly	X		Feebly (Shakily)	X	
Sceptically	X		Gruffly, Roughly	X		Ponderously	X	
Cynically	X		Grudgingly	X		as if announcing title of a play	X	
as if announcing the title of a play	X		Snappily	X		as if reading from a list of items	X	
as if reading from a list of items	X		Coldly	X		Nimbly, Delicately	X	
as if you might change your mind	X		Expansively	X		Sleepily	X	
Nimbly, Delicately	X		Giddily	X	X	Terrified	X	
Sleepily	X	X	Breathlessly	X		Histrionic	X	
Anxious	X		Hoarsely	X	X	Enraptured, Ecstatic	X	X	X
Terrified	X		Childishly	X		Menacing	X	X
Cheeky, Impertinent	X		Flowing	X		Aggressive	X	X
Supercilious, Conceited	X		Florid, Extravagant	X		Seductive, Enticing	X	X	X
Fiery	X	X	Liquid	X		Snappily	X	
As if to contradict someone	X	X	Wailing	X	X	(Rhythmically)	X	
Enraptured, Ecstatic	X	X	Raucous	X		(Tersely)	X	
Amazed, Astounded	X		Explosive	X	X	(Pitfully)	X	

Figure 13.5   Paralinguistic transformations of phonemic objects in *Red Bird*.

In general, however, the phonemes of language are not mouth symbols. Their dynamic morphology or energy contour does not represent either the object of action they stand for or anything about the immediate internal state of the utterer (as with expletives). In these cases, however, it is possible to impose a morphology on certain aspects of the phonemic object giving (or altering) meaning to it which might not be carried linguistically. In the work *Red Bird* the various phonemic objects contained in the phrase 'listen to reason' were spoken by a male and a female speaker in a number of different ways indicated by adverbs, in order to project such implications into the phonemic objects themselves (see Figure 13.5). In Berio's *Visage* similar paralinguistic 'meaning' is projected onto phonemic utterances.

It should also be noted that certain phonemic objects already act as signals, although they are not elements of language proper. Some of these have been called *vocal segregates* and examples are 'mm', usually meaning 'yes' and the 'tut' click implying 'how stupid' or 'fancy that'. The kiss, though not used in the phonetic structure of most languages, does, however, carry social connotations. Finally, it should be noted before we move onto a consideration of language-stream that phonemic objects may be organised sequentially into larger units which are yet not linguistic. A good example would be the 'Word-Machine' in *Red Bird* (see earlier in text).

Chapter 14

LANGUAGE STREAM AND PARALANGUAGE

The fall (bababadalgharaghtakamminarronnkonnbronntonner-
ronntuonnthunntrovarrhounawnskawntoohoohoordenenthur-
nuk!) of a once wallstraight oldparr is retaled early in bed and later
on life down through all christian minstrelsy.
(James Joyce, Finnegans Wake (Joyce 1939: 1))

'Twas brillig and the slithy toves
Did gyre and gimble in the wabe:
All mimsy were the borogoves,
And the mome raths outgrabe.
(Lewis Carroll, Jabberwocky (1872) (Carroll 1994: 28))

For a language utterance to convey its meaning, the linguistic signs need not reflect in any way the properties of the objects or activities to which they refer. There is nothing in common between the word 'red' and the property of redness. This is the famous Jacobsonian arbitrariness of the linguistic sign and is the assumption upon which most linguistic research is based. However, when we say that the linguistic sign *need* bear no relation to the signified, we are not saying that it *must* bear no relation. As we have seen in our analysis of phonemic objects, such relationships can be established in different ways in many cases.

The language stream itself conveys meaning in many ways (in many different sonic dimensions). Taking a minimalist view, we may describe the significant distinguishable elements of the speech stream purely in relation to the formants. Roughly speaking, with an unvoiced speech stream, vowels will be distinguished by specific formant structures and consonants by a combination of specific qualities and specific structures of change of these qualities. A typical speech act, however, is also characterised by a number of other properties relating to its rhythm and tempo and their articulation, its pitch and pitch articulation, its phonemic connectedness and so on. These other properties are also capable of conveying meaning and particularly of modifying the significance of the semantics that might be implied from a written version of the sentence. Furthermore, we can define sonic properties of the language stream which have nothing to do with any of this, for example, aspects determined by the particular physiology of the speaker.

From the point of view of sonic analysis, this distinction between language and paralanguage (as these other aspects have been called) is somewhat arbitrary. It is not based on a distinction between what is semantically meaningful and what is not, but on a distinction between what is captured in writing and what is not. This is only true of certain writing systems, however. In the Aztec codices sometimes the 'speech scroll' — the balloon issuing from the mouth of a character depicted — is specially elaborated to indicated paralinguistic aspects. In one instance (see Figure 14.1) ambassadors delivering speeches are shown with knives coming out of their mouths (left), whilst in another a Spaniard is shown talking to Aztecs and his speech scroll is decorated with feathers indicating the soft, smooth words he is using (right). Approaching these things from the point of view of sonic art, therefore, we will talk in terms of timbre fields and articulation fields which will be explained more fully below.

Comparing, for a moment, standard repertoire use of language and standard repertoire music, we may characterise the difference in the articulation of the sonic stream as follows: the melodic stream is pitch-disjunct and may be articulated by timbral colouration (either in the choice of instrumentation or within the internal morphology of the sound-objects of instruments). The language-stream is timbre-disjunct (bearing in mind the qualifications on the notion of vocal disjuncture mentioned in the previous chapter) and may be articulated by pitch inflections. It has been argued that a music based on the complex articulation of timbre could not be as sophisticated as that based on the articulation of pitch. However, if

Figure 14.1   Paralinguistic indicators in Aztec codices.

we investigate the language-stream, we will discover that the human brain has a truly amazing ability to generate and perceive rapid articulations of timbral quality. At certain points in the speech stream (particularly in diphthongs or within consonants) the removal of just one thirtieth of a second of sound is clearly noticeable (as the ear is crucially sensitive to change-continua). It is often argued that this perceptual ability is crucially linked to semantic understanding. If, however, we consider text-sound-art using essentially meaningless phonemic strings and take into consideration our discussion of mouth symbols and natural morphology of phonemes, plus our ability to perceive simultaneously a wide variety of characteristics of the speaker (age, status, regional accent, idiolect, physiological state, and attitude), it is clear that a sonic art based on the articulation of timbral characteristics may be quite as subtle as any pitch-lattice-based sonics.

The language-stream may therefore be thought of as a model for such a timbre-stream music. Such a music need not use the phonemic objects of languages or even confine itself to the timbral objects within the human repertoire. It need not be based fundamentally on the voiced/unvoiced distinction of the speech-stream (but might use some other kinds of timbral disjunction). It need not be pitch-stable (as the speech stream tends to be, remaining within a narrow range of pitch), nor need it confine itself to the tempo, rhythm and tempo and rhythm articulations typical in the speech-stream (for example we might use such human repertoire sound-objects as *s* or *X+* as sustained objects, inside which the formant area is being continuously filtered, or rapid multiplexes with a phonemic distribution statistically related (or not) to language in general or a specific language). Using the language-stream as a model, therefore, does not imply we are going to produce some kind of 'universal vocoder' form of musical discourse.

Conversely, any sound-stream which exhibits the articulation of formant areas within or close to the range of the tempo and rhythm of normal speech will be imprinted with the landscape *language*, hence a timbral organisation not deriving in any way from the human repertoire may make reference to and play with the landscape of the human voice and the notion of utterance.

Thirdly, we may look upon a particular language-string as a sound-object in its own right. In his commentary to *Ommagio a Joyce* (Berio 1959), Berio describes classifying the language strings into three types on the basis of their very general (external) properties. These are the *continuous* (e.g. sustained sibilants), the *periodic* (e.g. 'thnthnthn') and the *discontinuous* (e.g. 'Goodgod, henev erheard inall'). We can, however, work with the sonic properties of language-strings in a much more specific way.

Timbre field, phoneme field

In listening to (or working with) pitch-lattice music, it is often possible to define an entity known as a *harmonic field*. A sustained chord, of course, defines a harmonic field for as long as it is sustained. However, the crucial feature of a harmonic field is that we do not need to state all its pitch constituents simultaneously for us to be aware of its existence. Thus, the opening section of the Webern *Symphonie* is based on a harmonic field (Figure 14.2). The harmonic field is thus a property of a sequence of sounds, a property of inclusion in, and exclusion from, a set.

In the sphere of tonal music we may slightly redefine a harmonic field, such that the same note-name (e.g. C, E flat) in a different octave will

Figure 14.2 The symmetrical harmonic field in Webern's *Symphonie* op. 21.

be regarded as the same note. Our recognition that we are in a particular key relates to the definition of our harmonic field (in this new sense) corresponding to the seven-note scale which defines the key. Chromaticism within the key involves the expansion of the set of acceptable pitches (the harmonic field). Modulation involves a change in harmonic field. In this case, however, we might also consider the harmonic field of the entire piece which will be the entire set of twelve pitches making up the chromatic scale (or some sub-set of it). This in its turn is a sub-set of the set of pitches making up the quarter-tone scale and of the infinite set of pitches making up the continuum of pitch. We may thus focus in upon a piece on different time-scales and describe it in terms of the harmonic field defined by the sequential use of pitch.

It is easy to see how the concept of a field may be adopted for the spheres of timbre, timbre articulation, pitch articulation, phonemes and so on. At the most general level we can talk about the *timbre field* of a particular language. When listening to a language we do not understand, we will be particularly aware of this feature: in Japanese the extreme (very high and very low) formant areas used in some vowel production, in Dutch the salival fricatives (X+), in English the sense of articulatory (consonantal, dipthongal) continuity (compared with, for example, German). Such features in fact may often lie at the root of certain kinds of cultural prejudice where the timbral and articulatory aspects of the language are taken to indicate something about a spurious 'national character' of the entire group of speakers. This is essentially a confusion of the normal timbral field of a particular language with the attitudinal 'modulations' which may be applied to the normal timbre field of the native speaker's language.

Just as the definition of a harmonic field on a pitch lattice allows us to define chromaticism (the inclusion of pitches foreign to the harmonic field originally established), so the definition of a timbre field allows us to define 'chromaticism' or 'modulation' from normal language practice. Figure 14.3 gives a highly schematic representation of this idea. To do justice to the concept we would need a multi-dimensional space in which to draw this figure. However, from it we can see that a particular language will have a characteristic 'normal' set of timbre types, articulations, etc. and (even without understanding a language) we will be able to distinguish regional accents or idiolects (ways of speaking characteristic of the individual speaker) by their variation from this norm. Other variations from the norm, which might overlap with aspects of accent or idiolect, will indicate non-neutral modes of discourse (for example, anger or ridicule).

It is more interesting, however, to look at much more specific timbral fields. Thus, any short verbal utterance contains a particular set

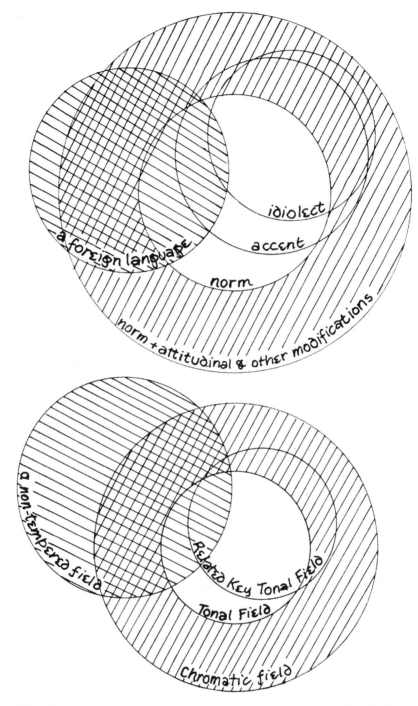

Figure 14.3 Timbre fired of a language and various subsets compared with a similar analysis for harmonic fields in tonal music.

of timbral objects, and these define a timbral field. We may explore the interrelationships amongst these objects, not only through their reordering in a linear text (an approach from poetry) but also in simultaneous and textural orderings (a choral approach). The objects may also be grouped into 'timbral-motifs' (which may, in fact, be words or phrases). Thus, just as Lutoslawski or Berio will define a harmonic field and a class of pitch-groupings (melodic motifs) simultaneously, it is possible to do exactly the same thing with timbre-stream material.

In Steve Reich's *Come Out* the phrase 'come out to show them' is used purely as a timbral motif. Several copies of the phrase are played initially in synchronisation and then gradually de-synchronised. As this happens, rhythmic and timbral patterns (due partly to phasing effects) are established, which arise directly out of the timbral properties of the sonic object 'come out to show them' (or rather the specific speech utterance of this phrase initially recorded on tape).

Aspects of variation and change amongst timbral fields may be observed in various text-sound pieces with no semantic content. Thus, in Schwitters' *Ursonata* (Schwitters 1993), for example in the 'fourth movement', we can see first of all that the overall timbral field is confined to a small number of phonemes — *Grimm, glimm, gnimm, bimbimm, bumm, bamm, Tilla, loola, tee* etc.. Next we notice that there are large-scale groupings, for example, we may divide *attack-vowel resonance-m* areas (*Grimm, bamm*) from *l-vowel resonance-l-vowel resonance* areas (*loola, luula, lalla*) and from *attack-vowel resonance* areas (*Tuii, tee, bee*). Within these areas we may make further subdivisions, for example, in the first section between areas stressing *g* and *i*, and areas stressing *b* and using a number of different vowel resonances (*u, i* and *a*).

All this differs from our perception of field characteristics in pitch-lattice music (apart from the obvious pitch-stream/timbre-stream distinction) in a number of ways which are, however, not intrinsic to text-sound composition. First of all, there is no counterpoint or chorusing. Secondly, there is no indication of rhythm (which might, however, be implied from the printed spacing) or tempo. Adding these, and other, dimensions we can imagine a sophisticated contrapuntal art based on the articulation of a multi-levelled timbre or timbre-motif (possibly phonemic) field structure.

These conceptions have a bearing on the construction of standard poetry. Here the timbral colouration of words may be a crucial aspect of the poetic form. Such features are usually divided into vowel correspondences (assonance) and more general correspondences usually involving consonants as well. From a sonic art point of view this distinction is either invalid (both are to do with timbral correspondences) or too narrow (there are many more than two classes of timbral objects). The correspondences between phonemic objects have a very long history in poetry, mainly in the form of rhyme. Some poets, such as Gerard Manley Hopkins, have placed particular stress upon this aspect of their writing and, in the book *Phonetic Music with Electronic Music*, Robson (1981) has developed a general theory of vowel harmony. If we free these considerations from linkage to a linear solo text, then poetry (even poetry deeply based in semantic meaning) and a choral or electro-acoustic art of timbral articulation meet, as pitch and harmonic field can be articulated independently of all these parameters. A vast new area of sonic art opens up before us which has previously been bypassed by the linguistic or pitch-lattice preoccupations of poets and musicians respectively.

Linguistic flow

In addition to the intrinsic properties of the timbral objects of a language-stream, the juxtaposition of particular kinds of objects determines a particular kind of 'flow'. Thus, the passage of one vowel to another need involve no alteration in the rate at which air is expelled from the lungs. A text which articulates vowels only can therefore be entirely smooth in its flow (apart from where the speaker needs to breath). Certain consonants also allow the air stream to continue, restricting or varying it only slightly, thus *m* and *n* momentarily divert the air stream through the nasal passages (only). *W* and *I* partially constrict the air flow for an instant whilst *v*, *z* and others do likewise but the constriction is slightly more intense, introducing noise turbulence momentarily into the air stream. Text may therefore be constructed exhibiting different properties of flow. Schwitters' "Tee tee tee tee" tends to invoke a set of air pulses, whilst "Bumm bimbimm bamm bimbimm" produces a kind of sawtooth articulation of the air flow, and "Tilla lalla" is essentially undulatory. Let us now consider the text extracts from Joyce's *Ulysses* which Berio chose for his *Omaggio a Joyce*[1]: "Deaf bald Pat brought pad knife took up" cuts up the air flow between each word. At the same time the use of the long vowels *a* in *bald*, *ou* in *brought*, *i* in *knife* suggests sustained, separated units and justifies to some extent Berio's attribution 'martellato' to this phrase (Berio 1959). "Chips, picking chips" is similarly discontinuous, but in this case all the vowels are short, suggesting the attribution 'staccato'. Finally, "A sail! a veil awave upon the waves" has in general the undulatory character of Schwitters' "Tilla lalla" which we might link by analogy with pitch portamento (see Figure 14.4).

---

[1] The original text is in Joyce (1960): 328–330.

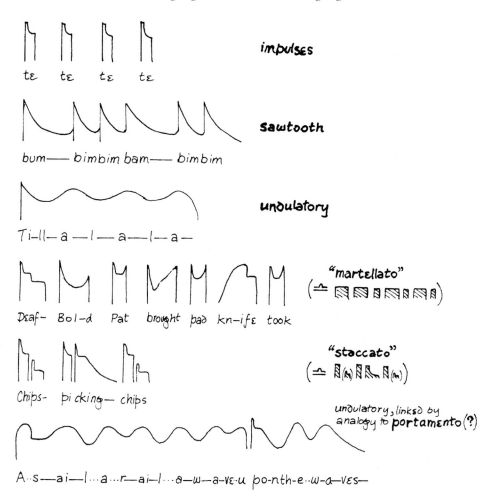

Figure 14.4 Linguistic (or aerodynamic) flow in Schwitters and Joyce.

In some lettrist poems an irregular staccato flow of air is implied by the stringing together of many consonants as in *Improvisations* by Jacqueline Tarkieltaub:

> *jtrsrndijvakaia. rdnstrklmndrnchtkrissvrichk!*
> *akrt! akrt! kh… kh…srk!*
> *rdinsrikarkdineirksrinirchvrstmnskrdrsismanris!*
> *fmjrkstnrsnichkezriksrmnsrnrguitrnsnierch!*
> *(quoted in Curtay 1974: 232)*

We might also point to certain general pitch characteristics of utterances at this stage: the sustained monotone with sudden articulations of the American tobacco auctioneer's spiel or the gradual rise in pitch of a horse-race commentary as the race nears its end (the siren effect) spring to mind. We will leave a more detailed consideration of pitch articulation to the section on paralanguage.

Semantics and cultural landscape

We are already approaching very close to the sphere of semantics which forms a universe of discourse separated from sonic art by the concept of the arbitrariness of the sign. For the text-sound-artist the link with linguistic semantics is a binding thread, even where it is negated. Sonic art perspectives will often be used as a foil to illuminate semantic content. There are numerous subtle ways in which semantic and sonic aspects of the language-stream may interact in a work of art. I wish to give a schematic outline of these here, not because I do not consider these things to be interesting, but because I have to draw the limits of what I write about at some point or I would be writing for ever!

First of all we should note that individual human languages, dialects, accents, cultural styles (for example, those indicative of class), special cultural forms (the archaic in religious observances, poetic forms, exultatory and ecstatic language), all have particular sonic aspects as well as cultural reference. Such features may be brought together and organised (for example, on tape) in terms of their (cultural) landscape properties, in terms of some kind of supra-linguistic scheme of reference or purely for their sonic properties (or of course all three or any degree or combination of these three, simultaneously).

The degree to which we recognise the semantic content of language will also alter the focus of our perception upon the language stream. Heard in 'normal' contexts, our native language will appear heavily semantic. A language which we know, but not well, will be heard in both semantic and timbral focus, whilst a language which we cannot speak or understand at all will be a largely timbral experience although, of course, mouth symbols and paralinguistic aspects of utterance may have some semantic impact upon us.

In terms of written text, we may accept extensions of vocabulary and even grammar as semantic:

> Spat — he mat and tried & trickered on the step and oostepped and peppered it a bit with long mouth sizzle reaching for the thirsts of Azmec Parterial alk-lips to mox and bramajambi babac up the Moon Citlapol — settle la tettle la pottle, la lune — Some kind of — Bong!
> (Jack Kerouac Old Angel Midnight quoted in Kostelanetz 1980: 18–19)

Mike walked in on the: attense of Chjazzus as they sittith softily sipping sweet okaykes H-flowered purrhushing 'eir goofhearty offan-on-beats, holding moisturize'-palmy sticks clad in clamp dresses of tissue d'arab, drinks in actionem fellandi promoting protolingamations e state of nascendi; completimented go!scene of hifibrow'n [...]
(Hans G. Helms Fa:m' Aniesgwow *quoted in Kostelanetz 1980: 20–21*)

Using standard conventions of grammar we may invent entirely new words which however appear to have quite clear semantic connotations:

'Twas brillig and the slithy toves
Did gyre and gimble in the wabe:
All mimsy were the borogoves
And the mome raths outgrabe."
(Lewis Carroll, Jabberwocky (1872) (Carroll 1994: 28))

Although almost half the words in this text are imaginary, it is quite clear from the context that *brillig* is a time of day,[2] a season or special occasion and that *toves* are some kind of creature. *Slithy* is interestingly constructed out of mouth symbols (relatable to both *slimy* and *slither*) whilst *gyre* we might relate semantically to the word *gyrate*.

In the computer-generated mock-Latin quotation quoted in Chapter 9, there are almost no real words but a non-speaker will accept the 'Latinness' of this text as the frequency of occurrence of certain phonemes and their typical ordering is reminiscent of Latin. In the poem of Hugo Ball quoted at the beginning of the previous chapter, although no known natural language is being used, we accept the utterance as linguistic because phonemes are organised into polysyllables and their statistical distribution has some similarities with typical languages. In the Schwitters *Ursonata*, however, the typical statistical distribution of phonemes in language is contradicted. We are beginning to enter into pure sonic art. Finally, the 'rdnstrklmndrnchtkrissvrichk!' utterance of lettrism severs our link with the phoneme and we approach the pure percussive sound-object 'tjak' of the rhythmic Ketchac monkey-chant of Bali.

Paralanguage of pitch and stress

The pitch and loudness of a natural speech act tend to remain quite close to a mean value. Around this value both pitch and loudness are articulated. Some of these articulations are conventional and contribute or qualify the meaning of the linguistic stream. In certain languages (such as Chinese) the perception of pitch is integral to the recognition of a particular phoneme. A phoneme otherwise having the same timbral characteristic will have a

---

[2] The Editor begged to differ, having believed all his life it was a state of the weather (*Ed.*).

different meaning according to whether it is spoken in a low, medium or high tessitura or with a rising pitch contour or a falling pitch contour. Pitch characteristics which are integral to the recognition of phonemes are known as *tonemes*. Pitch is also used in a less specific way to indicate the end of sentences (usually rising in French but falling in English), to indicate questions (rising at the end of the sentence in English) and so on.

Stress, which may be articulated by loudness difference or pitch difference, is also used as a conventional aspect of the language stream. Thus, in English, four levels of stress may be recognised: primary (1), secondary (2), tertiary (3), weak (4). For example: *hot food* (2, 1); *hotter* (1, 4); *hotel* (3, 1); *contents* (1, 3); *operate* (1, 4, 3); *operation* (1, 4, 3, 4). Stress is also distributed in a semantically significant way within phrases. Compare the difference in meaning of *don't do that* with the stress patterns (1, 4, 4), (2, 1, 4), (2, 4, 1), (4, 1, 2) or (4, 4, 1).

Such aspects of conventional paralinguistic pitch and stress cannot be completely divorced from even conventional musical practice. Thus, for example, classical Chinese word-setting must concern itself with the level or inflection of the tonemes. Certain languages tend to place the principal stress on the first syllable (and not on the second). Musically we might say that the language-stream lacks an anacrusis. This is most true of Finnish and Hungarian and the characteristic stress pattern of Hungarian carries through the folk music into the work of Bartok (the characteristic falling leap with the stress on the first note).

Beyond these features we may be able to distinguish certain overall characteristics of pitch (or stress) which are deviant from the normal mean value. The general range may be over-high or over-low or the range through which pitch is articulated may be over-wide. This may be a conventional aspect of accent as in the perceived 'sing-song' of Welsh English. Beyond a certain limit, however, an unusual tessitura or range of pitch-articulation will have more universal gestural significance. For example, the expression of anger is usually associated with high pitch and loudness, whilst low pitch, quietness (and possibly breathiness and smoothing of the air flow) may be associated with intimacy.

The melodic implications of intonation patterns may, in fact, be quite sophisticated. Istvan Anhalt (1984: 159) cites Fonagy and Magdics (1963) as having described in musical notation "what they perceive to be the melodic patterns of certain emotions or emotional attitudes: joy, tenderness, longing, coquetry, surprise, fear etc.". Even the simple question-pitch-inflection is, in fact, much more complicated and Kingdon (1958) has distinguished between "general, particular, alternative, asking for repetition, interrogative repetition, insistent and quizzical" intonation patterns for questions (cited in Anhalt 1984: 159).

Such paralinguistic aspects of pitch and stress have a bearing on the construction of vocal melody (and thence on melody in general). Thus, where a melodic line proceeds by wide leaps, particularly where this is outside a simple harmonic field, such as an arpeggio, and/or is associated with a freer speech-type of rhythmic articulation, we are likely to make the paralinguistic interpretation that the utterer is agitated, frightened or disturbed, or at least over-emphatically expressive (the 'Schoenberg effect').

The paralinguistic implications of pitch, tessitura and motion have clearly always had a strong influence on the practice of singing (consider for example Japanese *joruri* singing for the Bunraku puppet theatre, the late sixteenth century invention of recitative in Western Europe, etc.). Even where pitch is compositionally ordained to follow the most rigorous instrumentally conceived pitch-lattice logic, interpretation tends to input the paralinguistic gestures in the form of small articulations of pitch and stress. Schoenberg further extended these connections by his development of *Sprechstimme*. A schematic analysis of pitch usage (and its combination with timbral morphology) is indicated in Figure 14.5.

The use of pitch in any vocal utterance which is not clearly conventional language or conventional pitch-lattice music needs careful consideration. Curtay, in his lettrist compositions, specifies pitch in only the four (linguistically significant) registers, low, medium, high and very high, as he wishes to avoid any over-determination of the events by the logics of conventional music. I would consider this a much too simple view as may be evident from the analysis above. There is, however, a technical difficulty in integrating clearly-pitched material into a sonic structure which has previously contained no (stable) pitches; steady-state pitches tend to 'stick out like a sore thumb', producing a marked discontinuity in our perception unless they are introduced with great subtlety. It is clear that there are all sorts of degrees of balance between a sonic art fundamentally rooted in the relationships of fixed pitches (to which timbral characteristics are subservient) and a sonic art based on the sophisticated control of timbral possibilities (to which pitch characteristics are subservient). Although we may achieve transformations of structural organisation away from one pole and towards the other within a single sonic composition, it is important to be aware where the perceptual focus lies. This seems to be a problem both for conventional musicians (for example, in assessing timbrally articulated works based on a relatively fixed harmonic field) and for text-sound-artists anxious to abandon linguistic reference.

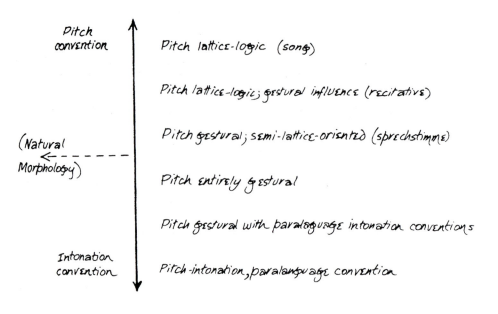

Pitch convention

Pitch lattice-logic (song)

Pitch lattice-logic; gestural influence (recitative)

Pitch gestural; semi-lattice-oriented (sprechstimme)

(Natural Morphology)

Pitch entirely gestural

Pitch gestural with paralanguage intonation conventions

Intonation convention

Pitch-intonation, paralanguage convention

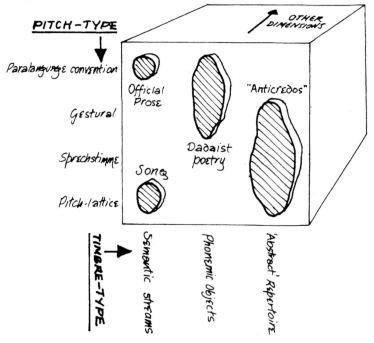

Figure 14.5   A schematic analysis of vocal pitch-usage.

Paralanguage and rhythm

A detailed discussion of the nature and implications of rhythmic organisation is outside the scope of this book. Just as with pitch and stress, the language stream has a characteristic average tempo and rhythm. We may guess that the typical tempo is in some way related to the speed of our ability to decode the signals and thence to our typical metabolic rate (it would appear that small birds have a higher metabolic rate, judging by the speed of articulation of their utterances which for us may congeal into timbral entities). Variations of tempo around this may be indicative of physiological state or mental attitude, or of cultural factors such as in the slow tempo of English Forest of Dean and American Alabama accents.

Each rhythm may be described as regularly irregular. In a normal speech-stream all syllables fall within a small range of possible durations. Within this range they vary according to conventional stress patterns, idiosyncratic or special semantic use of sustain-stress, or, within limits, randomly.

The tempo and rhythm of speech is undoubtedly one of the archetypal models for our physiological-intellectual interpretation of the meaning of rhythm, particularly irregular rhythm. It differs from the typical bipedal (or more generally bilateral, as with, for example, the heart) physiological rhythms of the body, in that it has no underlying regular pulse, but only an average rate of flow. Rhythmic fluctuations beyond a certain point (just as with extreme slow or fast tempi with bipedal-type rhythms) go beyond the scope of conventional paralinguistic interpretations and may be 'understood' in terms of more universal (and possibly extremal) gestural criteria (for example, agitation, terror, melancholy).

A sonic art perspective, however, brings a more precise conception of timing into play. Through performance practice deriving from music, or through computer control, we can stretch and alter the rhythmic characteristics of the language-stream so that they become, for example, unnaturally regular, unnaturally distributed in sustain-stress pattern, unnaturally fast or slow, unnaturally grouped in regular or evolving patterns and so on. In this way the perception of rhythm as an aspect of paralanguage can be extended or destroyed.

Paralanguage and morphology

As we have described previously, it is possible to use paralinguistic indicators to differentiate regional accent, status, idiolect and even the attitude of the speaker. Our interpretations are usually based upon the observation of a field of timbral types and morphologies and our ability to relate these to a known (typical) field. From a sonic art point of view we may be interested in working with any of these aspects of the language stream. For example we may collect, through recording, materials spoken by human voices with particular striking idiosyncratic characteristics. This would be akin to Fellini's technique of selecting his actors from amongst the general public in markets etc. for the particular idiosyncratic features of their faces or general appearance. With computer synthesis we may, in fact, construct a voice having a particular 'voice set' and control (e.g. gradually transform) these qualities, such that gender, age, health-image or body-image (all aspects of 'universal landscape') change. Alternatively, from a narrower linguistic viewpoint we might change status, regional origin or role (for example, sergeant major parade-ground voice-set, newspaper vendor voice-set).

We might also control the (semi-involuntary) physiological indicators known as 'vocal characterisers'[3] and 'vocal qualities'[4] on a general or moment-to-moment basis; vocal qualities such as pitch range, control and rhythmic smoothness (discussed previously), vocal hoarseness, general lip-openness, over- and under-voicing, slight or heavy breathiness, forceful or relaxed articulation control or thin or full resonance. As our landscape- and utterance-based interpretation of these para-linguistic features relates holistically to multi-dimensional fields and their articulation, the independent control over each aspect of the language stream which might be possible using computer technology combined with the electronic paralanguage of reverberation, echo, phasing, double-tracking, social-landscape distancing and yet-to-be-discovered techniques, opens up a truly mind-bending plethora of aesthetic possibilities.

---

[3] For example, laughing, giggling, snickering, crying, whimpering, sobbing, yelling, muffled whispering, muttering, moaning, groaning, whining, breaking, belching, yawning.

[4] From which we might deduce attitude; for example, anger, dominance, submission, intimacy, secrecy.

Chapter 15

THE GROUP

Personality, society

Once we begin to consider two or more utterances occurring in the same acoustic space, we enter into the realm of human interaction, whether it be viewed as 'theatre' (the projection of imaginary personas by actors) or the overhearing of real or imaginary situations (as might be the case in a tape composition). At this point landscape and utterance begin to blend. As we are dealing with the landscape of human society, we begin to pass over into the realm of theatre and a full consideration of all the implications of theatrical arts is beyond the scope of this book. I will merely attempt to give some flavour of the countless ramifications this connection has for sonic art. For anyone wishing to pursue this aspect further I would highly recommend the book *Alternative Voices* by Istvan Anhalt (1984). To some extent an utterance, particularly one which we can relate, no matter how distantly, to the language stream, projects the whole personality (or assumed persona) of the utterer which cannot be entirely understood in isolation from its social context. We may often infer from it a whole web of social situations, assumptions, meanings, attitudes, observances etc. which are not contained in the semantic content of the stream (if any) but implicit, pre-supposed or pointed to by it. The utterance implies the 'other' or 'them' or even implicates the listener as 'you' or 'them'. In sonic art we have the possibility of restructuring any aspect of these pointers.

In the monodic utterance, we may observe breaking, self-correction, incompletion, repetition, distortion of various kinds, filled pauses, retraced false-starts, stuttering, suppression, sudden interruptions, non-verbal expressives or the gradual disintegration of language itself. From our apprehension of the events we may relate them to internal soliloquy, glossolalic ecstasy, childhood pre- and early linguistic sound-play, monomania etc.. Or from the particular combination of semantics and paralanguage we may construct a social role or context; the monologue of the scientific address, the advertising hook line, the oratory of politics or demagoguery.

Individual interaction

Such contextual implications are focused and/or clarified in the communicative interaction of utterances. It is possible, even without the aid of semantic content to develop a subtle structure of social interaction, roles, power play, sexual encounters, group cohesion or anarchy. Ligeti's work *Nouvelles Aventures*, for three solo voices and small instrumental ensemble, does exactly this. Ligeti says of the piece —

> *All human affects, ritualised through forms of social intercourse, such as agreement and dissension, dominance and submission, sincerity and lie, arrogance, disobedience, the subtlest nuances of irony hidden behind a seeming consent, similarly high esteem that is concealed behind seeming disdain — all these, and still many more, can be exactly expressed through an a-semantic emotive artificial speech.*
>
> *Such a text should not be expected to define precisely any conceptual relationships, but ought to portray directly human emotions and modes of comportment in a way that despite the conceptual meaninglessness of the text, scenic instances [Momente] and actions could be perceived as being meaningful.*
>
> *An imaginary language, which makes human feelings and comportment communicable, must also be suitable for a work for the theatre, presuming that one regards the theatre as a pedestal for individual and social modes of comportment, as an essence [Konzentrat] of communication (and also that of isolation).*
>
> *The point of departure for the composition was a conceptualisation of relationships between affective modes of comportments, not an abstract structural plan. [...]*
>
> *It seems significant to me that there is no 'deeper meaning' hidden beyond the performed events. Despite the seeming absurdity and enigmatic character, the protagonists and the emotional and social situations are directly intelligible, and transparent. We do not find out what the story is about — and in a deeper sense there is, of course, no story, yet we quite precisely find out how the persons behaved and in what relationship towards each other they stand. (Ligeti quoted in Anhalt 1984: 91–2)[1]*

Clearly, percepts such as agreement, disagreement, dominance, submissiveness, solidarity, anarchy are aspects of the social landscape. Furthermore, attributes such as sincerity, lying, persistence or hesitation are more easily perceivable as such in a context in which utterances are exchanged. We may even make very fine distinctions in this context. For example, the performing together of actions which turn out to be too difficult (see the hocket in the Ligeti work) imply a desire for solidarity. All these features of the social landscape may be implied merely through the subtle control of paralinguistic signs and the relative similarity/ dissimilarity, coordination/non-coordination, loudness etc. of the individual utterances.

---

[1] Anhalt is here quoting from two articles originally in German. The English translation is presumably his (*Ed.*).

Back-tracking slightly we may regard this as a somewhat more refined articulation of what can already be observed in the communication of higher animals. There is an (understandable) fear of anthropomorphism in zoological studies which tends to veil the nature of communications in a kind of neutralist vocabulary. Translating from the various studies that have been done, we can discover a wide range of pre-semantic messages; Figure 15.1 illustrates some of these (many of which can, of course, be combined). With semantics human beings have expanded many of these areas into informal (courtship) and formal (political contest) rituals.

Within such landscapes of communication, we may observe or establish particular roles for the individual utterers ('initiator of actions', 'reinforcer of cohesion', 'disruptive influence' etc.) such roles may change, extend or develop. As all these complex interactions are, however, taking place in the field of sonic articulation, we can imagine extending this concept of role behaviour to the articulation of complex abstract sonic objects, thus developing an articulate sphere of musical discourse based on the logic of the landscape of utterance interaction but in which no utterers are present. From here we may go on to imagine landscapes in which both utterers and non-utterers appear to adopt roles relative to one another and communicate (in a sense the orchestra in many operas may be thought of as having a role, being a character within the ongoing drama). We may also imagine an interface between the natural morphology of sound-objects and the landscape of social utterance interaction (with or without utterers, or even recognisable sources).

A particular aspect of social interaction is, in fact, the failure or non-existence of communication. a sense of non-communicating co-existence can be enhanced in the virtual space of loudspeakers by the use of location cues (spatial position, reverberation etc.) and other devices to suggest the co-existence of two separate 'worlds'. Again, these concepts can be generalised to non-utterer, non-concrete situations; a sense of separate and non-interacting sonic streams may be established and then, for example, negated by the subsequent interaction of the materials. Such social 'readings' are particularly likely to affect our aesthetic perception where we use utterances in the sonic landscape.

Chorusing, co-ordination and mass

Amongst the various types of animal interaction discussed above, there is one particularly interesting group which I have labelled 'US'. These are signals made in a collective but uncoordinated manner by various members of the group which seem to have the function of binding the group together. They are not individual expressions of relationship or mutuality between

I-YOU

Neutral or Mutuality

Here I am, all is well
Here is parent; Here is child
Here is sibling

Sexuality

Solicitation
Come-on
Push-off

Dominance-Submission

Greeting a superior
Greeting a subordinate
Dominance threat
Appeasing a superior
Attack-call
Appeasement when attacked

I-THEM

Neutral or Antipathetic

I'm here. Who's that approaching?
We don't want any strangers around here!
Threat
Who's that over there in the distance?

I-US-THEM

Warning, minor danger from them
Warning, major danger from them
Help! minor danger from them
Help!! major danger from them

I-US

Mutual

Greetings
Help!
Danger!
Look at this!

Dominance

Follow me
Do as I indicate

US

Here we are together
This is our territory
Isn't this exciting!
Absolutely amazing!!

US-THEM

This is our territory, not yours!

Figure 15.1 Some pre-semantic messages of higher animals rendered in 'human'.

individual creatures, nor are they signals to the group about situation or circumstances, external threat or internal disobedience. Instead, they perform a quasi-ritualistic function. They express solidarity and may at the same time express a general group mood (e.g. excitement).

This solidarity chorusing behaviour can be observed in many species, from crickets and frogs to the group howl of wolves. A similar comment can be made about some of the one-to-one communications between individuals of equal status. As the call of any particular individual in these situations is, we might say, syntactically-semantically neutral (it does not refer to any specific or immediate cause of interest or anxiety in the environment or within the individual's 'psyche') it may become the element of a group syntax or semantics. In this way group calls which, as far as we can tell, have the gross function of affirming the solidarity (or even mere similarity) of the group may develop a degree of internal structure and co-ordination.

Thus, choruses of the spring peeper frog (*hyla crucifer*) have a characteristic structure with each chorus arising in the same manner time after time.

> *Typically [...] three frogs sing as a group and a large chorus seems to be nothing more than a number of these trios calling from the same breeding site. Furthermore, each of these trios develops in the same manner. The call is initiated by a single individual sounding the note of A for a varying number of times. After a brief rest, if he does not have an answer, he gives a trill. This trill apparently acts as a stimulus since it usually results in another individual starting to call on the note G#. When this happens the two individuals continue giving their respective notes — A, G#, A, G# etc. — for an indefinite number of times. If a third individual does not start calling, they stop their alternating calls, rest, and one of them — usually (and perhaps invariably) the one that is calling G# — gives the trill. At the sound of the trill, the third individual of the trio starts giving his call which is B. Thereafter, the three continue to call, each giving its respective note in the order indicated, A, G#, B, for an indefinite number of times.*
> (Goin, (orig. 1949) quoted in Bogert 1960: 209)

It is interesting to note that this 'group syntax' has already evolved in such a lowly creature. Furthermore, the normal functionalist approach to the explanation of all animal communications (for example, in terms of sexual bonding, status etc.) are difficult to apply when three individuals are involved! The bou-bou shrikes of East Africa —

> *[...] can sing in duet with such a rapid reaction time that unless an observer is actually standing between the two birds it is impossible to recognise that more than one bird is singing. [...] a pair of birds can elaborate a whole repertoire of duet patterns by which they can recognise one another in dense undergrowth and be distinguished from other pairs in the neighbourhood. In this species either sex can start or finish and either bird can sing the whole pattern alone in the absence of the partner. When the partner returns, the pair can either sing*

Figure 15.2   Examples of duet patterns of various African bou-bou shrikes where X and Y represent the two birds in the pair (after Thorpe and North (1965)).

> *in perfect unison or sing antiphonally again. Trio singing has also been observed [...]* (Hooker 1968: 333–334) (See Figure 15.2[2]).

Here, then, whatever the function or 'meaning' of the song, its syntax can be articulated by two or three creatures acting 'in concert'. In the music-making of groups of humans, this mutual solidarity function is implicit. It may be so distanced (within the structure of a larger society) that it is not immediately perceived as a function of the musical activity by the participants. Alternatively, the musical act may function specifically in that role (ritual function of music in group ceremonies). Because, however, many more levels of distancing are involved in human social communication and interaction, we may represent within the convention of group music-making the concept of disorder and strife as well as various sophistically-differentiated conceptions of social cohesion.

Renaissance imitative vocal polyphony, for example, presents a particular archetype of the relationship between the individual and the

---

[2] After Thorpe and North, 1965 quoted in Hooker 1968: 334.

group in the way in which the similar, but different, vocal lines are harmonically co-ordinated. The sense of balance and equality within harmony is quite distinct in its symbolic representation of the group from Bach's *Kyrie* in the *Mass in B minor*. Here a sense of co-ordination of utterance and planned development towards a final resolution is articulated over a framework of highly affective dissonance. The social metaphor is quite different.

And both of these differ quite markedly from choral works in which the voices are rhythmically (and perhaps harmonically) co-ordinated in their utterance, so we perceive only the group, or in which such groups are set off in antiphonal relationship to each other. The organisation of the group may point to specific group roles or functions within society, such as the simulated collective meditation by a group of individuals in Stockhausen's *Stimmung* or the quasi-religious action by a large group suggested in the *Introitus* of Ligeti's *Requiem*.

At the other extreme, particular types of rhythmic disco-ordination may present the group as a 'sea of humanity', a multitude or mob being manipulated or out of control. Even this social image has subtle ramifications. In his book, Anhalt (1984) gives some interesting insights into this. Thus, in the third movement of Lutoslawski's *Trois Poèmes d'Henri Michaux*, the composer uses a 'fan' effect where the chorus moves from rhythmic synchronisation to a swarm effect gradually. Anhalt describes this as "an allusion to the individual will, which seems to prevail over that of the collective [...]" (Anhalt 1984: 137). In the second movement, however, we experience 'raw force', 'aggression', 'mob behaviour', the shouts of a crowd, either semi-concerted or synchronised like the synchrony and asynchrony of the crowd cries at a great fight. Alternatively:

> The 'Kyrie' of Ligeti's Requiem *is a powerful showing of a mass of human beings, swirling and twisting in so many vocal currents, adding up to a turbulent sea of voices in which the identity of an individual is painfully and irrevocably submerged on account of the number of concurrently used similar melodic designs and overlapping registers. The canonic structures here have a 'blind leading the blind' character, conveying the cumulative affect of a hopeless predicament for the whole mass; [...]*
> (Anhalt 1984: 200[3])

With electro-acoustic projection of vocal sounds (microphones to loudspeakers), it is possible to establish imaginary images of the group. Thus, in *Vox-I*, one hears first of all a single undifferentiated timbre-stream; through gradual processes of division one begins to separate off the

---

[3] 'Affect' *sic* in last sentence of quote (*Ed.*).

'environment' from the 'utterance' and then, within the utterance, two and then four beings gradually emerge. Through various combinations of stream mixing and spatial motion these four beings may recombine or dissociate. Towards the end of the piece the four beings sing in unison (as opposed to being combined into a single-stream utterance) and the landscape itself takes on the articulation of speech.

Moving on to more sophisticated levels of social distancing and human group behaviour, the situation becomes increasingly complex and ramified and may include within itself subsidiary forms of group behaviour, such as music-making in religious observances, rallies or art events. Social landscape and utterance become intertwined in a multi-level sonic reality. We may begin to think of parody, incompetent performance, stylistic transformation and countless other levels of social signification. In universal sonic art freed of narrow preconceptions concerning the boundaries of artistic discourse, we may focus or defocus, manipulate, confuse or extend any or all of these levels of perception.

Coda

Chapter 16

BEYOND THE INSTRUMENT: SOUND-MODELS

The universal instrument

As stated at the beginning of this book, the theories and speculations it contains have been prompted by the development of the computer and its application to the field of music. As in all other fields, the computer can change our entire perspective on the way we do things because it is not a machine designed for a specific task but a tool which may be fashioned to fulfil any task which we can clearly specify. It is a metamachine. In particular, it offers the possibility of being a universal sonic instrument, a device with which we can model and produce any conceivable sound-object or organisation of sounds.

The limitations on its potential are partly due to our lack of acoustic understanding but primarily to our perceptual and aesthetic preconceptions about the nature of sonic art and its instruments. At its most elementary level these limitations could be seen in the small, digital packages available for music-making in the early 1980s. Even the fairly versatile Fairlight CMI had built into it the assumptions of instrumental fixity ('an instrument is a source of fixed timbre'), instrumental streaming (music is made up of streams of fixed timbre) and intervallic uniformity in scale structures. On smaller machines the software tended to make so many assumptions about what constituted a 'musical' sound-object that it was often easier to generate interesting sounds through 'misusing' the technology (for example, through aliasing effects).

There is, however, a deeper level at which most of the early 1980s digital technology was crucially limited. Its definition of an 'instrument' did not correspond with our perceptual reality. As listeners in the real world we do not tend to respond to each individual sound-object as an intrinsic entity and build up a Fourier analytic picture of it. We relate sound-objects to models and we may group many different sound-objects as examples of a particular model. Thus, for example, the spectrum (and its evolution) of a bass piano note is noticeably different from that of a high piano note — as sound-objects they are remarkably different yet we relate both of them to the sound-model 'piano' quite directly. The notion of sound-model corresponds very closely to the notion of intrinsic morphology put forward in earlier chapters.

The problem with both typical additive synthesis and FM synthesis applications is that they assume the sound-model is at the same level as the sound-object. Hence, once a particular sound-object has been built up by these techniques it can be reproduced at all levels of pitch and intensity to generate the percept of an instrument. In this sense, the technology is deeply influenced by the ideology of music springing from Western notation where timbre has been regarded as a secondary and fixed quality over which pitch and duration are articulated. Although, of course, we must have a physical understanding and representation of any sound in Fourier analytic terms to be able to achieve synthesis, this does not correspond directly to our perceptual processes.

From instruments to sound-models

The distinction between object and model may be understood more easily when we move into the field of sound-sources possessing a repertoire, such as the human voice. In this case the definition of one particular additive synthesis or FM spectral type is obviously totally useless (except, of course, if we wish to specify a different such type for every single vocal event in the stream). What we can, however, specify are various invariants which occur in the sound-source, for example, a description of the particular placing and spread of the formants of a particular voice and also typical articulation structures (the vocal attack-time, transition phenomena between formants and so on) and the general spectral typology (e.g. the shape of the individual glottal impulse).

All this, in fact, applies to standard musical instruments. As a simple example, it is already well-known that the spectral richness of a piano tone decreases with increasing frequency. This is a particularly simple law, but we might also specify the ways in which spectral envelope, pitch, jitter and amplitude envelope and fluctuations are correlated during various bowing actions.

This specification of (near-) invariants over a field of possible sounds is what I mean by a sound-model. It is a more general notion than the typical limited view suggested by the concept of 'musical instrument'. For example, we might model the rules which govern the relationship between spectral change, pitch change and loudness change in a metal sheet which is being flexed. Together with other invariants this will effectively specify the intrinsic morphology of the sound-model and the set of rules will govern the behaviour of the sound-model when we articulate it through some input device (which might be part of a program or a direct physiological-intellectual input; see below).

With the computer as sound-source, however, we are not confined to basing our sound-models on existing physical objects or systems. We may build a model of a technologically (or even physically) impossible object. We might specify the characteristics of the voice of an imaginary creature. Once, however, the sound-model is specified, we are free to change the invariants of its behaviour. We may transform it into an entirely different sound-model.

The crucial difference between building sound-models and building sound-objects is that the former preserves a clear and perceptually relevant distinction between intrinsic and imposed morphology. If we articulate the object within the rules specifying its invariants, we perceive an imposed articulation of the sound-model. If, however, we proceed with some process which changes those invariants, then we actually perceive the sound-model itself to change. The intrinsic morphology changes, the perceived source becomes 'something else'. This is crucial to our understanding of the perception of typical analogue synthesiser sounds. Largely because instrument-definitions on such synthesisers are based on sound-objects and not on sound-models, then no matter how we transform the sound-material, we tend to perceive it as coming from a synthesiser. It was not just a lack of detailing in the modelling of individual spectra in the voltage control synthesiser that made its sound-world characteristically 'synthesiser' but the more general lack of structuring in relation to perceptual sound-models. Some of these concerns may be illustrated with reference to the digital synthesis language *Chant*. Here the language makes a broad specification of the (semi-) invariants of the sound-model 'human voice', for example, the field of formant bands and their characteristics, typical values of vibrato, vibrato variations, jitter and so on. Composition with this language may be multi-levelled. At a gross level we may specify merely pitch, loudness, vowel type (*a*, *e* etc.), variations in type of vibrato, and so on. At a deeper level we may specify particular modifications of the formant bands (for example, to characterise a particular idiolect) with which we then compose. At yet another level we may wish to impose transformations on the formant bandwidths and the attack structures of individual events. This begins to interfere with the invariants and rules which govern the sound-model 'human voice' and by doing so we can generate sounds of bells, drums and so on. Defining classes of sound-objects at the level of sound-models, therefore, has a direct relationship with our perceptual categorisation of sound-events. Change the invariants and rules and one changes the perceived model.

At the time of writing (1983), *Chant* does not model most of the consonants. The modelling of such structures of articulation will be a key development in the evolution of the digital computer as a powerful tool for sonic art. Moreover, it should lead on to developing a modelling system for natural processes themselves. Perhaps some rigour may be brought to this through insights and mathematical techniques from differential topology. This would give a sound theoretical basis to the concept of natural morphology discussed in this book and allow us to have handles on the evolution of a sound process that corresponds to the critical parameters of the flow.

Given such powerful modelling systems, we may bring an imposed morphology to bear upon the sound-models through some kind of real-time or programmed input. The imposed fluctuations may then be made to articulate what remains a 'solid' (relatively stable mass) object (by changing the overall pitch level, loudness, loudness envelope, vibrato, vibrato width, vibrato steadiness, tremolo width and steadiness, jitter, etc. within certain limits) to 'liquefy' that object or a stream of objects (by articulating the spectral envelope and pitch contour, possibly in relation to one another, the typical event duration and density, the spread of pitch and so on), or merely to interact with its 'gaseous flow'. In the latter case I am not thinking of simple vocoder-type processes but some way of mapping bodily or vocal gestures into the flow properties of a sound (such as speed, density, turbulence etc.).

Imitation, transformation

In computer modelling there is a trade-off between flexibility and speed. If we are prepared to work within the constraints of a particular sound-model, we can generate results fairly quickly. Once, however, we decide to stretch or modify the basic models, we need to input much more information to the system and its musical productivity slows down. Another approach to the problem might be to begin with an existing real-world sound-object (such as the sound of our own voice) which we are able to experiment with and refine in real time before making a recording. Then, using powerful tools of analysis (particularly linear predictive coding or phase vocoder techniques), we may extract the perceptually distinct features of the recorded sound-object. Thus the package of analysis and resynthesis programs available at Stanford and IRCAM from the late 1970s (of which Andy Moorer was one of the main authors) made it possible not only to achieve this analysis but then to manipulate the parameters individually and to cross-synthesise. For example, once the pitch-information of a voice has been separated from the formant information it is possible to reconstitute the voice using different pitch information (or different formant information). Alternatively the pitch and/or formant information may be stretched or compressed in time. In fact, the dilating of time structure of complex sonic events such as occur in the speech stream or in 'fluid' sound-objects, gives us access to the detailed behaviour of sonic processes; a kind of sonic magnification. Using the programming power of the computer we may then reconstitute these objects with entirely different time-flow characteristics.

Finally, we may transfer the formant characteristics of one source onto another, the technique of cross-synthesis. For example, imposing the formant characteristics of a speech stream upon a bubbling fluid stream creates the perceptual model of a voice containing a stream. Alternatively, imposing the formant characteristics of the fluid stream upon the voice generates the sound-model of a stream in which a voice is contained. We might now perhaps take a voice generated by *Chant* which changes into a drum and then cross-synthesise this with the sound of a crowd. And, of course, the sources for cross-synthesis may themselves be imaginary sound-models.

Operational fields

At a larger-scale level the computer may allow us to analyse the detailed structure of large-scale events such as the behaviour of flocks of birds during an 'alarum', the detailed structure of semi-synchronous crowd chants, the textural structure of poured pebbles and so on. With or without this analysis, we can control in great detail the parameters of texture, from the standard harmonic and motivic field to timbral field, pitch-motion-type field etc. and subtle changes of all of these.

More significantly, however, we may group particular parameters and types of articulation into fields governed by rules. These *operational fields* may themselves be articulated through other inputs (physiological-intellectual performance behaviour or higher level rules) given by the composer. This grouping must be a very generalised facility so that the sonic artist can choose his field of focus upon the sound-materials. This might be in terms of harmonic fields, timbral fields, articulation types, paralinguistic fields, idiolectic features, spatial cues, linguistic grammaticality, natural morphological properties, sonic role-plays etc.. Only at this stage will the computer become a truly generalised tool for sonic art.

Human interfacing

The other crucial feature in the application of digital technology to sonic art is the development of sophisticated hardware and software tools to permit human physiological-intellectual performance behaviour to be transmitted as imposed morphology to the sound-models existing within the computer. This connects directly with the whole area of the evolution of musical instruments in their more conventional sense. We may anticipate in the not-too-distant future the development of a whole generation of digital sound-producing devices which are, to a greater or lesser extent, analogous with existing musical instruments (in fact some are already here). The keyboard synthesiser has been with us for a long time but now we are beginning to see the emergence of blown and bowed synthesisers which present themselves to the performer as analogues of conventional mechanical instruments but in which the sound-production is entirely electronic. The immediate advantage of this development is that we may, in fact, select the timbre that the instrument produces by varying the program. More significantly, perhaps, we may alter the way in which our various articulations of the string, air column etc. appear as articulations of the sound.

The concept of the transfer of parameters was already well-developed in the field of live electronics using analogue synthesisers. Thus, the arm motion speed, breath flow or, more typically, the resultant loudness variation, pitch variation and so on, could be monitored by various electronic devices (such as envelope followers, pitch-to-voltage converters etc.) generating a voltage proportional in some way to the magnitude of the input. The resultant voltages could then however be used to control any desired feature of the resulting sound. Amplitude might control pitch and pitch control amplitude. Both might control the parameters of a second instrument or more complex features of an evolving electronic sound-stream.

The analytic power of the computer at least potentially gives us the ability to monitor in several simultaneous dimensions the subtle details of performance behaviour. A sufficiently intelligent and fast machine should be able to sense parameters of breath flow, formant structure, glottal, tongue and lip vibrations, noise turbulence type and so on, separating these out so that the information from each can be applied to the control of different parameters of a sound-event. This sound-event may, of course, have nothing whatever in common with the characteristics of behaviour which generate the control information. Through practice, just as with the conventional instrument, we can imagine the performer developing a sophisticated co-ordination between his or her performance skills and the sonic output.

The design of sophisticated inputs has been one of the major weaknesses of the digital instrument revolution but with the generality of the computer there seems no reason why a whole range of multi-dimensionally sensitive input devices should not be developed. These might involve keyboards which were sensitive not only to which key was pressed but also to finger velocity and/or pressure and to lateral motion of the fingers (as in the analogue Buchla synthesisers) and these might be made much more interesting than the more common approaches have been, by adding devices allowing continuous contraction or expansion of the average interval size, the warping of intervallic uniformity (perhaps in a pre-programmed fashion), spectral change with register, linking attack velocity to, for example, timbral stability and duration rather than to loudness and so on. Bowed interfaces would be sensitive not only to pressure but also to speed of bowing, the width of bow to touch the string, the sul tasto-sul ponticello dimension, the temporal fluctuation of these things and so on. Even quadrapan and pedal devices might be redesigned. We might, for example, imagine a console with two quadrapan units which were also capable of moving in the up-down direction and two foot pedals which could be moved not only up and down but also from side to side and backwards-forwards. We might even use totally novel ways of inputting physiological-intellectual information, such as the monitoring of the many dimensions of facial gesture.

What, however, is clear above all else is that the internal architecture of sounds becomes both analytically and conceptually accessible and hence available for more or less precisely defined composition and, as our ability to monitor the subtleties of human intellectual-physiological gesture and transfer them onto sound-materials increases, our notion of what 'music' is must become much more generalised. It must embrace and systematically investigate areas that have traditionally been regarded as the legitimate property of psycho-acousticians, phoneticians, poets and sound-poets, of nature recordists and audio-zoologists, of naturalistic and 'effects'-based film-sound engineering and much more. Musicians will concern themselves with the affective and systematic ordering of timbre structure, sonic gesture, sound-landscape, the subtleties of psycho-linguistic and psycho-social cues and many other dimensions of the sound-universe, alongside the more traditional parameters of pitch and duration. The era of a new and more universal sonic art is only just beginning.

Postscript

It is clear that we are about to see a radical change in the nature of our civilisation. The impact of the computer, the universal metamachine, could, in a short time, destroy the whole basis for the work-ethic upon which most of our present-day materialist culture is built. We can expect a rough ride into this new world from the guardians of social orders which are no longer relevant but when we finally arrive we may at last find the arts playing a central role in the lives of the community in general, provided, that is, we do not manage to commit geno-suicide in the meantime.

The possibilities opened up for musical (and all other types of art) exploration are truly staggering. It is as if a magical dream has come true. We have the potential to make real any sound-event we can imagine. What will prevent us from getting to grips with this new situation is primarily our aesthetic preconceptions and lack of sensitivity. The effect of the former is obvious and has always been with us; the lack of sensitivity, however, may prove to be the most debilitating. The question is simply, if one can do absolutely anything, what precisely is worth doing? If it is not to be judged in terms of the pre-existing criteria of available musics, we must have enough personal musical integrity to admit that there is a distinction between the arbitrary manipulation of materials according to some preconceived plan and the construction or performance of valid sonic experiences. I hope this book might open up some new pathways without leading us into the sterile wasteland of formalism.

BIBLIOGRAPHY

Anhalt, I.
(1984) *Alternative Voices: Essays on contemporary vocal and choral composition* (Toronto, University of Toronto Press).

Ball, H.
(1974) *Flight Out of Time: A Dada Diary* (Elderfield, J., editor; Raimes, A., translator) (New York, Viking Press).

Barthes, R.
(1977) 'The Grain of the Voice'. In *Image-Music-Text* (Heath, S., translator) pp. 179–189 (London, Fontana/Collins).

Bastian, J.
(1968) 'Psychological perspectives'. In *Animal Communication* (Sebeok, T. A., editor) pp. 572–591 (Bloomington, Indiana University Press).

Bateson, G.
(1968) 'Redundancy and Coding'. In *Animal Communication* (Sebeok, T. A., editor) pp. 614–626 (Bloomington, Indiana University Press).

Berio, L.
(1959) 'Poesia e musica — un' esperienza". *Incontri Musicali 3* (1959): pp. 98ff also *Contrechamps 1* (1983) pp. 24–35 (French) and (extract in English) sleeve note to LP recording of *Omaggio a Joyce* (Vox Turnabout TV34177).
(1967) *Visage*: sleeve note to LP recording Vox Turnabout 34046S

Bogert, C. M.
(1960) 'The Influence Of Sound On The Behavior Of Amphibians and Reptiles'. In *Animal Sounds and Communication* (Lanyon, W. E. and Tavolga, W. N., editors) pp. 137-320 (Washington, American Institute of Biological Sciences).

Boulez, P.
(1971) *Boulez on Music Today* (London, Faber and Faber).

Busnel, R.-G.
(1968) 'Acoustic Communication'. In *Animal Communication* (Sebeok, T. A., editor) pp. 127–153 (Bloomington, Indiana University Press).

Carroll, L.
(1994) *Through the Looking Glass* (London, Penguin Books).

Chowning, J.
(1971) 'The Simulation of Moving Sound Sources'. *JAES* **19** pp. 2–6 (reprinted in *CMJ* **1(3)** pp. 48–52).

Curtay, J.-P.
(1974) *La poésie lettriste* (Paris, Seghers).
(1981) *Body Music 1* (Cassette with sleeve notes) (London, Audio Arts Editions).
(1983) *Lettrism, abstract poetry, mouth symbols and more …* (Unpublished manuscript).

Darwin, C.
(1965) *The Expression of the Emotions in Man and Animals* (University of Chicago Press).

Emmerson, S.
(1976) 'Luciano Berio talks to Simon Emmerson'. *Music and Musicians* (London) (May 1976) pp. 24–26.
(1982) *Analysis and the Composition of Electro-Acoustic Music* (London, City University (PhD thesis): University Microfilms International).

Erickson, R.
(1975) *Sound Structure in Music* (Berkeley, University of California Press).

Fónagy, I. and Magdics, K.
(1963) 'Emotional Patterns in Intonation and Music'. In *Festgabe für Otto von Essen* (Berlin, Akademie Verlag) pp. 293–326.

Goody, J. and Watt, I.
(1963) 'The Consequences of Literacy'. In *Comparitive Studies in Society and History* **5**.

Hall, D.
(1992) *Klee* (London: Phaidon Press).

Hayes, B.
(1983) 'A progress report on the fine art of turning literature into drivel'.
Scientific American **249(5)** pp. 16–24.

Helmholtz, H.
(1954) *On the Sensations of Tone as a Physiological Basis for the Theory of Music*
(New York, Dover).

Hiller, L.
(1981) 'Composing with Computers a Progress Report'. *CMJ* **5(4)** pp. 7–21.

Hopkins, G. M.
(1959) *The Journals and Papers of Gerard Manley Hopkins* (House, H. and
Storey, G., editors.) (Oxford University Press).

Hooker, B. I.
(1968) 'Birds'. In *Animal Communication* (Sebeok, T. A., editor) pp. 311–337.
(Bloomington, Indiana University Press).

Isou, I.
(1947) *Introduction à une nouvelle poésie et une nouvelle musique* (Paris,
Gallimard).

Joyce, J.
(1939) *Finnegans Wake* (London, Faber and Faber).
(1960) *Ulysses* (London, Bodley Head).

Kaufmann, W.
(1967) *Musical Notations of the Orient* (Bloomington, Indiana University Press).

Kingdon, R.
(1958) *The Groundwork of English Intonation* (London, Longman).

Kostelanetz, R.
(1980) *Text-Sound Texts* (New York, William Morrow and Company).

Langer, S.K.
(1953) *Feeling and Form* (London, Routledge and Kegan Paul).

Lévi-Strauss, C.
(1970) *The Raw and the Cooked* (London, Cape).

McAdams, S.
(1982) 'Spectral Fusion and the Creation of Auditory Images'. In *Music, Mind and Brain* (Clynes, M., editor) (New York, Plenum Press) pp. 279–298.

Marler, P.
(1965) 'Communication in Monkeys and Apes'. In *Primate Behavior: Field Studies of Monkeys and Apes* (DeVore, I., editor.) (New York, Holt, Reinhart and Winston) pp. 544–584.

Motherwell, R.
(1989) *The Dada Painters and Poets: An Anthology* (Harvard University Press).

Nicholson, E. M. and Koch, L.
(1946) *Songs of Wild Birds* (London).

Pauli, H.
(1971) *Für wen komponieren Sie eigentlich?* (Frankfurt a.M., Fischer).

Robson, E.
(1981) *Phonetic Music with Electronic Music* (Parker Ford, Pa., Primary Press).

Rodet, X., Potard, Y. and Barrière. J.-B.
(1984) 'The CHANT Project: From the Synthesis of the Singing Voice to Synthesis in General'. *CMJ* **8(3)** pp. 15–31.

Rowell, T. E.
(1962) 'Agonistic Noises of the Rhesus Monkey (Macaca mulatta)'. *Symposium of the Zoological Society of London* **8** pp. 91–6.

Rowell, T. E. and Hinde, R. A.
(1962) 'Vocal Communication by the Rhesus Monkey (Macaca mulatta)'. *Proceedings of the Zoological Society of London* **138** pp. 279–294.

San Diego Extended Vocal Techniques Group
(1974) *Index to a Recorded Lexicon of Extended Vocal Techniques* (San Diego, Center for Music Experiment and Related Research).

Schaeffer, P.
(1966) *Traité de Objets Musicaux* (Paris, Du Seuil).

Schaeffer, P., Reibel, G. and Ferreyra, B.
(1983) *Solfège de l'objet sonore* (Paris, INA/GRM).
(Three cassettes with accompanying text (original LP version 1966)).

Schafer, R. M.
(1969) *The New Soundscape* (BMI, Canada/Universal Edition).
(1977) *The Tuning of the World* (New York, Knopf).

Schouten, J. F., Ritsma, R. J. and Cardozo, B. L.
(1962) 'Pitch of the Residue'. *JASA* **34(8/2)** pp. 1418–1424.

Schwitters, K.
(1993) *Poems, Performance Pieces, Proses, Plays, Poetics* (Rothenberg, J. and Joris, P. editors/translators) (Philadelphia, Temple University Press).

Shepherd, J., Virden, P., Vulliamy, G. and Wishart, T.
(1977) *Whose Music? A Sociology of Musical Languages* (London, Latimer).

Stuckenschmidt, H. H.
(1959) *Arnold Schoenberg* (London, Calder).

Thom, R.
(1975) *Sructural Stability and Morphogenesis* (Reading, Mass., W. A. Benjamin).

Thompson, D'A. W.
(1961) *On Growth and Form* (Cambridge University Press).

Thorpe, W. H. and North, M. E. W.
(1965) 'Origin and significance of the power of vocal imitation: with special reference to the antiphonal singing of birds'. *Nature* **208** pp. 219–222.

Weber, M.
(1958) *The Rational and Social Foundations of Music* (Martindale, Riedel and Neuwirth, translators) (Carbondale, Southern Illinois University Press).

Wessel, D.
(1979) 'Timbre Space as a Musical Control Structure'. *CMJ* **3(2)** pp. 45–52.

Wishart, T.
(1979) *Book of Lost Voices* (York, Wishart (private publication)).

Xenakis, I.
(1971) *Formalised Music* (Bloomington, Indiana UP).
[Revised edition: Stuyvesant, Pendragon Press (1992)].

MUSIC EXAMPLES

This book is about *listening*. Trevor Wishart insists that only the ear can validate or criticise music composition. His original lectures and plan for this book included recordings of a vast array of musical examples from many sources. Copyright problems have made the assemblage of a complete accompanying recording prohibitively difficult.

What has been included on the accompanying CD are the otherwise unobtainable extended vocal materials recorded by Trevor Wishart himself and extracts of other of his works to illustrate the arguments of the text. In addition regenerated acoustic and psychoacoustic examples have been included. The CD track/index is given in the left-hand margin.

Within the current constraints of copyright law the author and editor invite the reader to construct an ideal series of music examples from the following list of commercial recordings which will be referred to in the text by the example numbers indicated. This book makes most sense if the reader has assembled these music examples and listens to them at the relevant point in the text. All entries are CDs unless marked as LP or Cassette. Where the author has made reference to specific sounds, transformations etc. timings are given with respect to the actual recording cited, whereas where reference is to a general style or approach no specific timings are given. For well known works of which several recordings are easily available none is specifically cited. (Where no source is cited the example may be found on the accompanying CD.)

The author repeated music examples in his original lectures. He also grouped sounds into a single Example when they were intended to be directly compared. These aspects have been preserved in the text and the sequence below.

The following are reproduced with permission: Example 3.5 (Jean-Claude Risset); Example 3.20 (Roger Reynolds); Example 4.1 (David Wessel); Examples 5.1 and 7.8 (Jean-Baptiste Barrière).

Chapter 1

	Ex. 1.1:	Denis Smalley: *Pentes* [8.10–10.52].
		[Ode Record Co. Ltd. (New Zealand): CD MANU 1433]
[1.01]	Ex. 1.2:	Trevor Wishart: *Musical Box* from *Menagerie* [0.00–1.20].
		[YES Records (York): (LP) YES 8]
	Ex. 1.3:	Iannis Xenakis: *Concret PH II*.
		[Nonesuch (NY): (LP) H-71246]
	Ex. 1.4:	Michael McNabb: *Dreamsong* [8.08–9.11].
		[Mobile Fidelity Sound Lab: MFCD 818]
	Ex. 1.5:	Goon Show: *Napoleon's Piano*.
		[BBC Radio Collection (London): (Cassette) ZBBC 1016 (ISBN (0563) 225440)]
	Ex. 1.6:	Bernard Parmegiani: *Etude élastique* from *De Natura Sonorum* [0.50–1.36].
		[INA/GRM (Paris): INA C3001]
	Ex. 1.7:	Luciano Berio: *Omaggio a Joyce* [0.00–1.00].
		[BVHaast (Amsterdam): CD 9109]
	Ex. 1.8:	Richard Coldman: *Fret buzz* [1.25–2.40].
		[Incus Records (UK): (LP) Incus 31]

Chapter 2

Ex. 2.1:	Japanese *Joruri* singing (*gidayu* style) (e.g. Takemoto Tsunatayu: *Kiyari Ondo*).
	[King Record Co. Ltd. (Japan): KICH 2008]
Ex. 2.2:	North Indian singing (e.g. Sulochana Brahaspati: *Khyal (Raga Bilaskhani Todi)*).
	[Nimbus (UK): NI 5305)
Ex. 2.3:	Jazz singing (e.g. Billy Holliday: *Lady Sings the Blues*).
	[Verve (Polygram): 823 246–2]
Ex. 2.4:	Josef Haydn: *Dona nobis pacem* from *Missa in Tempore Belli* (*'Paukenmesse'*)
Ex. 2.5:	Japanese shakuhachi playing (e.g. Kohachiro Miyati: *Shika no Tone*).
	[Elektra Nonesuch: 7559–72076-2]
Ex. 2.6:	A classical chamber work (using wind instruments) (e.g. Antoine Reicha: Wind Quintet in D major op. 91 no. 3).
	[Hyperion Records Ltd. (UK): CDA66268]
Ex. 2.7:	Traditional jazz (e.g. Louis Armstrong and His Hot Five: *West End Blues*).
	[BBC Enterprizes (UK): BBC CD 597]

Chapter 3

The music examples from chapter 3 may be found on the accompanying CD; except Example 3.5 they have been resynthesised based on models generated originally by the Groupe de Recherches Musicales.

[11.01] Ex. 3.16: Vibraphone sound: (a) normal (b) with attack cut (3 versions).

[12.01] Ex. 3.17: Flute note: (a) with attack cut (b) normal.

[12.02] Ex. 3.18: Trumpet note: (a) with attack cut (b) normal.

[13.01] Ex. 3.19: The influence of onset synchrony on coherence.

[14.01] Ex. 3.20: Splitting an aural image into two (Roger Reynolds).

[15.01] Ex. 3.21: Different sound objects from a single source (metal sheet and a taut string).

[16.01] Ex. 3.22: Sound of definite *mass*: resistance to filtering and its transposition.

[17.01] Ex. 3.23: *Grain* illustrated with electronic impulses.

[17.02] Ex. 3.24: *Grain* illustrated for a bassoon note.

[18.01] Ex. 3.25: Speed up of melody into grain: (a) descending scale (b) irregular melodic pattern.

[19.01] Ex. 3.26: Speed up of string of speech sounds approaches speech multiplex.

Chapter 4

[20.01] Ex. 4.1: Two sequences based on David Wessel's researches into timbre space.

Chapter 5

[21.01] Ex. 5.1: *Chant* example: transformation from bell to male voice.

[22.01] Ex. 5.2: Trevor Wishart: *Red Bird* transformation '(Li)-sss-(ten)' to birdsong (1.26–1.42).
[October Music: Oct 001]

[23.01] Ex. 5.3: A typical vocally-produced multiplex.

[24.01] Ex. 5.4: As 5.3 but the field characteristic of the multiplex changes with time.

Chapter 6

[25.01] Ex. 6.1: Trevor Wishart: *Anna's Magic Garden* (2.50–3.31).
[Overhear Music (UK): Ohm001]

Ex. 6.2: Bernard Parmegiani: *Etude élastique* from *De Natura Sonorum* [0.45–1.36].
[INA/GRM (Paris): INA C3001]

Ex. 6.3: Luciano Berio: *Visage* (0.45–2.15).
[BVHaast (Amsterdam): CD 9109]

[26.01] Ex. 6.4: Trevor Wishart: *Anticredos* (unspatialised extract from Wishart studio demo version) [unpublished].

Chapter 7

Ex. 7.1: Witold Lutoslawski: *Trois Poèmes d'Henri Michaux* (II: *Le grand combat*) (2.20–3.50).
[Polskie Nagrania (Poland): PNCD041]

Ex. 7.2: Clément Janequin: *Le Chant des Oyseaulx*.
[Harmonia Mundi (France): HMC 901099]

Ex. 7.3: Ludwig van Beethoven: Symphony No.6 (*Pastorale*) (II: *Scene at the brook* (entry of Nightingale (bar 129) to the end)).

Ex. 7.4: Karlheinz Stockhausen: *Trans* (opening 2.00).
[Stockhausen Verlag (Germany): Stockhausen 19]

Ex. 7.5: Bernard Parmegiani: *Matières induites* (3.30-) + *Ondes croisées* (–0.40) from *De Natura Sonorum*.
[INA/GRM (Paris): INA C3001]

Ex. 7.6: Goon Show: *Napoleon's Piano*.
[BBC Radio Collection (London): (Cassette) ZBBC 1016 (ISBN (0563) 225440)]

[27.01] Ex. 7.7: Trevor Wishart: *Automusic* (extract).
[Unpublished[1]]

[28.01] Ex. 7.8: *Chant* example: transformation from bell to male voice.

[29.01] Ex. 7.9: Trevor Wishart: *Red Bird* book/door slam (23.00–24.50).
[October Music: Oct 001]

[30.01] Ex. 7.10: Trevor Wishart: *Red Bird* lisss/birds (1.26–1.42).
[October Music: Oct 001]

Ex. 7.11: Alvin Lucier: *I am sitting in a room*.
[Sacramento: Composer/Performer Edition: (LP) 'Source Record Number Three' (in: *Source: music of the avant garde* (Double issue 7/8 (1970)]

Ex. 7.12: Luc Ferrari: *Presque Rien No. 1*.
[Deutsche Grammophon: (LP) 2561 041]

Ex. 7.13: Larry Wendt: *From Frogs*.
['Poésie Sonore Internationale' (Jean-Michel Place, France) (Cassette) 10007]

Ex. 7.14: Michael McNabb: *Dreamsong* (0.00–1.20).
[Mobile Fidelity Sound Lab: MFCD 818]

[31.01] Ex. 7.15: Trevor Wishart: *Musical Box* from *Menagerie* (0.00–1.20).
[YES Records (York): (LP) YES 8]

[32.01] Ex. 7.16: Trevor Wishart: *Still Life* from *Menagerie* (1.00–3.02).
[YES Records (York): (LP) YES 8]

Ex. 7.17: Karlheinz Stockhausen: *Gesang der Jünglinge* (5.10–6.30).
[Stockhausen Verlag (Germany): Stockhausen 3]

Ex. 7.18: Luciano Berio: *Visage* (6.54–7.32).
[BVHaast (Amsterdam): CD 9109]

Chapter 8

Examples 8.1–8.12, from Trevor Wishart's *Red Bird* are all found on the accompanying CD. The whole work is found on October Music (UK): Oct 001.

[33.01] Ex. 8.1:   Sound-image 'bellows/water-pump' (20.26–22.20).
[34.01] Ex. 8.2:   'Listen to reason' transformation (4.01–5.31).
[35.01] Ex. 8.3:   Garden landscape (11.00–12.12).
[36.01] Ex. 8.4:   Reason landscape (37.42–39.09).
[37.01] Ex. 8.5:   Animal-like sound images (a) emerge from the background (15.02–16.30), (b) take on articulation of words (16.57–17.57) and (c) gesturally interact with the bird sounds (18.06–18.44).
[38.01] Ex. 8.6:   Bird cadenza (33.15–34.27).
[39.01] Ex. 8.7:   Word machine (20.25–20.42).
[40.01] Ex. 8.8:   Phonemes as flocking birds (25.52–26.36).
[41.01] Ex. 8.9:   'Rea' transformation to bark (5.01–5.23).
[42.01] Ex. 8.10:   '-ble' bursts out into bubbling (4.06–4.14).
[43.01] Ex. 8.11:   Ambiguous machinery/animal landscape: (a) a 'glimpse' of the animal sounds out of context (38.18–38.25) and (b) placed in context (37.47–38.34).
[44.01] Ex. 8.12:   'Rea' transformation to clock: (a) to texture (4.30–4.44 and 6.07–6.31), (b) from texture to short reverberated attack (27.13–28.38 and 29.04–29.10) and (c) from attack to clock tick (30.49–30.53 and 31.45–32.45).

Chapter 10

         Ex. 10.1:   Jean Sibelius: Symphony No.4 (III: bars B+6 to C).

Chapter 11

         Ex. 11.1:   Arnold Schoenberg: *Erwartung* (bars 146–157).
[45.01] Ex. 11.2:   Comparison of the simulated signals of the Great Northern Diver (Loon), the wolf, the whale and the red squirrel.

Chapter 12

The sound examples from Chapter 12 were all performed by Trevor Wishart and are to be found on the accompanying CD.

The glottis and windpipe

[46.01] Ex. 12.1:   Glottal vibrations (vibrating larynx): iterated impulses (unpitched).
[46.02] Ex. 12.2:   Glottal vibrations (vibrating larynx): normal rate of vibration (pitched).
[46.03] Ex. 12.3:   Windpipe vibration caused by forcible exhalation from lungs: below the larynx.
[46.04] Ex. 12.4:   Windpipe vibration caused by forcible exhalation from lungs: above the larynx.
[47.01] Ex. 12.5:   As 12.3.
[47.02] Ex. 12.6:   The same (as 12.3) combined with the sound of the larynx.
[47.03] Ex. 12.7:   As 12.4.
[47.04] Ex. 12.8:   The same (as 12.4) combined with the sound of the larynx.
[47.05] Ex. 12.9:   Octave division (normal pitch followed by division).

The tongue

[48.01] Ex. 12.10: Tongue vibrations: tip at front of mouth.
[48.02] Ex. 12.11: Tongue vibrations: tip onto soft palate.
[48.03] Ex. 12.12: Tongue vibrations: tip strongly retroflexed.
[49.01] Ex. 12.13: Rolled 'r' with arched tongue middle mouth.
[49.02] Ex. 12.14: Rolled 'r' with arched tongue back of mouth.
[49.03] Ex. 12.15: Rolled 'r' with arched tongue against uvula (snoring).
[49.04] Ex. 12.16: Rolled 'r' with arched tongue brought into sung pitch range.

The lips and cheeks

[50.01] Ex. 12.17: Lip vibration: normal.
[50.02] Ex. 12.18: Lip vibration: folded towards teeth.
[50.03] Ex. 12.19: Lip vibration: strongly pouted outwards.
[50.04] Ex. 12.20: Use of hands to assist production of long lip notes.
[50.05] Ex. 12.21: Lip oscillation variations.
[50.06] Ex. 12.22: Two independent lip oscillations.
[51.01] Ex. 12.23: Cheek vibration with pitch variation controlled by hands.
[51.02] Ex. 12.24: Sub-audio cheek vibration.
[51.03] Ex. 12.25: Independent cheek vibrations (with resultant beats).

Filters

Filtered noise and whistles

Double and treble production

[57.05] Ex. 12.50: Tongue vibration (uvula *U*) combined with glottal sounds (3 variants).
[58.01] Ex. 12.51: Combinations of lip and glottis vibrations.
[58.02] Ex. 12.52: Combinations of cheek and glottis vibrations.
[58.03] Ex. 12.53: Combinations of noise sounds and glottis vibrations.
[58.04] Ex. 12.54: Combination with intermodulation of (a) ordinary whistling with singing compared with (b) high *s*-whistle with low glottal sounds.
[58.05] Ex. 12.55: Two simultaneous tongue vibrations.
[58.06] Ex. 12.56: Combination of lip and tongue vibrations (with intermodulation).
[59.01] Ex. 12.57: Cheek and tongue vibrations.
[59.02] Ex. 12.58: Noise and tongue vibrations.
[59.03] Ex. 12.59: Lips and arched tongue vibrations.
[59.04] Ex. 12.60: Cheeks and arched tongue vibrations.
[60.01] Ex. 12.61: Noise and arched tongue vibrations.
[60.02] Ex. 12.62: Whistle and arched tongue vibrations.
[60.03] Ex. 12.63: Noise and uvular vibration of tongue.
[60.04] Ex. 12.64: Noise and lip vibrations.
[61.01] Ex. 12.65: Whistle and lip vibrations ('trimphone').
[61.02] Ex. 12.66: Simultaneous noise, tongue, lip, glottis vibrations independently articulated.
[61.03] Ex. 12.67: Glottis and tongue vibration through pouted lips ('trumpet').

Air stream and other effects

[62.01] Ex. 12.68: 'Wamp', 'half-wamp' and 'quarter-wamp'.
[62.02] Ex. 12.69: Half-lunged multiphonic.
[62.03] Ex. 12.70: Unlunged whistle.
[63.01] Ex. 12.71: Manual-diaphragm flutter (continuous sound).
[63.02] Ex. 12.72: Manual-diaphragm drumming (short staccato sounds).
[63.03] Ex. 12.73: Shake-head flutter (pitched and noise versions).
[63.04] Ex. 12.74: Drum-glottis flutter.
[63.05] Ex. 12.75: Shake-body flutter.
[64.01] Ex. 12.76: Drum-cheeks flutter.
[64.02] Ex. 12.77: Strum-lips flutter.
[64.03] Ex. 12.78: Strum-nose flutter.
[64.04] Ex. 12.79: Diaphragm flutter with tongue vibration.
[64.05] Ex. 12.80: Diaphragm flutter with lip vibration.

[65.01] Ex. 12.81: Ululation.
[65.02] Ex. 12.82: Ululation across break in voice.
[65.03] Ex. 12.83: Ululation with high depth ('laugh').

Water effects

[66.01] Ex. 12.84: Arched tongue vibration with saliva/water.
[66.02] Ex. 12.85: *X*/water.
[66.03] Ex. 12.86: Filtered *X*/water.
[66.04] Ex. 12.87: Filtered half-lunged *X*/water.
[66.05] Ex. 12.88: *K*-plosive + *X*/water ('children's gunshot').
[66.06] Ex. 12.89: Filtered half-lunged *X*/water: plosive staccato production.
[67.01] Ex. 12.90: Filtered half-lunged *X*/water: plosive staccato production + tongue-tip vibration.
[67.02] Ex. 12.91: Unvoiced/water sounds with pitch content.
[67.03] Ex. 12.92: Inhaled lip vibration (normal then water behind lips).
[67.04] Ex. 12.93: Inhaled air stream with water around sides of tongue.

Transformations (exhaled sustainable sounds)

[68.01] Ex. 12.94: Tongue oscillation transformations.
[68.02] Ex. 12.95: As 94 adding and subtracting water.
[69.01] Ex. 12.96: Pitched production: transformations between lunged and half-lunged.
[69.02] Ex. 12.97: Pitched production: transformations between under- and over-breathed.
[70.01] Ex. 12.98: Pitched production: transformations between normal and fluttered.
[70.02] Ex. 12.99: Transformation from tongue to lip vibration.

Inhaled sounds

[71.01] Ex. 12.100: Inhaled lip vibrations: tones, pulses, multiphonics.
[71.02] Ex. 12.101: As 100 + control with heals of hands.
[71.03] Ex. 12.102: Inhaled tongue vibration (retroflex position).
[71.04] Ex. 12.103: Inhaled tongue vibration (uvula position).
[72.01] Ex. 12.104: Inhaled pure tones.
[72.02] Ex. 12.105: Inhaled click trains.
[72.03] Ex. 12.106: Inhaled sub-harmonics.
[72.04] Ex. 12.107: Inhaled complex multiphonics.

[72.05] Ex. 12.108: Inhaled unstable complex vibration.
[72.06] Ex. 12.109: Inhaled unstable complex vibration with filtering.

Pulses

[73.01] Ex. 12.110: Epiglottis pulses.
[73.02] Ex. 12.111: Arched tongue pulses (rear, centre and front).
[73.03] Ex. 12.112: Tip of tongue pulses (from retroflexed to further forward).
[73.04] Ex. 12.113: Tongue/teeth and tongue/ top lip pulses.
[73.05] Ex. 12.114: Teeth and lips pulses.
[73.06] Ex. 12.115: Lips pulses.
[74.01] Ex. 12.116: Pulses *k* and *t*: lunged, half lunged, unlunged.
[74.02] Ex. 12.117: Plosive half-lunged *d*.
[74.03] Ex. 12.118: Plosive half-lunged *p*.
[74.04] Ex. 12.119: Plosive unlunged *p*.

Voiced pulses

[75.01] Ex. 12.120: Pulse *d* (lunged) with secondary voicing and breath.
[75.02] Ex. 12.121: As 120: other types of voicing (windpipe, tongue vibration, whistle).
[75.03] Ex. 12.122: Pulse *k* (lunged): variation of airstream content.
[75.04] Ex. 12.123: Pulse *k* (lunged): variation of airstream type.
[75.05] Ex. 12.124: Pulse *k* (lunged): airstream glissando.
[75.06] Ex. 12.125: Plosive air stream effect (suppression of original pulse).

Pulses with stops, buzzes, filtering

[76.01] Ex. 12.126: Plosive *d* (unvoiced, voiced) compared with addition of *g*-stop (*d(g)!*) (unvoiced, voiced).
[76.02] Ex. 12.127: Plosive *d* with addition of *p*-stop (*d(p)!*).
[76.03] Ex. 12.128: Drum imitation (*d(g)!* with glottal vibration).
[76.04] Ex. 12.129: *H*-stream stopped with *ch* and *k*.
[76.05] Ex. 12.130: S-stream stopped with *p*.
[76.06] Ex. 12.131: Slap tongue (unlunged *t*), slap teeth pulses.
[77.01] Ex. 12.132: Buzzed lips: lunged.
[77.02] Ex. 12.133: Buzzed lips: half lunged.
[77.03] Ex. 12.134: Buzzed lips: unlunged.
[77.04] Ex. 12.135: As 134 with air exhalation.
[77.05] Ex. 12.136: Manually initiated lip pulses.

[78.01] Ex. 12.137: Pulse (unlunged *k*) with oral filtering.
[78.02] Ex. 12.138: Pulse (unlunged *p*) resonance control through pouting.
[78.03] Ex. 12.139: Plosive click with filter glissando.

Simultaneous and alternated pulses

[79.01] Ex. 12.140: Simultaneous pulses *g* + *k*.
[79.02] Ex. 12.141: Simultaneous pulses *t* + *k*.
[79.03] Ex. 12.142: Pulse alternation *tktk*…: lunged.
[79.04] Ex. 12.143: Pulse alternation *tktk*…: half-lunged.
[79.05] Ex. 12.144: Pulse alternation *tktk*…: unlunged.
[79.06] Ex. 12.145: Pulse alternation *gthgth*…: unlunged.
[80.01] Ex. 12.146: Pulse alternation *ptpt*…: lunged.
[80.02] Ex. 12.147   Pulse alternation *ptpt*…: half-lunged.
[80.03] Ex. 12.148   Pulse alternation *ptpt*…: unlunged.
[80.04] Ex. 12.149: Manual iteration lip pulses: lunged.
[80.05] Ex. 12.150   Manual iteration lip pulses: unlunged.

Pulses (clicks and combinations)

[81.01] Ex. 12.151: Pulse during inhalation at epiglottis.
[81.02] Ex. 12.152: Unlunged click: lateral tongue movement.
[81.03] Ex. 12.153: Unlunged click: vertical tongue movement (*kl*).
[81.04] Ex. 12.154: Unlunged click: plosive vertical tongue movement.
[81.05] Ex. 12.155: Unlunged *t*- or *tut*-click.
[81.06] Ex. 12.156: Unlunged *th*-click.
[82.01] Ex. 12.157: Kiss (short) with various degrees of lip pouting.
[82.02] Ex. 12.158: Plosive + kiss combination.
[82.03] Ex. 12.159: Lateral + kiss combination.

Transitionals and percussives

[83.01] Ex. 12.160: Consonant transitions between harmonics of a given
                       glottal pitch: *m*, *n*, *ng*, 'deep' *ng*.
[84.01] Ex. 12.161: Iterations of transitionals: *mnmn*… and *n-ng-n-ng*…
[85.01] Ex. 12.162: Hand clap with mouth as variable resonator.
[85.02] Ex. 12.163: Tapping teeth with mouth as variable resonator.
[85.03] Ex. 12.164: Popping finger out of closed lips.
[85.04] Ex. 12.165: Manual expulsion of air from cheeks through lips.
[85.05] Ex. 12.166: 'Water drop'.

Multiplexes and complex articulations

[86.01]   Ex. 12.167: Multiplex combinations: *pkʃlgr* + *X*+ (lunged and half-lunged) + lip-flabber.
[86.02]   Ex. 12.168: As 167 + tongue movement.
[86.03]   Ex. 12.169: As 168 + glottal glissando.

Chapter 13

[87.01]   Ex. 13.1:   Birdsong trills slowed down.

---

[1] Original commissioned broadcast BBC2 Television (*Sounds Different*: 'Music Outside') 1980.

MUSIC REFERENCES

The following works are referred to in the text in addition to those specified by the author as music examples for audition (see above). For electroacoustic works recording details are given otherwise the publisher of the score.

Davies, Hugh (with Hans-Karsten Raeke)
Klangbilder [(CD) Klangwerkstatt Edition (Mannheim) SM 500 135 D]

Ferneyhough, Brian
Second String Quartet [Peters Edition]
Time and Motion Study III [Peters Edition]

Ferrari, Luc
Music Promenade [(LP) Wergo 60046]

IRCAM
IRCAM un portrait [(LP) Centre Georges Pompidou (Paris) IRCAM 001]

Ligeti, György
Nouvelles Aventures [Peters Edition]
Requiem [Peters Edition]

La Barbara, Joan
Voice is the original instrument [(LP) Wizard Records (New York) RVW 2266]

Reich, Steve
Come Out [(CD) Elektra Nonesuch 979 169–2)

Schaeffer, Pierre; Reibel, Guy and Ferreyra, Beatriz
Solfège de l'objet sonore [(3 Cassettes) INA/GRM (Paris) 4001–3 sc]

Schoenberg, Arnold
Erwartung [Universal Edition]
Pierrot Lunaire [Universal Edition]

Smalley, Denis
Orouboros [Unpublished]

Stockhausen, Karlheinz
Mikrophonie I [Universal Edition]
Hymnen [(CD) Stockhausen Verlag 10]
Telemusik [(CD) Stockhausen Verlag 9]
Stimmung [Universal Edition]

Wishart, Trevor
Anticredos [(CD) October Music (UK) Oct 001]]
Tuba Mirum [Wishart (York)]
Vox I [(CD) Virgin Classics (UK) VC 7 91108-2]

INDEX

Other titles in the Contemporary Music Studies series:

Volume 11
John Cage's Theatre Pieces: Notations and Performances
William Fetterman

Volume 12
On Sonic Art
Trevor Wishart

Volume 13
Soviet Film M̶   ̶ ̶ ̶ ̶ ̶ ̶urvey
Tatio̶

Vol̶
Sch̶   ̶istoric Encounter
Edit̶

Vol̶
Itali̶
Ray̶

Vol̶
The   ̶ic — A Henry Cowell Symposium
Edit̶

Vol̶
Giar̶   ̶piero (1882–1973):
The   ̶d Music of a Wayward Genius
John̶

Volume 18
Jani Christou – The Works and Temperament of a Greek Composer of Our Time
Anna M. Lucciano

Volume 19
Harry Partch – An Anthology of Critical Perspectives
Edited by David Dunn

Volume 20
Readings in Music and Artificial Intelligence
Edited by Eduardo Reck Miranda